NEW YORK
ALIEN RESIDENTS,

1825-1848

Compiled by

KENNETH SCOTT

&

ROSANNE CONWAY

CLEARFIELD COMPANY
REPRINTS & REMAINDERS

Reprinted for Clearfield Company, Inc. by
Genealogical Publishing Co. Inc.
Baltimore, MD 1991

Library of Congress Catalogue Card Number 78-57005
International Standard Book Number 0-8063-0814-1

Made in the United States of America

Introduction

IN THE COLONIAL PERIOD an alien who came to England or one of the English colonies could neither hold nor bequeath real property; if he acquired such, it escheated to the Crown upon his demise. Naturally, many aliens in New York sought to obtain the right to hold, dispose of, inherit and bequeath land. This privilege might be secured in England by denization granted by the king or by naturalization through an act of Parliament, while in New York it might be obtained by an act of the Provincial Assembly or, only up to 1700, by denization granted by the governor.[1]

After the Revolution the real estate of a resident alien escheated to the State of New York instead of to the Crown upon his demise, and he had no right to acquire, hold, convey, inherit or bequeath land except by act of the legislature. To deal with this problem the New York Legislature, on April 21, 1825, passed "An Act to enable resident Aliens to take and hold Real Estate and for other purposes."[2] In brief, the Act required an alien to make deposition that "he is a resident in, and intends always to reside in the United States, and to become a citizen thereof as soon as he can be naturalized; and that he has taken such incipient measures as the laws of the United States require, to enable him to obtain naturalization." Further, such alien was to have no power to lease any real estate held in virtue of the Act until he became naturalized. Such alien, moreover, was not to be capable of taking or holding lands which might have descended or been devised or conveyed to him before his having become such resident and having made the required deposition.

By the Act of 1825 the alien's deposition must be filed in a book or books in the office of the Secretary of State of New York.

---

[1] Kenneth Scott and Kenn Stryker-Rodda, *Denizations, Naturalizations and Oaths of Allegiance in Colonial New York* (Baltimore: Genealogical Publishing Co., 1975), pp. v-vi. Both before and after the Act of April 21, 1825 aliens were enabled to take and hold real estate by acts in which they were specifically named.

[2] *Laws of the State of New York*, 1825, pp. 427 and 432. See also *Revised Statutes of the State of New York* (Albany: Packard and Van Benthuysen, 1836), pp. 715-716.

A fee of fifty cents was allowed for the recording. The Act provided that, if after six years the alien had not been naturalized or was not then a resident of the United States, his lands should be vested in the people of New York as though the law had not been made.

The aliens' depositions, now in the New York State Library in Albany, are a valuable source for genealogical research for the following reasons: the alien's place of residence, regularly by county and often by village, town or city, is stated; country of birth, sometimes with name of county or department, is often given; date of birth, the age when the alien arrived in the United States, or when he deposed, is occasionally recorded; date of arrival in America may be found; status of a woman (single, married or widowed) is usually set forth, as is the name of a husband, with his trade or profession; rarely, the maiden name of a married woman is reported; in a few instances filing on behalf of children is made by a parent; finally, the status of a resident alien is very often recorded, giving evidence of an enormous variety of occupations.

Places of origin appear frequently: Great Britain or the United Kingdom or, more specifically, England, Ireland, Scotland, Wales, Cornwall, the Isle of Wight and the Isle of Man; Upper and Lower Canada, New Brunswick and Newfoundland; France, Italy, Belgium, the Netherlands, Switzerland, the Roman States, Piedmont, Sweden, Denmark, Poland, Sardinia and Hungary; Germany, or, more specifically, Prussia, Hessen, Hessen Darmstadt, Hessen Kassel, Wuertemberg, Bavaria, Hanover, Nassau, Westphalia, Saxony, Waldeck and the cities of Hamburg, Bremen and Frankfurt am Main; the West Indies, Cuba, Jamaica, St. Croix and Barbados.

The first four volumes of depositions, covering the years 1825-1848, contain information about some 4,260 resident aliens. In a very few instances it has been difficult to determine a name, for the clerk made some letters, u and n, for example, in the same way. Many of the resident aliens were illiterate and must have given information orally, all of which resulted in unorthodox spellings, especially in the case of Irish names of towns or villages. At the end of each item the date of the deposition is here given.

It is hoped that this book will provide valuable genealogical data and call attention to the fifty-four volumes of depositions in the New York State Library, a source of information hitherto little used and, in general, unknown to most researchers.

The compilers of this volume are indebted to Aurelia G. Scott, who proofread the typescript, Joan Sanger, who corrected errors in typing, and Peter Christoph, who secured microfilm of the first four volumes of depositions.

KENNETH SCOTT

ROSANNE CONWAY

ABBOTT
  William, of NYC - 28 Sept. 1836
ABELING
  Charles, of Canajoharie, Montgomery Co., native of Germany -
    18 Aug. 1834
ABENDROTH/ABANDROTH
  William, of Albany - 29 Dec. 1832
ABERNETHY
  Henry, of Brooklyn, Kings Co. - 18 Sept. 1845
ABERT
  Martin, of Wayne Co. - 28 Sept. 1830
ACKER
  Jacob, of Williamsburgh, Kings Co. - 14 July 1846
ACKERLY
  George, of NYC - 21 June 1836
ACKERMAN
  Christian Gottlieb, of Buffalo, Erie Co. - 29 June 1843
ADAMS
  Benjamin, of NYC - 9 Jan. 1835
  Catharine, of Utica, Oneida Co. - 24 Dec. 1844
  George, of NYC, native of Eng., for last 13 years res. of NYC -
    6 May 1830
  John, of Buffalo, Erie Co. - Mar. 1830
  Thomas, of Utica - 10 Feb. 1842
  Thomas, of Evans, Erie Co. - 16 Feb. 1843
  Thomas R., of Watertown, Jefferson Co. - 1 Aug. 1840
ADDIS
  John B., of Bushwick, Kings Co. - 6 July 1846
AIGUIER
  Jean Baptiste, of NYC, late of France - 29 Apr. 1829
AINSLIE
  John, of Meredith, Delaware Co. - 6 Jan. 1836
AITCHSON
  Robert, of NYC - 4 Mar. 1836
AITKIN
  Robert, of NYC, carpenter - 23 June 1841
AKAM
  John, of Chautauque, Chautauque Co. - 27 June 1835
AKERMAN
  John George, of Buffalo, Erie Co., formerly of Wuertemberg,
    Germany - 10 Dec. 1845
AKHURST
  James, of Schaghticoke, Rensselaer Co., baker - 17 Nov. 1836
  James Henry, of Brooklyn, Kings Co., born in Kent Co., Eng.,
    about 1817; came to U.S. in 1836 - 19 Aug. 1844
AKRILL
  John, of NYC - 7 Nov. 1835
ALANSON
  Arthur, of Canajoharie, Montgomery Co. - 31 Oct. 1837
ALCOTT
  Jeremiah, of Otsego Co. - 20 June 1832
ALDINGER
  Michael, of Fairfield, Herkimer Co. - 2 Feb. 1836
ALDRICH
  David, of Buffalo, Erie Co. - 8 Aug. 1835
ALEXANDER
  Hezekiah, of City and Co. of Albany - 26 July 1836
  John, of Burlington, Otsego Co. - 14 Oct. 1834
  Samuel, of Oswegatchie, St. Lawrence Co., late of Eng. -
    2 Apr. 1835
ALLAN
  Robert, of Phelps, Ontario Co. - 8 July 1831
ALLCHIN
  Charles, of Onondaga Co. - 26 Feb. 1839

New York Alien Residents, 1825-1848

ALLEN
  Barbara, of NYC, single woman - 5 Nov. 1842
  George, of Albany - 4 Dec. 1835
  Isaac, of Canajoharie, Montgomery Co., late of Blackston, York
    Co., Eng.; arrived U.S. 10 June 1834 - 31 Mar. 1835
  John, of Harmony, Chautauque Co. - 7 Mar. 1837
  Richard Paine, of Rochester, Monroe Co. - 17 Dec. 1836
  Robert, of Onondaga Co. - 2 Dec. 1836
  Samuel, of Lawrens, Otsego Co. - 29 Mar. 1832
  Thomas, of Canajoharie, Montgomery Co. - 28 Apr. 1836
  Thomas, of Onondaga Co. - 3 Dec. 1836
  William, of Canajoharie, Montgomery Co. - 15 Aug. 1833
ALLERTHOM
  John, of Niagara Co., native of Yorkshire, Eng., for past six
    years res. of U.S. - 3 Feb. 1845
ALLISON
  Andrew, of Tyrone, Steuben Co., subject of U.K. - 4 Jan. 1830
ALLISPACH
  Ida (wife of John C. Allispach), of NYC - 22 Sept. 1845
  John C., of NYC, merchant - 15 Oct. 1840
ALLNALL
  John, of Evans, Erie Co., British subject - 27 Aug. 1845
ALLSTADT
  Mary Magdalin (wife of John C. Allstadt), of NYC - 2 Oct. 1845
ALVEY
  Samuel, of Kings Co. - 27 June 1836
AMBROSE
  William C., of Westchester Co., British subject - 21 Dec. 1843
AMHIRST
  Walter, of Oneida Co. - 7 July 1830
ANDER
  William, of Boston, Erie Co.; emigrated from U.K. 1830 - 25 Mar.
    1836
ANDERSON
  David, of NYC, merchant, born in Scotland; took incipient mea-
    sures at Philadelphia on 25 Jan. 1823
  William, of NYC, gentleman, res. for about 5 or 6 years at 114
    Spring St. - 3 Oct. 1838
ANDREWS
  John R., of NYC - 22 Dec. 1840
ANGUS
  Jane, of Albany - 10 Feb. 1835
ANNA
  Jacob, of West Turin, Lewis Co. - 11 Dec. 1843
  Maria Smith, of West Turin, Lewis Co. - 11 Dec. 1843
ANNON
  Thomas, of Deerfield, Oneida Co., native of Ire; took incipient
    measures in Court of Oyer and Terminer in Utica - 7 Oct. 1836
ANSELL
  John, of Onondaga Co., native of G.B. - 12 Feb. 1833
ANSTICE
  Moses, of NYC - 27 Oct. 1832
ANTHONY
  Samuel, of Albany Co. - 30 Aug. 1847
ANTONINI
  Josephine, of NYC - 22 Sept. 1845
APP
  Jeremiah, of Utica, Oneida Co., native of Baden in Kingdom of
    Prussia - 26 Oct. 1837
APPLEYARD
  Thomas, of Brooklyn, Kings Co. - 7 Apr. 1843
ARBERTINT/ORBERTINT
  Huger, of Lyme, Jefferson Co. - 25 Feb. 1835
ARBUCKLE
  Joseph, of Montgomery, Orange Co., late of U.K. - 22 Mar. 1832

ARBUCKLE (continued)
  Thomas, of Montgomery, Orange Co., late of U.K. - 29 Dec. 1831
ARCHARD
  Henry, of Hastings, Westchester Co., shoemaker, but now in NYC -
    9 June 1846
ARMAND
  Marie, of NYC - 7 Sept. 1835
ARMENT
  George, of Verona, Oneida Co.; declared intent 19 Apr. 1843 -
    19 Nov. 1843
ARMISTEAD
  Francis, of Cayuga Co. - 2 Apr. 1847
ARMITAGE
  William, of Wayne Co. - 22 Sept. 1835
ARMOUR
  John, of Flatbush, Kings Co. - 16 July 1847
ARMSTEAD
  David, of Venice, Cayuga Co. - 17 Feb. 1845
ARMSTRONG
  John, of NYC, boarding-house keeper - 29 May 1824
  John, of NYC, carman, late of U.K. - 4 Jan. 1826
  John, of Walkill, Orange Co., native of Ire. - 17 Feb. 1829
  Mary (wife of John Armstrong, carman), of NYC - 23 Apr. 1834
  Thomas, residing at corner of Middagh and Kirk's Sts., Brooklyn,
    Kings Co., clock- and watchmaker - 15 Nov. 1843
  William, of NYC, gardener - 31 Jan. 1835
ARNOLD
  Henrietta Hearn (wife of Aaron Arnold, merchant), of NYC, for-
    merly of the Isle of Wight - 4 Aug. 1830
  Henry, of NYC, tailor - 7 Sept. 1836
  John, of Albany - 30 June 1838
ARROWSMITH
  Thomas, of Onondaga Co. - 9 Nov. 1840
ARTHUR
  Alexander, of Utica, Oneida Co., gentleman - 29 Aug. 1833
ARTOIS
  Anton, of NYC, gentleman - 11 Apr. 1835
ASH
  Ellen, for several years res. of Vernon, Oneida Co. - 24 Sept.,
    1846
  Joseph N., of NYC, plumber - 4 June 1842
ASHFIELD
  James, of Brooklyn, Kings Co. - 21 Mar. 1836
ASPINALL
  Charles, of Dutchess Co., for several years res. of U.S. - 25 Nov.
    1845
ATHERTON
  Charles, of NYC, late of U.K. - 22 July 1844
  Samuel, of NYC - 15 Apr. 1846
ATHOW
  Brett, of Rensselaer Co. - 25 Sept. 1838
ATKIN
  John, of Cayuga Co. - 22 Nov. 1831
ATKINS
  Mary, of Lansingburgh, Rensselaer Co. - 5 Apr. 1845
ATKINSON
  Bateman, of Kings Co. - 11 July 1836
  James, of Onondaga Co. - 22 Sept. 1835
  Sarah, of Scriba, Oswego Co. - 14 Dec. 1843
AUSTICK
  Samuel, of Otsego, Otsego Co., formerly of Leeds, Yorkshire,
    Eng. - Feb. 1829
AUSTIN
  Henry, of Sing Sing, Westchester Co. - 28 Nov. 1839
  John, of Onondaga Co. - 5 Oct. 1846

AUSTIN (continued)
  Thomas, of NYC - 24 Dec. 1834
  Thomas, of Poughkeepsie, Dutchess Co., late of Cambridgeshire,
    Eng. - 28 Apr. 1835
  Thomas, of NYC - 28 Mar. 1839
AUTHIER
  Joachim, of Albany - 3 June 1845
AVENELL
  Charles, of Columbia, Herkimer Co. - 13 Jan. 1842
AVERY
  George, of Buffalo, Erie Co., born in Eng., long res. of Black
    Rock, Erie Co. - 6 Apr. 1844
AVEZZANA/AVERZZANA
  Joseph, of NYC - 13 Feb. 1835
AVILA
  John, of Brooklyn, Kings Co. - 15 Aug. 1834
  Samuel, of Brooklyn, Kings Co. - 15 Aug. 1834
AVIS
  James K., of Westfield, Richmond Co. - 5 June 1845
AYLARD
  John, of NYC, carpenter - 30 June 1836

BABBAGE
  Richard, of Genesee Co. - 4 Feb. 1834
BACH
  Cloude, of Lewis Co. - 7 June 1842
BACHE
  Jacob, of Sheldon, Genesee Co., French subject - 27 Mar. 1839
BACHMAN
  Carl Frederick, of Croghan, Lewis Co. - 23 Sept. 1843
BACKER
  Daniel, of Wayne Co. - 28 Sept. 1830
BACON
  William, of Monroe Co. - 4 Dec. 1832
BAGE
  Robert, of NYC, hat manufacturer - 21 July 1834
BAHRET
  Jacob, of NYC, residing at No. 241 Rivington St., tailor - 18
    Nov. 1836
BAILEY
  Andrew, of Albany - 4 Nov. 1830
  James, of Hudson, Columbia Co. - 15 Mar. 1841
BAILLY
  Martin, of NYC, farmer, late of village of Gordoeyon, Dept. of
    Meurthe, France - 1 Nov. 1833
BAILY
  David, of Boston, Erie Co. - 22 Mar. 1832
BAIRD
  Arthur, of Canandaigua, Ontario Co. - 20 June 1837
BAISLEY
  Nancy, of NYC, late of the Netherlands - 13 Apr. 1830
BAKER
  Edward, of Utica, Oneida Co., lately from Worth, Kent Co., Eng. -
    14 Mar. 1831
  George, of Lewis Co. - 26 May 1842
  M.C., of NYC - 22 Oct. 1847
  Samuel, of Newcastle, Westchester Co. - 7 Mar. 1842
  Thomas, of Oswego, Oswego Co. - 21 Apr. 1836
  William, of Oneida Co., native of Fulkston, Kent Co., Eng. - 10
    Dec. 1832
BALL
  Thomas, of Saratoga, Saratoga Co. - (sworn in Rensselaer Co.) 2
    Jan. 1843
BALLANTINE
  James, of Williamsburgh, Kings Co., shoemaker - 19 Jan. 1847

New York Alien Residents, 1825-1848

BALANTINE (continued)
Robert, of Albany - 5 Feb. 1830
BALLER
John, of Troy - 14 Sept. 1831
BALLEY
Mary, several years res. of Brooklyn, Kings Co. - (sworn in NYC)
25 Oct. 1845
BALS
George, of Orleans, Jefferson Co., native of Hess, Germany - 24
July 1833
BALSAR
Margaret, of NYC - 24 Oct. 1846
BALZ
John Phillip, of Jefferson Co., born in Duchy of Hesse Darm-
stadt - 14 Jan. 1835
BANGE
Francis, of Lewis Co. - 12 July 1836
BANISTER
James, of Middlefield, Otsego Co., formerly of Stockport, Chester
Co., Eng. - 12 Oct. 1840
BANT
Johanna, of NYC - 28 Oct. 1835
BARBERICK
Agnes, of Irondequoit, Monroe Co. - 13 Oct. 1841
BARBEY
Andrew, of Brooklyn, Kings Co., born in Saarlouis, France, but
now situated in Prussia - 3 June 1839
BARKER
John, of Springfield, Otsego Co. - 17 May 1831
Marmaduke, of Onondaga Co. - 27 Feb. 1834
William G., of Walworth, Wayne Co., born 25 July 1809 in Adol-
phus, Lenox Co., Upper Canada; arrived in U.S. 27 Dec. 1833 -
6 Apr. 1840
BARLING
John, of NYC, chemist - 14 June 1832
BARLOW
Edward, of NYC - 24 Oct. 1847
BARNARD
Thomas, of NYC, gold-refiner - 9 Aug. 1839
BARNES
Charles, of Fishkill, Dutchess Co. - (sworn at Newburgh, Orange
Co.) 26 Apr. 1838
Edward, of Allegheny Co. - 25 July 1835
John, of NYC - 11 Oct. 1837
Mary (wife of John Barnes, comedian), of NYC - 3 Nov. 1837
Samuel C., of Brooklyn, Kings Co. - 22 Apr. 1837
BARNS
Hurdman, of Canandaigua, Ontario Co. - 21 May 1844
BAROWSKY
Charles Edward, of NYC, Prussian subject - 28 Nov. 1826
BARR
Nathaniel, of Newburgh, Orange Co. - 31 Oct. 1838
BARRATT
John, of Orange Co., late of Stapleford, Nottinghamshire, Eng. -
4 Nov. 1829
John, of Poughkeepsie, Dutchess Co., formerly of Nottinghamshire,
Eng. - 3 May 1845
BARRETT
Edward, of NYC, late res. of Bath, Eng. - 21 June 1836
BARRNETT
William, of Oswegatchie, St. Lawrence Co. - 5 Jan. 1830
BARRON
Joseph, of NYC, furrier - 26 Nov. 1828
BARROW
Robert, of Albany, late of London, Eng. - 17 Sept. 1832

BARRY
 Mary (wife of Richard Barry), of NYC - 27 Sept. 1844
 Thomas, of Chautauque Co. - 25 June 1847
BARTELLEMY
 Pierre F., of Lyme, Jefferson Co. - 25 Feb. 1835
BARTHOLMA
 George, of Brighton, Monroe Co. - 6 Nov. 1837
BARTOL
 Emma J. (wife of Barnabas H. Bartol and daughter of Edward Welch-
   man), of NYC, formerly of Kineton, Eng., where she was born on
   2 Apr. 1821); her father, with all his family, removed to the
   U.S. in Aug. 1839; her father died 20 Mar. 1845 - 24 June 1846
BARTON
 James, of Stockholm, St. Lawrence Co. - 21 June 1828
BARTOW
 Ellis, of NYC - 1 June 1846
BASHALL
 Jean David, of Mexico, Oswego Co. - 2 Feb. 1831
 Jean George, of Mexico, Oswego Co. - 2 Feb. 1831
BASKERVILLE
 Mary Ann (wife of William Baskerville), of NYC, native of Ire. -
   24 Sept. 1840; another entry states that she came to the U.S.
   in 1836 and was sworn 7 Nov. 1840
 William, of NYC, native of Ire., came to U.S. in 1836 - 7 Nov.
   1840; another item states he was sworn 24 Sept. 1840
BASSETT
 Alexander, of NYC - 24 Nov. 1834
 John, of New Lisbon, Otsego Co. - 11 Oct. 1836
BASSOTTI
 Constantino, of NYC, late of Italy, turner - 10 Feb. 1836
BASTABLE
 Stephen, of Onondaga Co. - 28 Sept. 1836
BATCHERS
 Daniel, of Madison, Madison Co., born in Co. of Sussex, Eng.,
   aged 29 on 2 Jan. 1832 - Oct. 1831
BATEMAN
 Edward, of Albany - 3 Sept. 1832
 Joseph F, of NYC, brass finisher - 14 Apr. 1834
BATES
 Thomas, of Buffalo, Erie Co. - 11 Nov. 1834
BATH
 Richard P., of Buffalo, Erie Co.; emigrated from G.B. in 1830 -
   21 Mar. 1836
BATSON
 John, of Otsego Co. - 25 Oct. 1831
 Josiah, of Cherry Valley, Otsego Co. - 3 Feb. 1830
 Thomas Chew, of Otsego Co. - 25 Oct. 1831
BATTIN; see BUTTIN
BAULY
 Charles, of Jefferson Co. - 31 Oct. 1836
BAUMLER
 John, of NYC - 15 Oct. 1838
BAVIN
 Richard, of Oneida Co., formerly of Calverton, Buckinghamshire,
   Eng. - 7 Aug. 1840
BAXTER
 William, of Brooklyn, Kings Co., born in U.K. - 20 Mar. 1837
BAYARD
 Peter, of NYC - 26 Nov. 1836
BAYER
 Louis, of NYC, doing business in Fulton St. - 8 June 1836
 Michael, of Irondequoit, Monroe Co. - 3 Sept. 1847
BAYERLEY/BYERLEY/BYERLY
 Samuel, of NYC, merchant - 13 Feb. 1835

New York Alien Residents, 1825-1848

BAYLIS
  Charles, of Otsego, native of G.B. - 12 May 1830
BEACH
  Thomas, of NYC - 5 May 1846
BEAK
  Charles, of Onondaga, Onondaga Co. - 8 Feb. 1847
BEAL
  John, of Onondaga Co. - 27 Aug. 1834
BEALES
  John Charles, of NYC, physician - 4 June 1836
BEAMAN
  Jane (wife of Benjamin Beaman), of NYC - 6 July 1846
BEARD
  Henry, of Albany Co. - 16 Dec. 1847
BEARSLEY/BASELEY
  Samuel, of Kings Co. - 17 July 1835
BEARTY
  Alexander, of New Berlin, Chenango Co. - Feb. 1831
BEATTIÉ
  John, of Hannibal, Oswego Co. - 31 Jan. 1840
  Nelson, of Syracuse, Onondaga Co. - 28 Sept. 1838
  Walter, of Cortland Co. - 31 Jan. 1848
  William, of Orleans, Jefferson Co. - 15 May 1835
BEATTY
  Robert, of NYC, born in Ire.; subsequently resided on Island of
    St. Croix and became a Danish subject; arrived in U.S. in July
    1841 - 20 Sept. 1842
BEAVAN
  Thomas, of Albany - 29 Aug. 1844
BEAVER
  John, of NYC, painter - 11 Aug. 1841
BECAR
  Noel J., of NYC, merchant, French subject - 16 Oct. 1824
BECHET
  Claudius C., of NYC, late of France - 22 June 1836
BECK
  James, of NYC, born in Scotland, member of firm of James Beck &
    Co. - 18 Feb. 1846
  John, of NYC, born in Eng.; came to NYC 27 Oct. 1827 - 11 May 1831
  John Philip, of Rochester, Monroe Co. - 12 Oct. 1837
  John S., of NYC - 23 May 1834
BECKER
  Daniel, of Frankford, Herkimer Co. - 4 Jan. 1836
BECKET
  Francis, of NYC, native of France - 2 July 1834
BECKWITH
  George, of Sangerfield, Oneida Co. - 12 Sept. 1831
  Joseph, of Sangerfield, Oneida Co. - 12 Sept. 1831
BEDNATSKY
  John Frederick, of Lewis Co. - 20 Sept. 1831
BEDOINE
  Claude, of Albany - 3 Dec. 1833
BEELMAN
  John M., of Brooklyn, Kings Co. - 11 Feb. 1834
BEER
  James, of NYC, house-carpenter, late of Eng. - 26 Feb. 1827
BEGUIN
  John Lewis, of NYC - 18 May 1835
BEHAN
  Susan, of Syracuse, Onondaga Co. - 14 Apr. 1845
  Thomas, of Rochester, Monroe Co. - 14 May 1835
BEIRNE
  Michael O., of Cortland Co. - 15 Feb. 1838
BEITTER
  Dorothy, of Buffalo, Erie Co. - 3 June 1839

BEKLE/BEKEL
  Barbara, of Erie Co. - 13 Mar. 1835
BELL
  Catharine J. (wife of John Bell, of NYC, baker), of NYC - 26 Oct.
    1847
  Samuel, of Queensbury, Warren Co. - 13 Mar. 1835
  Thomas, of NYC, merchant - 23 Aug. 1825
BELLAMY
  Joseph M., of NYC, collector, born in Eng.; arrived in NYC from
    Europe in 1824 - 12 Feb. 1830
BELLER
  John, of Williamsburgh, Kings Co. - 16 July 1846
BELLEW
  Thomas, of Watertown, Jefferson Co. - 7 Nov. 1833
BELLOW
  James, of Albany - 16 Oct. 1830
BELMONT
  August, of NYC - 20 Apr. 1846
BEMIS
  Edward, of Rochester, Monroe Co. - 17 Dec. 1836
BENFIELD
  Nathaniel, of Eaton, Madison Co. - 17 May 1843
BENNETT
  Edward W., of Buffalo, Erie Co. - 11 July 1835
  Elizabeth (wife of Andrew H. Bennett), of NYC - 11 Mar. 1846
  Henrietta Agnes, of NYC - 30 Jan. 1845
  Henry, of Allegheny Co. - 26 June 1832
  James Gordon, of NYC - 30 Jan. 1845
  John, of Allegheny Co. - 26 June 1832
  John, of Wayne Co. - 23 May 1832
  Philip, Jr., of NYC - 4 Jan. 1831
  Samuel, of Richmond Co.; declaration of intent 28 Jan. 1842 -
    12 Mar. 1845
  Sarah (wife of Thomas Bennett, of NYC), of NYC - 29 Mar. 1845
  William, of Allegheny Co. - 26 June 1832
BENNETTS
  Louedy, of Sweden, Monroe Co., where has resided nearly 3 years
    past; was born in Co. of Cornwall, G. B.; removed to U. S.
    1 July 1832 - 9 May 1844
BENNIE
  John, of Homer, Cortland Co. - 6 Feb. 1834
BENSON
  Berkett, of Erie Co., lately come to U.S. - 14 Mar. 1836
  Michael, of Erie Co. - 8 June 1832
BENTLEY
  John, of Lockport, Niagara Co. - 3 June 1836
  Joseph, of Onondaga Co. - 7 Nov. 1838
  William, of Niagara Co. - 10 Feb. 1836
BERANEK/BERANECK
  George, of Rochester, Monroe Co. - 17 Oct. 1844
BERGER
  Pierre Alexis, of NYC, native of Lyons, France - 8 Apr. 1840
BERGOUZIE/ BERGONZIE
  Eugene, of NYC - 19 Apr. 1834
BERNARD
  Jean, of Le Ray, Jefferson Co., born at Frederic Fontaine, France,
    in 1800; removed to New York in 1830 - 22 Mar. 1842
BERNHARD
  George, of Wayne Co. - 28 Sept. 1836
BEROUD
  Paul, of NYC - 26 Oct. 1846
BERRILL
  John A., of Sangersfield, Oneida Co. - 11 Mar. 1842
BERRINGER
  Jacob, of Albany - 12 Sept. 1835

8

BERSH
  Joseph, of Buffalo, Erie Co. - 22 Aug. 1831
BERSHOUD
  Louis, of Lewis Co. - 21 June 1836
BESHER
  John, of Lancaster, Erie Co. - 31 Oct. 1840
BEST
  Francis, of Onondaga Co. - 25 Aug. 1836
  John, of Onondaga Co. - 25 Aug. 1836
  William, of Onondaga Co. - 25 Aug. 1836
BETZ
  Frederick, of Erie Co., native of Lieblos in the Chur Dukedom of
    Hessen, Germany - 30 Aug. 1844
BEURELE
  Charles, of Buffalo, Erie Co. - 27 Aug. 1835
BEVAN
  Edward, of NYC - 16 Dec. 1833
BEYER
  George H., of NYC - 11 June 1846
BIABOT
  Pierre, of NYC - 24 June 1840
BICAR
  John, of ÑYC, carpenter - 1 May 1832
BICKELHAUPT
  Peter, of NYC, milkman - 13 Oct. 1845
BIDDELE
  Joseph, of Lockport, Niagara Co. - 11 Mar. 1846
BIDDLE
  William, of NYC - 29 Aug. 1833
BIDEN
  John, of Rochester, Monroe Co. - 23 Mar. 1847
BIEHN
  Lorenz, of NYC - 24 Dec. 1844
BIEHU
  Margaretha, of NYC - 9 Nov. 1843
BIELLE
  John Baptiste Joseph, of NYC, box-maker - 9 Sept. 1831
BIGDEN
  Robert, of Erie Co. - 12 Dec. 1826
BIGGS
  John, of Dunkirk, Chautauque Co., native of Scotland - 9 Apr.
    1831
  Peter, of Elmira, Chemung Co. - 8 Aug. 1842
BILDERSEE
  Isaac, of NYC, late of the U.K. - 2 Sept. 1843
BILLIN
  Charles, of NYC - 2 Sept. 1847
BILLING
  Samuel, of NYC - 2 Sept. 1847
BINDEN
  John, of Genesee Co. - 4 Feb. 1834
BINTZ
  Francis, of Lewis Co. - 16 May 1840
  Michael, of Lewis Co. - 16 May 1840
BIRCH
  Rachel, of NYC - 3 Aug. 1833
BIRDEE
  Harry, of Marcellus, Onondaga Co. - 31 Jan. 1848
BIRKIN
  Thomas W., of Hamilton, Madison Co., native of G.B. - 4 Feb. 1834
BIRMINGHAM
  Andrew, of Rockland Co. - 8 Feb. 1837
BIRNIE
  Alexander, of Hastings, Westchester Co. - 24 Apr. 1843

New York Alien Residents, 1825-1848

BISANTZ
  Jacob, of Erie Co. - 19 Mar. 1832
  John, of Erie Co. - 19 Mar. 1832
BISDEE
  Edward, of Skaneateles,Onondaga Co. - 27 Dec. 1831
  Thomas Orlando, of Onondaga Co. - 6 Oct. 1835
BISHOP
  Edward W., of City and Co. of Albany - 7 Sept. 1836
  Mary (wife of Edward W. Bishop, of NYC, counsellor at law), of
    NYC - 28 Jan. 1845
BISSOU
  Alexander Theodore, of NYC - 27 Dec. 1841
BLACK
  Thomas G., of Buffalo, Erie Co., native of London, Eng.; migrated
    to U.S. in Mar. 1832 - 31 July 1835
  William, of Brooklyn, Kings Co. - 1 Aug. 1837
BLACKBURN
  John, of Hartland, Niagara Co. - 16 Oct. 1846
  Thomas, of Hartland, Niagara Co. - 19 Oct. 1846
BLACKSTOCK
  James, of NYC - 20 Feb. 1832
BLADE/BLAID
  Richard, of Pamelia, Jefferson Co. - 24 Apr. 1837
BLAIR
  Alexander, of NYC - 1 Dec. 1845
  Henry B., of NYC - 2 Mar. 1843
BLAKE
  William, of Herkimer, Herkimer Co. - 15 Feb. 1832
BLANC(or BLANE?)
  Eugene, of Le Roy, Jefferson Co. - 28 Dec. 1831
BLEECKER
  Sebastena Cornelia (daughter of Dirk Mentz, dec'd), of Albany Co.,
    born in the Netherlands - 30 Sept. 1847
BLENSLEY
  James, of NYC, carpenter - 14 July 1836
BLEOO
  John, of Queens Co. - 15 Sept. 1843
BLISS
  Theodore C., of NYC, merchant, doing business at No. 12 Platt St. -
    18 Aug. 1836
BLOTT
  Benjamin, of Richmond Co. - 17 June 1843
  Thomas, of Montgomery Co., formerly of Co. of Northampton, Eng. -
    30 Mar. 1831
BLOUDAN
  Anthony, of Jefferson Co. - 12 Sept. 1842
BLUM
  Abraham, of NYC, merchant, subject of Prussia, res. of NYC past
    4 years - 17 May 1838
BLUMER
  Gabriel, of Onondaga Co. - 19 Dec. 1837
BLY
  James, of Clarkstown, Rockland Co. - 7 Jan. 1847
BLYTH
  John, of Wayne Co. - 26 Jan. 1831
BOASE
  John, of Canandaigua, Ontario Co. - 20 May 1831
BOCHMELER
  Henry, of Wayne Co. - 26 Sept. 1833
BODELL
  Samuel, of Pamelia, Jefferson Co. - 24 Dec. 1832
BODEN
  Augustus F., of NYC - 30 Dec. 1835
  William F., of NYC - 30 Dec. 1835

BOESE
  Ann (widow of Henry Boese, late of NYC), of NYC - 30 Sept. 1844
BOEUF
  Joseph, of NYC, teacher - 30 Dec. 1833
BOGART
  David D., of Troy, Rensselaer Co. - 5 June 1845
BOHANA
  Thomas, of NYC - 24 May 1831
BOIZARD
  Eustache Napoleon, of NYC - 10 May 1834
BOLAM
  John, of Burlington, Otsego Co. - 24 Sept. 1835
BOLL
  Daniel, of NYC - 10 Dec. 1841
  Samuel Daniel, of Rochester, Monroe Co. - 14 Apr. 1836
BOLLE (or BROLL?)
  Peter Samuel, of Rochester, Monroe Co. - 28 Mar. 1836
BOLLIN
  John, of Niagara, Niagara Co. - 7 Oct. 1844
BOLTON
  George, of Vernon, Oneida Co. - 16 June 1834
  George, of Onondaga Co. - 7 Oct. 1834
  Mathias, of NYC - 4 Jan. 1847
BOMMER
  George, of Kings Co.; came from France in Aug. 1839 - 21 Feb. 1845
BONICHON
  Benoist/Benvit, of NYC - 10 Nov. 1825
BONNAR
  James, of Burlington, Otsego Co. - 15 Sept. 1834
BONNARD
  Louis, of NYC, late of France - 3 Oct. 1846
BONNEFOND
  John Baptiste, of Paulina Hancock Twp., Delaware Co. - 24 Sept.
    1840
BONNEFOUX
  Laurent, of NYC - 4 Apr. 1836
BONNETT
  Thomas, of Barre, Orleans Co. - 28 Jan. 1839
BONSOR
  Jane (wife of Joseph Bonsor), of NYC - 23 Nov. 1842
BOOT
  Harriet, of Buffalo, Erie Co., subject of U.K. - 1 Feb. 1840
BOUCHER
  Alfred, of NYC - 31 Oct. 1839
BOULES
  Leonard, of Jefferson Co. - 23 Dec. 1836
BOWEN
  Mary, of NYC - 28 Dec. 1845
  Patrick, of Mamaroneck, Westchester Co., farmer - 1 Mar. 1832
BOWLEY
  Thomas, of Watervliet, Albany Co. - (sworn in Rensselaer Co.) 13
    Dec. 1845
  William, of Watervliet, Albany Co. - 13 Dec. 1845
BOWMAN
  Roger, of Stanford, Dutchess Co. - 11 Feb. 1832
BOWN
  Mathias, of Westfield, Richmond Co., gardener - 30 Mar. 1847
BOX
  John, Jr., of Richmond, Oswego Co. - 10 Jan. 1838
BOYCE
  William, of Williamsburgh, Kings Co., carpenter - 24 Dec. 1831
BOYD
  Alexander, of Poughkeepsie, Dutchess Co., formerly of Ayrshire,
    Scotland - 15 Jan. 1842
  Duncan, of Sullivan Co. - 26 Jan. 1842

BOYD (continued)
  John, of Sullivan Co., carpenter - 20 Nov. 1841
  Thomas William, of NYC - 7 June 1846
BOYL
  Dominic, of Salina, Onondaga Co. - 13 Mar. 1830
BOYLAN
  John D., of NYC, gentleman - 5 June 1829
BOYLE
  Barney, of Brooklyn, Kings Co., oilcloth manufacturer - 26 Mar.
    1828
  Edward, of Brooklyn, Kings Co. - 5 Nov. 1825
BOYLES
  James, of Pike, Allegheny Co., subject of U.K. - (sworn in Genesee
    Co.) 26 Mar. 1839
BOYNE
  Phillip, of Auburn, Cayuga Co. - 28 May 1846
BRABHAM
  Joseph, of NYC, late of U.K. - 16 June 1835
BRABO
  Joaquin Duran, of NYC, merchant - 7 Sept. 1827
BRACONIER
  George, of Wayne Co. - 26 Sept. 1833
  Philip, of Wayne Co. - 26 Sept. 1833
BRADFORD
  George, of Farmington, Ontario Co. - 14 Aug. 1846
  Robert, of Onondaga Co. - 4 Dec. 1837
BRADLEY
  Hugh, of Rochester, Monroe Co. - 8 May 1839
  William, of City of Albany - 4 Jan. 1836
BRADY
  John, of Kings Co. - 15 June 1829
  Patrick, of Kings Co. - 15 June 1829
  Philip, of Dryden, Tompkins Co., late of Co. Caven, Ulster, Ire. -
    19 May 1834
  William, of Winfield, Herkimer Co. - 4 Sept. 1832
BRAEM
  Rudolph, of Brooklyn, Kings Co. - 2 May 1838
BRAINE
  John Josiah, of NYC - 3 Jan. 1845
BRAITHWAITE
  Robert, of Rochester, Monroe Co.; emigrated to U. S. in 1831 -
    5 Oct. 1835
BRAKEFIELD
  James, of Schenectady Co. - 9 Oct. 1838
  John, of Schenectady Co. - 9 Oct. 1838
  Louisa, of Schenectady Co. - 9 Oct. 1838
  Mary, of Schenectady Co. - 9 Oct. 1838
  Mary Ann, of Schenectady Co. - 9 Oct. 1838
BRAMLEY
  Thomas, of Newburgh, Orange Co. - 25 May 1842
BRANCHE
  Jean, of Lyme, Jefferson Co., late of France - 16 May 1832
BRANDON
  Isaac L., of NYC, merchant - 3 Apr. 1829
  Joseph, of NYC, born in London, Eng.; first came to NYC in
    Nov. of 1826; he remained about 1 year; then he went away
    on business; he returned to NYC in Jan. of 1829 - 1 Aug.
    1829
BRANDRETH
  Benjamin, of NYC, physician - 3 Aug. 1836
BRANIFF
  Thomas, of NYC - 30 Jan. 1836
BRANNON
  Christopher, of NYC, mason - 27 July 1827

BRASS
  David, of Pike, Allegheny Co. - 5 May 1843
BRATLEY
  Benjamin, of Hamilton, Oneida Co. - 6 July 1838
BRAYLEY
  Joseph, of Hartland, Niagara Co., late of Devonshire, Eng. - 11
    Feb. 1835
BREADY
  James, of NYC, drayman - 1 June 1827
BRECKEL
  Lodowick, of Sag Harbour, Suffolk Co. - 30 May 1840
BRECKONS
  John, of Albion, Oswego Co., native of Witheril, Cumberland Co.,
    U.K. - 15 Sept. 1835
BREEN
  Mores, of City and Co. of Albany; declaration of intent 31 Oct.
    1846 - 5 Nov. 1847
BREITENBECKER
  Lewis, of Gorham, Ontario Co., age 45, native of Dept. of Lower
    Rhine, France, res. of U.S. for about 5 years - 20 Aug. 1833
BREKENSHAW
  Richard, of Palmyra, Wayne Co. - 25 Dec. 1838
BREMEYER
  George William, of NYC - 3 Aug. 1840
BRENNAN
  Thomas, of Florence, Oneida Co. - 11 Dec. 1826
BRENNEN
  Andrew, of Rochester, Monroe Co., subject of G.B. - 20 Jan. 1848
BRENON
  Claude, of Turin, Lewis Co. - 26 July 1836
BRENT
  Benjamin, of Buffalo, Erie Co. - 4 Oct. 1843
BRETEY
  Elizabeth, of Buffalo, Erie Co. - 4 Dec. 1838
BREWIN
  Edward, of Thompson, Sullivan Co., age 24; came from G.B. to N.Y.
    in 1818 - 16 June 1831
BRICE
  Elizabeth, of Brooklyn, Kings Co., born in Pontefract, York Co.,
    Eng., on 21 Aug. 1814; came to U.S. 8 Oct. 1830 - 1 Aug. 1844
  John, of Brooklyn, Kings Co. - 9 June 1834
BRIDGE
  John, of Allen, Allegheny Co. - 28 Apr. 1837
BRIDGER
  Edward, of Sing Sing, Westchester Co. - 31 May 1834
  James, of Troy, Rensselaer Co, free white person, age 27 and up-
    wards- 15 Mar. 1830
BRIENS
  Owen, of Onondaga Co. - 17 Oct. 1839
BRIGGS
  William, of Greenport, Columbia Co. - 22 Oct. 1846
  William, of Greenport, Columbia Co. - 2 Nov. 1846
BRIGHT
  Edward, of Utica, Oneida Co. - 6 Apr. 1831
BRIGHTMAN
  James, of NYC - 24 Apr. 1834
BRILL
  Henry, of Minden, Montgomery Co. - 22 Sept. 1837
BRINKWORTH
  William, of NYC, shoemaker - 15 May 1826
BRINNEN
  John, of Minden, Montgomery Co. - 5 Dec. 1838
BRISTOW
  Thomas, of Brooklyn - 4 Apr. 1832

BRITONNIERE
  Auguste, of Brooklyn, Kings Co., gardener, French citizen - 22
    May 1830
BRITTAIN
  Hugh, of NYC, cartman - 6 Dec. 1827
BROADFOOT
  James, of Erie Co. - 11 Dec. 1835
BROADHURST
  Mary (wife of Charles Broadhurst), of NYC - 5 Sept. 1845
BROCKSBANK
  William, of Hudson, Columbia Co., native of Skelton, Yorkshire,
    Eng. - 13 Aug. 1836
BRODIE
  John, Jr., of NYC, slater - 27 June 1831
BRODRICK
  Michael, of Albany - 5 Dec. 1840
BROLL; see BOLLE
BRONNER
  Christian, of Erie Co., age 24 - 30 Mar. 1830
  Philip, of Erie Co., age 23 - 30 Mar. 1830
BROOKER
  William, of Oswego,Tioga Co. but at present in NYC - 15 Nov. 1825
BROOKS
  Charles, of Otsego Co. - 30 May 1836
  Thomas, of Dutchess Co., native of Yorkshire, Eng. - 5 June 1834
  Thomas, of Galen, Wayne Co., British subject - 23 Sept. 1840
BROSNAHAN
  Daniel, of Troy, Rensselaer Co. - 24 Oct. 1846
BROTHERS
  Lewis, of Albany - 29 Oct. 1835
BROUGHTON
  Edward, of Brooklyn, Kings Co., late of G.B. - 20 Apr. 1826
BROUSSEAN
  Joseph, of Saratoga Springs, Saratoga Co. - 26 Apr. 1841
BROWN
  Andrew, of NYC - 19 Apr. 1845
  Ann (wife of Peter A. Brown), of NYC - 25 May 1847
  Catharine, of Brooklyn, Kings Co. - 12 Sept. 1837
  Eliza (wife of Jesse Brown, of NYC), of NYC - 1 Mar. 1838
  Hugh, of NYC - 23 Apr. 1844
  James, of Oneida Co., native of Glangere, Suffolk Co., Eng. - 10
    Dec. 1832
  James, of Albany Co. - 18 Oct. 1847
  James E., of Lewis Co. - 21 Sept. 1830
  John, of NYC, weaver - 10 Aug. 1830
  John, of NYC, milkman - 29 Oct. 1836
  John, of Albany - 1 May 1839
  John P., of NYC, victualler - 15 Oct. 1835
  Joseph, of NYC - 22 July 1835
  Joseph P., of Troy, Rensselaer Co. - 12 Jan. 1836
  Matilda, of Brooklyn, Kings Co., widow - 23 Jan. 1830
  Robert, of Wayne Co. - 25 Jan. 1832
  Thomas, of NYC, native of Eng.; came to State of N.Y. in 1822 -
    13 Oct. 1836
  William, of Troy, Rensselaer Co. - 10 May 1836
  William, of Newburgh, Orange Co., British subject - 27 Apr. 1839
  William, of Aurelius, Cayuga Co., where he has resided since
    Sept. 1844, born in Co. of Westmoreland, Eng., age now 25; he
    came to U.S. in 1843 - 13 Sept. 1847
  William Henry, of NYC - 14 Mar. 1834
  William P., of Buffalo, Erie Co. - 29 Apr. 1833
  William Thomas, of NYC - 2 Sept. 1834
BRUCCIANI
  Nicola, of NYC; made declaration of intent and sworn 30 Jan.
    1844

New York Alien Residents, 1825-1848

BRUCE
  David, of Rochester, Monroe Co. - 26 Jan. 1847
BRUCKNER
  Christopher, of NYC, merchant, late of Germany - 3 Feb. 1835
BRUE
  Eugene, of NYC, merchant - 5 Feb. 1847
  Marie Catharine (wife of Eugene Brue), of NYC - 6 Feb. 1847
BRUNCK
  Francis Charles, of Wayne Co. - 26 Sept. 1834
BRUNT
  Robert, of NYC, cartman - 5 Mar. 1827
BRYANT
  Charles, of Onondaga Co., native of Eng.; arrived in U.S. 20 May
    1836 - 13 Nov. 1845
BRYDEN
  John, of Kirkland, Oneida Co. - 18 Feb. 1843
BRYSON
  John, of Montgomery, Orange Co. - 24 Sept. 1832
BUBEAR
  William, of NYC, labourer - 20 Sept. 1827
BUCHANAN
  Alexander, of NYC, dyer - 3 Apr. 1835
  Margaret (widow of James Buchanan), of NYC - 13 Nov. 1846
BUCHOZ
  Louis R., of NYC, watch-casemaker - 11 June 1834
BUCKHOUT
  George, of NYC - 5 Apr. 1837
BUCKINGHAM
  Thomas, of Plattsburgh, Clinton Co. - 11 May 1837
BUCKLAND
  John W., of Buffalo, Erie Co., late of London, Eng. - 19 Mar. 1836
BUCKLEY
  John, of Java, Genesee Co., subject of U.K. - 6 Dec. 1838
  William, of NYC - 22 Aug. 1837
BUDDLE
  John, of Canajoharie, Montgomery Co., born citizen of G.B. - 26
    Jan. 1832
BUERGER
  Ernst Moritz, of Buffalo, Erie Co. - 20 Oct. 1844
BUHRE
  Conrad, of NYC, gardener, born in Prussian Minden, Prussia; made
    declaration of intent on 4 Jan. 1838 - 12 Jan. 1838
BUHRING
  John, of Sheldon, Genesee Co. - 2 Feb. 1836
BULL
  William, of Sing Sing, Westchester Co. - 28 May 1832
  William, of NYC - 21 Mar. 1836
BULLIONS/BULLIOUS
  Peter, of NYC - 18 Oct. 1847
BULLOCK
  William, Jr., of Evans, Erie Co. - 17 Aug. 1836
BULLYMORE
  Thomas, of Buffalo, Erie Co., British subject; took incipient
    measures on 18 Aug. 1844 - 17 May 1845
BULYED
  Francis, of Wayne Co. - 27 Nov. 1831
BUNN
  William, of Ontario Co. - 15 Oct. 1846
BURDEN
  Joseph W., of NYC, ship chandler - 10 Oct. 1842
  Maria (wife of Joseph W. Burden, of Williamsburgh, Kings Co., late
    of NYC, merchant) - (sworn in NYC) 16 Aug. 1844
BURDETT
  Charles, of NYC, rule manufacturer - 20 Jan. 1848

15

BURDGE
  William, of Brooklyn, Kings Co., British subject - 25 May 1843
BURGESS
  John, of Bushwick, Kings Co., farmer - 22 Dec. 1830
BURGERT
  Henry, of NYC, baker - 21 May 1827
BURK
  James, of NYC, late of Ire., res. of NYC since 1817 when he came
    from Ire. - 10 Apr. 1827
  John, of Onondaga Co. - 19 Mar. 1839
  William, of De Kalb, St. Lawrence Co., born in Ire.; removed to
    U.S. in 1825 - 16 June 1836
BURKE
  Lawrence, of Flushing, Queens Co., house-carpenter, born on Is.
    of Newfoundland - 11 Aug. 1840
  Myles, of NYC, gentleman - 24 May 1831
  Richard, of NYC - 28 Oct. 1845
BURLIN
  Henry, of Buffalo, Erie Co. - 29 Nov. 1847
BURNE
  Percy, of Monroe Co. - 13 Apr. 1836
BURNETT
  William, of NYC - 1 June 1831
BURNS
  Michael, of Lewis Co. - 21 Sept. 1830
  Peter, of NYC, manufacturer - 9 Nov. 1825
  Thomas, of Onondaga Co. - 13 Mar. 1838
BURRELL
  Catharine Rodon, of NYC - 10 Sept. 1839
  Susan Jane, of NYC - 10 Sept. 1839
BURRIDGE
  Joseph, of NYC - 12 Jan. 1848
BURRILL
  George Pratt, of NYC - 19 Aug. 1839
BURROWS
  John, of NYC - 1 Oct. 1845
  Thomas, of NYC, merchant, residing at 242 Stanton St. - 10 May
    1844
BURT
  William, of Wayne Co. - 28 Jan. 1840
BURTON
  John, of NYC - 25 Apr. 1832
  William, of Hudson, Columbia Co. - 13 Dec. 1841
BURY
  Lewis, of Laurens, Otsego Co. - 14 Sept. 1837
BUSBY
  John, of NYC - 24 Aug. 1835
BUSCHER
  George, of Onondaga Co. - 28 Nov. 1835
BUSER
  George, of Kings Co. - 27 Aug. 1838
BUSH
  George Martin, of Buffalo, Erie Co. - 3 Sept. 1831
  Jean Michel, of Lewis Co. - 31 Aug. 1838
  John, of Watson, Lewis Co. - 25 July 1840
  Michael, of Watson, Lewis Co. - 25 July 1840
BUSHE
  Elizabeth (wife of George Bushe, of NYC, physician) - 11 May 1837
  George, of NYC - 18 Apr. 1836
BUSKETT
  Charles Thomas, of Erie Co. - 12 Dec. 1826
BUSS
  Jesse, of NYC, baker - 21 Mar. 1828
BUTCHER
  Samuel, of NYC, formerly of Eng. - 27 Dec. 1826

New York Alien Residents, 1825-1848

BUTT
  John, of NYC, late of U.K. - 30 June 1830
BUTTERWORTH
  Archibald H., of NYC - 4 Mar. 1837
BUTTIN/BATTIN
  Joseph, of Denmark, Lewis Co. - 6 Jan. 1836
BUTTLE
  Robert, of NYC - 20 Feb. 1837
BYERS
  David D., of NYC - 29 June 1830
BYRNE
  Andrew, of NYC, house-carpenter; made declaration of intent 6
    Aug. 1823 - 15 Oct. 1827
  Andrew, of NYC - 10 Feb. 1842
  Charles, of NYC, tailor - 18 Jan. 1826
  Martin, of Brooklyn, Kings Co. - 17 Dec. 1847
  Walter, of NYC, merchant - 1 Dec. 1826
  William F., of Onondaga Co. - 24 Sept. 1838
BYRNES
  Elizabeth, of Lenox, Madison Co., born in Ire. - 25 Sept. 1834
  Patrick, of NYC, laborer - 24 Apr. 1828
BYRNS
  Felix, of Cambridge, Washington Co. - 24 Mar. 1831

CABRE
  John, of NYC, rigger and stevedore - 1 Nov. 1825
CACKETT/CAXKETT
  Charles, of Otsego Co. - 15 Apr. 1833
CAHILL
  Eliza, of Brooklyn, Kings Co., native of Ire. - 10 Sept. 1842
CAIRD
  James, of Antwerp, Jefferson Co. - 16 Nov. 1831
CALDER
  James, of NYC - 28 Feb. 1846
CALDERWOOD
  David, of Perth, Fulton Co. - (sworn in Albany) 11 Nov. 1843
CALDWALL
  William, of Freetown, Cortland Co. - 30 Jan. 1833
CALDWELL
  James G., of Freetown, Cortland Co. - 28 Jan. 1834
  Sarah, of Rochester, Monroe Co., British subject, res. of U.S.
    for past 18 years - 8 Apr. 1839
CALEN/CALIN
  Xavier, of Lyme, Jefferson Co. - 13 Jan. 1843
CALL
  Charles, of Wayne Co. - 29 Jan. 1834
CALLAN
  Francis, of NYC, labourer - 6 June 1827
CALLENDER
  David, of Albany - 14 Sept. 1830
CALLIGHAN
  Michael, of Williamsburgh, Kings Co., native of Ire. - 26 Apr.
    1845
CALLIS
  Thomas, of NYC - 7 Apr. 1832
CALVERT
  Henry, of Kings Co. - 22 June 1836
CAMBERS
  William, of Orleans Co. - 18 May 1835
CAMERON
  James, of Rockland Co. - 8 Apr. 1837
CAMP
  Ellen (wife of Charles Camp), of NYC - 22 Apr. 1845
CAMPBELL
  Andrew, of NYC - 30 Aug. 1847
  Catharine, of NYC, late of Co. Derry, Ire. - 23 May 1844

17

CAMPBELL (continued)
 Francis, of NYC, residing at 162 Houston St., blacksmith - 6 Feb. 1837
 George, of Rochester, Monroe Co.; emigrated to U.S. in 1813 - 5 Oct. 1825
 Isabella, of NYC, late of Co. Derry, Ire. - 23 May 1844
 James, of NYC, stone-cutter - 3 Apr. 1826
 James, of NYC, formerly of Ire. - 2 Mar. 1843
 James, of Watertown, Jefferson Co. - 30 Mar. 1843
 James, of Hudson, Columbia Co. - 16 May 1828
 James, of Le Roy, Genesee Co., born in Perthshire, Scotland; emigrated to U.S. in 1814 - 5 Feb. 1831
 James, of German Flatts, Herkimer Co. - 24 May 1831
 John, of Ghent, Columbia Co. - 5 Apr. 1830
 John, of Rochester, Monroe Co. - 7 Feb. 1839
 John, of Mohawk, Montgomery Co. - 11 Jan. 1842
 Margaret, of NYC, widow - 8 Feb. 1837
 Mary, of Ogdensburgh, St. Lawrence Co. - 6 Aug. 1836
 Mary, of NYC, late of Co. Derry, Ire. - 23 May 1844
 Peter, of Castleton, Richmond Co. - 25 Dec. 1830
CAMPION
 Catharine (widow of Patrick Campion), of NYC, formerly of Queens Co., Ire. - 6 Apr. 1836
CAMUS
 George Frederick, of NYC, French subject - 3 Nov. 1847
CANDA
 Charles, of NYC - 13 July 1839
CANDY
 Abraham D., of Easthampton, Suffolk Co., gentleman - 13 Oct. 1829
CANNING
 Edward W., of NYC, merchant, doing business at 21 Platt St. - 18 Aug. 1836
CANTLING
 Timothy, of Albany - 27 May 1844
CANTWELL
 John, of NYC - 28 May 1846
CAPENER
 William, of Dutchess Co. - 17 June 1836
CAPFOR
 Andrew, of Lewis Co. - 20 Sept. 1831
CARDWELL
 Alexander, of Ogdensburgh, town of Oswegatchie, St. Lawrence Co. - 3 Mar. 1842
CARL
 Joseph, of Albany - 13 Oct. 1846
CARLE
 Luke, of NYC, born in Ire., res. of NYC since 1824 - 8 Aug. 1827
CARLISLE
 Elizabeth, of NYC - 16 Nov. 1847
CARLON
 Patrick, of Albany - 19 Aug. 1835
CARMICHAEL
 Margaret (widow of Daniel Carmichael, late of Williamsburgh, gentleman, dec'd, formerly of NYC, grocer), of Williamsburgh, Kings Co. - 30 May 1842
CARMODY
 Richard J., of Albany - 24 Jan. 1842
CARNEY
 James, of Brooklyn, Kings Co., grocer; had declared intention 9 June 1821 - 28 July 1825
CARR
 Robert, of Geneva, Ontario Co. - 28 May 1840
 William, of Tyrone, Steuben Co., subject of U.K. - 3 Feb. 1830
CARROLL
 John, of NYC - 17 May 1834

CARROLL (continued)
  Lawrence, of Rochester, Monroe Co., born in Tullamore, Kings Co.,
    Ire.; arrived in U.S. 6 Jan. 1838 - 15 Oct. 1847
  Peter, of Flatbush, Kings Co. - 28 Feb. 1837
  William, of Buffalo, Erie Co. - 29 Mar. 1832
CARSE
  Robert, of NYC, late of U.K. - 30 Nov. 1842
CARTER
  Henry, of Newtown, Queens Co., cabinetmaker, late of U.K. - 23
    Feb. 1836
  James, of NYC, late of Portsmouth, Eng. - 29 Jan. 1827
  John, of Kingston, Ulster Co. - 22 Jan. 1839
  Robert, of Yates Co., native of Eng. - 9 Feb. 1833
  Robert, of NYC - 2 Nov. 1844
CARTWRIGHT
  Daniel, of Wayne Co. - 25 Jan. 1843
  William, of Northfield, Richmond Co. - 23 Feb. 1847
CASSEMAN
  William, of Lewis Co. - 21 Sept. 1830
CASSIDY
  Francis, of NYC, farmer - 3 Apr. 1832
  Patrick, of Kings Co. - 3 Mar. 1842
CASTELLO
  David, of NYC, merchant - 8 Jan. 1835
CASTEL ROTTO
  John Ferdinand, of NYC, subject of Germany - 26 Oct. 1824
CASTLES
  Michael, of NYC - 16 July 1834
CASTLETON
  John, of Erie Co. - 8 Dec. 1835
CASWELL
  Dominico, of Buffalo, Erie Co. - 17 Mar. 1830; also 29 Dec. 1831
CATHCART
  Anna, of NYC - 24 Feb. 1844
  James, of Haverstraw, Rockland Co. - 19 Oct. 1847
CATTON
  John, of Wayne Co. - 26 Jan. 1831
CAVAN
  Ann (wife of William Cavan), of NYC - 4 Apr. 1844
CAVANNA
  Augustus, of NYC - 15 Nov. 1833
CAZET
  Ernest, of NYC - 10 Apr. 1844
CENEDER
  Peter, of Lewis Co. - 20 Sept. 1831'
CERAGIOLI
  Bartolomeo, of NYC - 27 Feb. 1833
  Charles, of NYC - 27 Feb. 1833
CEVORE
  Francis, of Diana, Lewis Co. - 20 Apr. 1837
CHABAN
  Laurent, of Williamsburgh, Kings Co., glass-cutter - (sworn in
    NYC) 3 June 1846
CHABERT
  Xavier, of NYC - 8 Sept. 1832
CHADERTON
  Thomas, of NYC, British subject - 4 May 1837
CHALLACOMBE
  John, of Albany Co. - 29 Oct. 1838
CHALLONER
  George, of Erie Co., native of Co. of Chester, Eng. - 4 Feb. 1845
  John, of Erie Co., native of Co. of Chester, Eng. - 4 Feb. 1845
  Sampson, of Erie Co., native of Co. of Chester, Eng. - 4 Feb. 1845
  Sampson, Jr., of Erie Co., native of Co. of Chester, Eng. - 4
    Feb. 1845

CHAMBERS
  Robert, of Rochester, Monroe Co. - 28 Dec. 1847
  Sarah (wife of John W. Chambers), of NYC - 6 Mar. 1847
CHANTRILL
  Matthew, of Winfield, Herkimer Co. - 17 Dec. 1838
CHAPLIN
  William, of Castleton, Richmond Co., formerly of Norfolk, Eng. -
    17 Apr. 1841
CHAPMAN
  George, res. of Hartland, Niagara Co., for past 5 years - 1 Sept.
    1835
  Henry Thomas, of Brooklyn, Kings Co. - (sworn in NYC) 2 May 1844
CHAPPELL
  Samuel, of Middlebury, Genesee Co. - 14 Feb. 1839
CHARLES
  Andrew, of Angelica, Allegheny Co., free white person, age 23 and
    upwards; arrived in U.S. within past 4 years - 16 Feb. 1830
  David, of Marcey, Oneida Co. - 28 Jan. 1848
  Robert, of Angelica, Allegheny Co. - 4 Feb. 1837
CHASSELET
  Pierre Alexandre, of NYC, manufacturer - 28 Oct. 1833
CHATTERTON
  Nathan, res. of Rhode Island (sworn in Albany) 10 June 1847
CHAVELL
  Martha, of NYC, late of Eng., widow - 29 Nov. 1836
CHEESE
  Edmund, of Canajoharie, Montgomery Co., native of G.B. - 3 Nov.
    1832
CHEESMAN
  James, of Fort Edward, Washington Co., grocer and merchant - 20
    Feb. 1835
CHEEVERS
  William, of NYC - 15 Mar. 1844
CHELLBORG
  Albert, of Brooklyn, Kings Co. - 8 May 1844
CHERRY
  Robert, of Ontario Co. - 1 June 1846
CHICK/CHINCK
  Thomas, of Batavia, Genesee Co., subject of G.B. - 16 June 1840
CHISHOLM
  Walter, of NYC - 6 May 1843
CHRISTIAN
  William, of Wilna, Jefferson Co., native of Isle of Man - 14 Nov.
    1839
CHRISTIE
  Elizabeth (wife of Robert Christie, of NYC), of NYC, native of
    Scotland - 12 May 1845
  James, of Seneca, Ontario Co. - 29 Sept. 1838
  Robert, of NYC; made declaration of intent in Marine Court on 19
    Apr. 1836 - 27 Apr. 1836
CHRISTOPHERS
  Thomas S., of NYC - 4 June 1836
CHRISTY
  John Joseph, of NYC, farmer - 31 Mar. 1832
CHURCHILL
  Otis, of Albany, native of West Bolton, Stanstead Co., Lower Ca-
    nada - 11 Mar. 1841
CHYNOWETH
  William, of Rochester, Monroe Co. - 16 Mar. 1837
CLAFFEY
  Peter, of Mendon, Monroe Co. - 5 Mar. 1841
CLAGUE
  John, of Utica, Oneida Co., British subject - 1 Aug. 1840
CLANCY
  John, of Onondaga Co. - 26 Nov. 1838

CLAPHAM
  Samuel, of NYC - 6 Mar. 1837
CLARK
  Ann, of Albany - 21 Apr. 1845
  Edward, of NYC - 10 Oct. 1836
  James, of Rochester, Monroe Co. - 27 Apr. 1835
  James, of Albany, Albany Co. - 5 Oct. 1847
  John, of City and Co. of Albany, late of U.K. - 23 Nov. 1836
  John, of Newburgh, Orange Co., formerly of Worcestershire, Eng. -
    15 Apr. 1842
CLARKE
  Joshua, of NYC, stucco-plasterer - 9 Sept. 1833
  Josiah, of NYC, subject of U.K. - 24 Oct. 1828
  Michael, of NYC, late of U.K. - 29 Apr. 1837
  William, of Albany Co. - 7 Nov. 1846
CLARKSON
  Francis, of NYC - 20 June 1844
  George, of Norfolk, St. Lawrence Co. - 8 Nov. 1833
CLAXTON
  William, of Poughkeepsie, Dutchess Co. - 27 Nov. 1845
CLAY
  William, of Onondaga Co., born in G.B. - 28 Nov. 1832
CLEARY
  Thomas, of NYC, born in Ire., age 37, merchant; emigrated from
    Halifax, Nova Scotia - 5 May 1827
CLEEVE
  Charles, of NYC, physician - 10 Apr. 1826
CLEGG
  Hannah (wife of James Clegg), of NYC - 5 June 1847
  James, of NYC - 5 June 1847
CLEMENCE
  Thomas of City of Albany - 20 Jan. 1837
CLEMENTS
  John, of NYC - 20 Aug. 1836
CLINDINEN
  Joseph, of Wayne Co. - 5 Oct. 1830
CLOYDE
  John, res. of Troy, Rensselaer Co., sine 12 Apr. 1830 - 16 Mar.
    1832
CLUCAS
  Henry, of NYC - 11 May 1847
COATS/COATES
  Thomas, of Sangerfield, Oneida Co. - 24 Feb. 1845
COATSWORTH
  Joseph, of Buffalo, Erie Co. - 3 Mar. 1835
COBHAM
  George Ashworth, of NYC, late of G.B. - 21 Apr. 1835
COCAGNE
  Nicholas, of Lyme, Jefferson Co. - 25 Feb. 1835
COCHRAN
  Andrew George Cobbett, of Buffalo, Erie Co. - 9 Apr. 1835
  James H., of Newstead, Erie Co. - (sworn in Genesee Co.) 21 Mar.
    1842
  John, of NYC - 23 Nov. 1835
  Robert, of Ripley, Chautauque Co., subject of G.B. - 24 June 1828
  William, of Buffalo, Erie Co. - 24 Sept. 1835
COCHRANE
  William, of NYC, merchant - 16 Feb. 1828
COCK
  Matthias/Matthew, of Niagara Co., born in France - 30 Mar. 1842
CODLING
  George, of NYC - 5 Aug. 1847
COEHEN
  Henry, of Watertown, Jefferson Co. - 28 Mar. 1843

21

COEY
  William John, of NYC, packing-boxmaker - 4 Jan. 1833
COHEN
  Dinah (wife of Samuel Cohen), of NYC - 6 May 1846
  Levi, of NYC - 20 Feb. 1847
COLE
  John, of Buffalo, Erie Co. - 24 Sept. 1836
  Robert, of Oswego, Tioga Co. - 15 June 1836
COLEMAN
  Alexander, of Flatbush, Kings Co. - (sworn in NYC) 26 Oct. 1844
  Daniel, of Flatbush, Kings Co. - (sworn in NYC) 2 Nov. 1844
COLLETTE
  Lambert Nicholas, of Erie Co. - 26 Aug. 1835
COLLIER/CALLIER
  Nicholas, of Albany Co. - 2 July 1835
COLLINS
  Elizabeth, of NYC - 28 June 1847
  John, of Monroe Co. - 8 Feb. 1836
  Luke, of Onondaga Co. - 8 Apr. 1837
  Stanton, of Syracuse, Onondaga Co. - 22 Nov. 1845
COLLUM
  John, of Albany - 3 June 1844
COLVILL
  David G., of Erie Co. - 5 June 1835
COMBE
  Michel, of Attica, Oneida Co., late of Paris, France - 6 Oct.
    1825
COMMAY
  Dudley, of NYC, late of Ire. - 25 Feb. 1836
COMPTON
  John, of NYC, farmer - 21 Mar. 1837
CONDERT
  Charles, of NYC - 22 June 1835
CONLEY
  Catharine, of Brooklyn, Kings Co. - 29 May 1847
  John, of Wayne Co. - 1 Oct. 1830
CONNELLY
  James, of Greece, Monroe Co. - 16 Jan. 1836
  Michael, of Amsterdam, Montgomery Co. - 7 Mar. 1844
CONNOLLY
  Charles M., of NYC - 10 July 1834
CONRAD
  Jacob, of Rochester, Monroe Co. - 4 Sept. 1839
CONREY
  Francis, of NYC, formerly of Ire. - 21 June 1826
CONROY
  Catharine, of NYC - 3 Apr. 1844
  Michael, of NYC, porter - 23 Nov. 1833
  Thomas, of NYC - 10 Aug. 1832
CONSADINE
  Edmund, of Richmond Co. - (sworn in NYC) 6 Aug. 1842
CONWAY
  Ann (widow of John Conway, late of NYC), of NYC, born in Eng. -
    5 May 1845
  James, for past 5 years res. of NYC - 5 Apr. 1844
COOK
  Thomas, of Franklin, Delaware Co. - 14 Jan. 1836
COOKE
  James, of Oneida Co., formerly of Newton, Co. of Cheshire, Eng. -
    14 Mar. 1831
  Robert, of Oneida Co., formerly of Newton, Co. of Cheshire, Eng. -
    14 Mar. 1831
  Robert, of NYC - 28 Dec. 1839
  Robert, of NYC - 26 Oct. 1847
  Thomas, of Brooklyn, Kings Co. - 9 Jan. 1835

New York Alien Residents, 1825-1848

COONRADT
  George, of Onondaga Co. - 26 Aug. 1836
COOPER
  Martha, of Kings Co. - 24 Sept. 1836
  Michael, of Troy, Rensselaer Co. - 14 Apr. 1837
  William, of NYC, livery-stable keeper - 25 May 1835
COPSON
  Daniel, of Kings Co. - 16 June 1834
CORD
  John, of Rochester, Monroe Co. - 2 Jan. 1847
CORKEY
  Samuel, of NYC, gardener - 14 Jan. 1841
CORKRIN
  Peter, of NYC, dealer - 2 Sept. 1831
CORLIN
  James, of Brooklyn, fur-dresser - 4 Aug. 1825
CORMODY
  Michael, of German Flatts, Herkimer Co., native of Ire. - 22 Aug.
    1842
CORNAIRE
  Simeon, of Lyme, Jefferson Co. - 25 Feb. 1835
CORNELIUS
  Francis, of Greenbush, Rensselaer Co. - 23 Dec. 1836
  John, of Greenbush, Rensselaer Co. - 23 Dec. 1836
CORNELL
  Margaret, of Troy, Rensselaer Co. - 30 Nov. 1846
CORNER
  Samuel, of Beekmantown, Clinton Co. - 2 Oct. 1832
CORNES
  George, of Oneida Co., native of Co. of Kent, Eng.; came to U.S.
    on 6 May 1827 - 10 Mar. 1831
CORNOCK
  Joseph, of Albany - 17 Jan. 1835
CORNWALL
  James, of Delaware Co., late of London, Eng. - 14 Sept. 1835
CORNWELL
  Sarah, of Brooklyn, Kings Co., born in Pontefract, Co. of York,
    Eng., on 1 Apr. 1813; came to U.S. on 8 Oct. 1830 - 1 Aug. 1844
CORREA
  Emanuel Alvares, of NYC - 31 July 1837
  Sarah, of NYC, late of Island of Jamaica - 8 Feb. 1827
COSGRIFF
  James, of Lewis Co. - 21 Sept. 1830
COSGROVE
  Teresa (widow of Patrick Cosgrove), of NYC - 13 Sept. 1845
COSTIGAN
  Michael, of Brooklyn, Kings Co. - 16 Jan. 1829
COTCHER
  John, of Albany - 20 Apr. 1846
COTTER (or COLTER?)
  Oliver, of Albany - 10 Feb. 1831
COTTRAM (or COTTNAM or COTTMAN?)
  John, of Albany - 10 Feb. 1831
COUGHLAN
  Patrick, of Troy, Rensselaer Co. - 26 Feb. 1842
  Thomas, of Canajoharie, Montgomery Co., native of G.B. - 16 Aug.
    1834
COULTAS
  William, of Wayne Co. - 24 Jan. 1831
COURAN
  Peter, of Onondaga Co. - 5 Dec. 1838
COURROSIER/COURVOSIER/COURVOISIER
  Adela, of NYC - 27 Nov. 1834
COURT
  Henry C., of Pamelia, Jefferson Co., born in Eng. - 2 June 1841

COURTNEY
  John, of NYC, lately resident of Geneva, Ontario Co., in the family of Gideon Lee, Esq. - 28 Oct. 1839
COWDRAY
  William, of Columbia Co. - 31 Oct. 1831
COWEN
  John, of Brownville, Jefferson Co., age 36 - 19 Nov. 1836
COX
  Benjamin, of Albany Co. - 31 Oct. 1846
  Edward P., of Buffalo, Erie Co. - 29 Nov. 1847
  John, of NYC, merchant, res. of the several years past 10 Mar. 1827
  Joseph, of NYC, merchant - 10 Mar. 1827
COXON
  Joseph, of NYC - 10 Oct. 1847
COY
  Henry, of NYC - 28 Oct. 1845
COYL
  Patrick H., of Leyden, Lewis Co. - 26 Sept. 1846
COYLE
  Sarah (wife of Andrew Coyle), of NYC, native of U.K. - 25 Oct. 1844
COYNE
  James, of NYC, formerly of Co. Armagh, Ire. - 1 Sept. 1840
CRAFT
  George, of Rochester, Monroe Co. - 24 May 1836
CRAIG
  Andrew, of Troy, Rensselaer Co. - 9 Feb. 1838
  Joseph, of NYC, painter and glazier - 25 June 1833
  William, of Livingston Co. - 1 Oct. 1833
CRALLIN
  Thomas, of Buffalo, Erie Co., born Isle of Man - 27 July 1832
CRAMER
  John Adam, of Buffalo, Erie Co. - 22 Aug. 1831
CRAMP
  James, of Vienna, Oneida Co. - 13 Apr. 1831
  Samuel, of NYC - 9 Sept. 1846
CRANE
  Catharine R., of NYC - 21 June 1844
  Edward, of Utica, Oneida Co. - 13 Aug. 1828
CRANSHAW
  Joseph, of Lewis Co. - 16 Feb. 1839
CRAVEN
  Richard, of Westmoreland, Oneida Co. - 25 Mar. 1831
CRAWFORD
  Jane, of Oswego Co. - 23 Oct. 1839
  Peter, of Buffalo, Erie Co. - 2 Apr. 1833
CREAGH
  Bartholomew, of Brooklyn, Kings Co. - 5 May 1836
CREIGHTON
  Frederick, of firm of Bliss and Creighton, watchmakers, doing business at 42 Fulton St., NYC - 25 Mar. 1836
CREOLE
  Joseph, of Batavia, Genesee Co. - 3 Feb. 1841
CRERAR
  Agnes, of NYC - 28 Apr. 1834
CRIDGE
  John, of Troy, Rensselaer Co., late of Parish of Thulbur, Somerset Co., Eng.; he migrated to U.S. in 1832 - 12 Aug. 1835
CRIDLAND
  Charles R., of Buffalo, Erie Co. - 24 June 1835
CRITCHELL
  James, of Gates, Monroe Co. - 10 Nov. 1846
CROCE
  Gaetano, of NYC - 8 July 1836

CROCKER
  George, of Stafford, Genesee Co. - 4 Feb. 1841
  Stephen, of Albany Co. - 27 Oct. 1838
CROISSANT
  Frederick, of Le Roy, Jefferson Co., born at Frederick Fontaine,
    France, in 1784; removed to New York in 1828 - 11 Dec. 1835
  George, of Le Roy, Jefferson Co. - 3 Dec. 1833
  John, of Le Roy, Jefferson Co., born at Frederick Fontaine, France,
    in 1816; removed to U.S. in 1828 - 11 Dec. 1835
  Pierre, of Le Roy, Jefferson Co., born at Frederick Fontaine,
    France, in 1799; removed to New York in June 1833 - 4 Mar. 1840
CROMMENANCE/CROMMANCE
  Henry Dominque, of NYC - 16 Jan. 1835
CROOK
  Richard L., of NYC - 22 Sept. 1847
CROOKE
  Robert, of NYC, merchant - 2 Nov. 1847
CROSIER
  William, of Albion, Oswego Co. - 16 Mar. 1831
CROSSLEY
  William, of Rochester, Monroe Co. - 25 Sept. 1843
CROSTON
  Alice, of NYC, widow - 2 Mar. 1831
CROUCH
  Levi, of Albany - 1 Apr. 1842
CROWTHER
  William, of Westchester Co. - 29 Jan. 1838
CRUISE
  Anna Maria Russell, of NYC - 1 Nov. 1841
  Patrick Russell, of NYC, late of G.B. - 30 Sept. 1830
CRUMMEY/CRUMMIE
  Andrew, of Troy, Rensselaer Co. - 12 June 1837
  John, of Albany - 1 May 1845
CRUMP
  Benjamin, of Buffalo, Erie Co. - 21 Nov. 1834
CRYSLER
  Ralph M., of Rochester, Monroe Co., born in Niagara Twp., Niagara
    District, Prov. of Upper Canada, on 22 Dec. 1796; arrived in
    U.S. 23 Sept. 1839 - 6 Apr. 1841
CUDIHY
  John, of NYC - 19 Mar. 1832
CUDLIPP
  David, of NYC - 18 Nov. 1825
CUENIN
  Jean Baptiste, of NYC - 24 Feb. 1832
CUFF
  John, of NYC - 24 Jan. 1834
CULL
  William, of Stafford, Genesee Co. - 19 Oct. 1839
CULLEN
  John, of Albany - 9 Dec. 1839
CUMING
  Robert, of Erie Co. - 3 Dec. 1834
CUMMING
  Ann, of Kings Co. - 25 Feb. 1837
  Thomas, of NYC - 13 Apr. 1831
CUMMINGS
  John, of Ulster Co., native of Kilkenny Co., Ire. - 18 Dec. 1832
  Williams, of NYC - 29 Sept. 1836
CUMMINS
  John, of Kingston, Ulster Co. - 10 June 1834
  Michael, of Utica, Oneida Co. - 20 Dec. 1832
CUNLIFF/CUNLIFFE
  Simon, of Albany - 17 Sept. 1830

CUNNINGHAM
  James, of NYC, grocer - 7 Jan. 1834
  James, of NYC, engineer - 22 Feb. 1834
  James, of Wayne Co. - 21 Nov. 1838
  John, of Westport, Essex Co., born in hamlet of French Park, town
    of Boyne, Co. of Rosscommon, Ire., age 36 - 27 Sept. 1843
  Robert, of Albany Co. - 24 Mar. 1831
  William, of NYC, coppersmith - 17 Jan. 1827
  William, of Schenectady, Schenectady Co. - 11 Mar. 1831
  William, of Kings Co. - 14 Feb. 1834
CUROW
  Thomas, of Brooklyn, Kings Co. - 17 June 1835
CURRAN
  John H., of Lewis Co., native of Ire., age 32 - 18 Apr. 1832
  Patrick, of NYC, res. of said city for past 2 years - 27 May 1839
CURREN
  Mary Eliza (wife of John Curren, late widow of James Kemgan), of
    NYC; she believes she was born in State of New York - 28 Mar.
    1844
CURREY
  David, of Porter, Niagara Co. - 7 Nov. 1845
  James, of Orange Co. - 14 Dec. 1840
CURRIE
  James, of Poughkeepsie, Dutchess Co., formerly of Derry, Ire. -
    9 June 1845
  Samuel, of Poughkeepsie, Dutchess Co. - 6 Nov. 1835
CURRY
  John, of Le Roy, Jefferson Co. - 3 Feb. 1840
  Michael, of Wayne Co. - 24 Sept. 1835
CUSACK
  Edward, of Monroe Co. - 13 Dec. 1847
CUTHBERT
  George, of Brooklyn, Kings Co. - 8 Dec. 1847
CUTHBERTSON
  Daniel, of NYC, merchant - 19 Oct. 1841
CUTTING
  John, of Oswego, Oswego Co. - (sworn in Monroe Co.) 21 Dec. 1846
  William, of Auburn, Cayuga Co., British subject - 28 Sept. 1846
CUYLER
  John, of NYC - 27 July 1839
CZAKERT
  Peter, of Rochester, Monroe Co. - 24 May 1838
DAFTER
  Moses, of Oswegatchie, St. Lawrence Co.- 25 May 1831
DAILY
  James, of Ogdensburgh, St. Lawrence Co. - 16 Jan. 1833
DALBY
  Joseph, of Buffalo, Erie Co. - 13 Mar. 1837
DALE
  George, of Niagara Co. - 12 Jan. 1836
  William, of Manlius, Onondaga Co., lately come from Eng. - 27
    Aug. 1831
  William, of Fort Plain, Montgomery Co. - 9 Mar. 1836
DALGAS
  Henry, of NYC - Jan. 1846
DALLERY
  Charles Henry, of Williamsburgh, Kings Co. - (sworn in NYC) 14
    June 1847
DALTON, Elizabeth (wife of James T. Dalton), of NYC - 18 Oct. 1847
DALY
  Winniford (widow of Thomas Daly), of NYC, born in Ire. - 21 Nov.
    1840
DAMEREL
  George, of NYC, iron-founder - 23 Mar. 1826

DAMERUM
  William, of Richmond Co. - 20 Oct. 1834
DANCY/DANCEY
  Frederick, of Penfield, Monroe Co. - 29 Dec. 1846
DANNE
  Joseph, of NYC, merchant - 8 Mar. 1839
DANNEFELSER
  Adam, of Brooklyn, Kings Co. - 26 Mar. 1836
DANVERGNE
  Peter, of NYC - 25 Sept. 1840
DARBY
  George Frederick, of NYC, merchant - 3 May 1837
DARLING
  John, of Andes, Delaware Co., native of Scotland - 13 Sept. 1832
DASMOND
  John, of Henrietta, Monroe Co. - 3 Apr. 1837
DAVEY
  John, of Orange Co. - 3 Oct. 1840
DAVID
  Jonathan, of Onondaga Co. - 29 May 1839
DAVIDSON
  Agnes, of Albany, born in Paisley, Co. of Renfrew, Scotland, age
    now about 40 - 13 Jan. 1841
  Charles, of Pavilion, Genesee Co. - 29 Jan. 1844
  James, of NYC, slater - 23 July 1831
  Jeanette (wife of John Davidson, of Albany), of Albany; her mai-
    den name was Mc Laren; she was born in town of Callender, the
    parish of Callender, Co. of Perth; age now about 42 - 13 Feb.
    1841
DAVIES
  David, of Marcy, Oneida Co. - 8 July 1834
  David, of NYC - 6 May 1846
  Thomas, of Utica, Oneida Co. - 31 Mar. 1831
DAVIS
  Ann, of NYC - 9 Oct. 1839
  Ann, of NYC - 29 May 1844
  Catharine, of NYC, single woman - 18 July 1844
  David, of NYC, broker - 26 Feb. 1827
  Edward, of Ravenswood, Newtown, Queens Co. - 13 May 1837
  Evan, of Trenton, Oneida Co., farmer - 28 Apr. 1832
  Henry, of Rensselaer Co. - 16 Nov. 1835
  Henry, of Brooklyn, Kings Co. - 31 Mar. 1842
  John, of Brooklyn, Kings Co. - 9 Sept. 1828
  John, of Plainfield, Otsego Co., res. of the state for 15 years -
    14 Mar. 1835
  Richard, of Turin, Lewis Co. - 8 Apr. 1825
  Samuel E., of NYC, formerly of London, Eng. - 30 Apr. 1829
  Samuel Strangman, of Henrietta, Monroe Co. - 20 Jan. 1832
  Shadrach, of NYC, mason - 30 Jan. 1827
  Thomas, of Winfield, Herkimer Co., res. of New York State for
    past 20 years - 9 Nov. 1831
  Thomas, of Utica, Oneida Co., res. of New York State for past
    4 years - 18 Aug. 1846
  William, of Onondaga Co. - 22 Aug. 1836
  William, of Kings Co. - 17 Sept. 1837
DAVISON
  John, of NYC - 16 Nov. 1837
  Robert, of Westfield, Chautauque Co., British subject - 12 Feb.
    1830
  William, of NYC, formerly of Eng. - 17 Oct. 1836
DAWSON
  Jervis, of NYC - 30 July 1845
DAY
  Joseph, of Kings Co. - 3 May 1836
  Joseph, of Lockport, Niagara Co. - 4 Feb. 1837

DAYS
    Isaac, of Watervliet, Albany Co. - 12 Mar. 1839
DEACON/DEACAN
    Benjamin A., of Niagara Co. - 19 Feb. 1836
DEAN
    Henry H., of Turin, Lewis Co. - 19 Sept. 1834
    James, of NYC, late of Bolton Le Moores, Co. of Lancaster, Eng. -
        30 Dec. 1835
    Thomas, of NYC, formerly of Eng. - 27 Dec. 1826
DEANE
    Elizabeth (widow of Joseph Deane), of NYC - 7 Dec. 1846
DEBENHAM
    James, of Kings Co. - 14 Sept. 1837
DE CHACON
    Georgiano (widow of Pablo De Chacon), of NYC - 23 Apr. 1846
DECHSLER
    Francis, of Sheldon, Wyoming Co. - 28 Sept. 1841
DE CONRAD
    Arnold, of NYC, native of Germany - 16 June 1843
DEERANT
    Isaac, of Onondaga Co. - 23 May 1839
DEERING
    William, of Erie Co. - 27 Dec. 1841
DE FLIEGER
    Cornelius, of Rochester, Monroe Co., late from the Netherlands -
        20 June 1844
DE GARCIA
    Agustina Gonzalez (wife of John P. Garcia, merchant), of NYC -
        6 Mar. 1835
DEHANT
    Jacques, of Lyme, Jefferson Co. - 25 Feb. 1835
DEITZ
    Mois, of NYC - 13 Dec. 1847
    Rosa (wife of Mois Deitz), of NYC - 13 Dec. 1847
DE LA CADENA
    Mariano Velasques, of NYC, translator - 24 Aug. 1826
DELAFOLIE
    Francis Alexis/Elixis, of Le Roy, Jefferson Co. - 15 Nov. 1834
DELANY/DELANEY
    James, of Sand Lake, Rensselaer Co. - 4 Nov. 1834
    Thomas, of Westmoreland, Oneida Co. - 3 Jan. 1835
DE LA SALLE
    Theophile, of Fowler, St. Lawrence Co., formerly of France; he
        came to U.S. about 1 Oct. 1835 - 21 Sept. 1837
DELBRIDGE
    James, of Rochester, Monroe Co. - 21 June 1843
DELEHANTY
    Johanna (widow of Michael Delehanty and daughter of Daniel Cleary,
        dec'd), of Albany - 24 May 1838
DELILE
    Louis, of NYC, mariner - 19 May 1830
DELMONICO
    Laurent, of NYC - 21 Apr. 1838
DE LYNES
    George, of NYC, merchant - 24 Apr. 1825
D(E)MACKOWICK/D(E)MACKAWICK
    William Charles, of NYC - 23 Mar. 1835
DEMANGE
    Jean Baptiste, of Albany, lately of France - 11 May 1835
DEMING
    Ann, of Trenton, Oneida Co. - 16 Oct. 1840
DE MOTT
    Richard, of NYC - 27 Sept. 1832
DEMPSEY
    Edward, of Ogdensburgh, Oswegatchie, St. Lawrence Co. - 3 Mar. 1842

DEMPSEY (continued)
  James, of NYC, formerly of Monenarigg, Co. of Wexford, Ire. - 5
    Nov. 1825
  James, of West Turin, Lewis Co. - 23 Nov. 1842
DE NANTEIUL/DE NANTEUL
  Augustus, of NYC - 2 July 1835
DENAZ
  Francis, of Albany - 23 June 1842
DENHAM
  Christopher Richard, of Lockport, Niagara Co. - 14 Sept. 1836
  James, of De Witt, Onondaga Co. - 25 Feb. 1845
DENNIGAN
  Catharine, of Buffalo, Erie Co., citizen of U.K. - 17 Dec. 1847
DENNIS
  William, of Brooklyn, Kings Co. - 8 July 1834
DENNISTON
  Hans, of NYC - 21 Sept. 1836
DENT
  Robert, of Clinton Co., late of Yorkshire, Eng. - 8 Aug. 1825
DEPOIRE
  Napoleon, of Lyme, Jefferson Co. - 2 June 1835
DERAISMES/DERAISME/DERASMIES
  John Francis Joseph, of NYC, merchant - 17 May 1833
DERFURE
  John, of Canajoharie, Montgomery Co. - 31 Aug. 1841
DE ROUS
  Jules, of NYC - 20 May 1843
DE ST. CROIX
  Benjamin, of Poughkeepsie, Dutchess Co., druggist - 14 Aug. 1829
DESEAMUS
  Joseph, of NYC, painter - 4 June 1827
DESEVRE
  Hyacinth, of Watertown, Jefferson Co., native of Montreal, Lower
    Canada - 9 Nov. 1842
DETHERIDGE
  Isaac, of Schoharie Co. - 17 Feb. 1847
DETTMER/DETTINER?
  Augustus, of Minden, Montgomery Co. - 14 Feb. 1838
DEVAN
  Patrick, of Orange Co. - 7 Jan. 1833
DEVLIN
  Daniel, of NYC, merchant - 26 Feb. 1844
  John, of NYC, cartman, late of Ire. - 3 Feb. 1826
DEVYR
  Thomas A., of Williamsburgh, Kings Co. - 19 July 1843
DEWEY
  Henry, of Onondaga Co. - 9 Oct. 1835
DEWHIRST
  John, of Rochester, Monroe Co. - 12 June 1832
DE ZALDO
  Ramon, of NYC - 4 Dec. 1843
DEZENGREMELLE/DIZENGREMEL
  Remy, of Lyme, Jefferson Co. - 25 Feb. 1835
  Remy Prosper, of Lyme, Jefferson Co. - 2 June 1835
DIAPER
  Frederick, of NYC, architect - 11 May 1846
DIBOLT
  Magdalena (wife of Francis Vogelweill, supposed to be dead), of
    NYC - 25 Aug. 1843
DICK
  John, of Brooklyn, Kings Co., born in Scotland, age 63 - 26 May
    1845
  John, of Kings Co., born in Scotland - 24 Apr. 1845
DICKINSON
  Thomas, of NYC, farmer, late of U.K. - 12 June 1832

New York Alien Residents, 1825-1848

DICKSON
  William, of Mount Pleasant, Westchester Co. - 22 May 1832
DILLEN
  Matthew, of Huntington, Suffolk Co., late of Co. of Galway, Ire. -
    24 Jan. 1838
DILLON
  Michael, of Chemung Co. - 1 Mar. 1837
DILVERT
  Daniel, of Easton, Washington Co., native of Mallow, Co. of Cork,
    Ire. - 5 Feb. 1845
DIMBLEBY/DIMBLELY
  John, of Trenton, Oneida Co. - 2 Apr. 1831
  John, Jr., of Trenton, Oneida Co. - 12 Apr. 1831
DIMM
  Henry, of NYC, shoemaker - 5 Apr. 1847
DINGFELTER
  Andrew, of Canajoharie, Montgomery Co. - 31 Aug. 1841
DINSMORE
  John, of Brooklyn, Kings Co. - 20 July 1842
DISABELL
  Francis, of Gibbons Ville, Albany Co. - 5 Nov. 1832
DITENBECK
  Jacob, of Lewis Co. - 20 Sept. 1831
DIXON
  Ellen, of NYC - 20 Sept. 1844
  John, of Ontario Co. - 23 May 1833
DOAT
  George, of Erie Co. - 31 Mar. 1835
DOBSON
  Henry, of Brooklyn, Kings Co. - 9 Nov. 1835
DOCTEUR
  Joseph, of Lyme, Jefferson Co. - 18 Jan. 1843
DODD
  John B., of NYC - 3 Oct. 1825
  John B., of NYC - 12 June 1832
DOELLER
  Godfrey, of Erie Co., native of Schwagenau, Prussia; came to U.S.
    on 22 Aug. 1844 - 30 Aug. 1844
DOERING
  John, of NYC, sugar-baker - 13 Mar. 1830
DOERR
  Jacob, of Erie Co., native of Buedingen, Grand Duchy of Hessen
    Darmstadt; came to U.S. on 4 Oct. 1843 - 30 Aug. 1844
DOLAN
  Frances (wife of Thomas Dolan), of NYC - 30 June 1846
  Michael, of NYC, mason - 25 Sept. 1826
  Thomas, of Erie Co. - 9 Mar. 1836
DOMINICK
  James, of NYC, carpenter - 11 Jan. 1830
DOMNIQUE
  Francis, of NYC, jeweller - 6 May 1840
DONALDSON/DONELDSON
  James, of NYC - 22 May 1833
DONELEY
  Bernard/Bernerd, of Lewis Co. - 21 Sept. 1830
DONNELLY
  Hugh, of Williamsburgh, Kings Co. - 9 Dec. 1845
  Letitia, of Castleton, Richmond Co., spinster - 6 Oct. 1842
  Patrick, of NYC, residing at 132 16th St., laborer - 12 July 1843
  Sarah (widow of Patrick Donnelly), of NYC - 10 Nov. 1847
  Thomas, of NYC, where he has resided past 7 years; declared his
    intent 9 Mar. 1822 - Jan. 1822
DONOHO
  John, of NYC - 23 Apr. 1838

30

DOPF
  George, of Buffalo, Erie Co. - 20 Oct. 1843
DORAN
  James, of Poughkeepsie, Dutchess Co., formerly of Co. of Down,
    Ire. - 23 Sept. 1842
  Paul, of NYC - 10 Apr. 1845
DORBAUN
  Andrew, of Canajoharie, Montgomery Co., formerly subject of
    Prussia; came to U.S. on 28 June 1834 and has resided in Cana-
    joharie since 2 July 1834 - 24 Sept. 1838
DORD
  Claudius, of NYC - 26 May 1847
DORE
  George, of Otsego, Otsego Co. - 17 Feb. 1846
  Robert B., of NYC, drayman, late of U.K. - 8 Dec. 1825
DORLER
  James, of NYC - 24 Aug. 1835
DORTIE
  Sebastien C., of NYC - 5 May 1837
DOUGAL
  John, of Andes, Delaware Co., native of Scotland - 29 Aug. 1833
DOUGHERTY
  Charles, of Juhelville, Jefferson Co., born in Ire. - 15 Oct.
    1841
  Mary (wife of Edward Dougherty), of New Windsor, Orange Co. - 3
    Oct. 1836
  Robert, of Turin, Lewis Co. - 23 Aug. 1836
  William, of Deerfield, Oneida Co., native of Ire. - 10 July 1828
DOUGLAS
  Andrew, of NYC, native of Scotland, for several years res. of the
    U.S. - 3 May 1827
DOUGLAS/DOUGLASS
  Eliza Graham, of the Douglas farms, near Flushing on Long Is-
    land - (sworn in Kings Co.) 7 Mar. 1839
DOVE
  Charles, of Potsdam, Lawrence Co. - 2 Mar. 1837
DOWN
  Edward, of Onondaga Co. - 27 Feb. 1834
  George, of Onondaga Co. - 24 Aug. 1840
  John, of Albany Co. - 27 Oct. 1838
  Richard, of Oakfield, Genesee Co. - 13 Sept. 1843
DOWNEY
  Thomas, of Newstead, Erie Co. - 5 Dec. 1831
  William, of Newstead, Erie Co. - 5 Dec. 1831
DOWNING
  Elizabeth, of Brooklyn, Kings Co., subject of U.K. - 17 Apr.
    1844
  John, of Troy, Rensselaer Co. - 8 May 1841
  John, of Sangerfield, Oneida Co. - 30 Sept. 1841
DOYLE
  George, of NYC, house-carpenter - 12 Aug. 1835
  John, of Hoosick, Rensselaer Co. - 7 June 1837
DRAPER
  Benjamin, of Lockport, Niagara Co., native of Yorkshire, Eng.,
    age now 33; two years ago the first of May last past he be-
    came a resident of Lockport - 9 June 1841
  Benjamin, of Kinderhook, Columbia Co. - 15 Feb. 1844
  John William, of NYC, physician and professor of chemistry in
    the university of said city - 10 June 1842
  William, of Kings Co. - 29 Sept. 1836
DREWETT
  John W., of Rochester, Monroe Co. - 4 Nov. 1839
DRISCOLL
  Patrick, of NYC, butcher - 29 July 1847

New York Alien Residents, 1825-1848

DRIVER
  Isabella (widow of John R. Driver), of NYC - 4 Sept. 1844
DRUAULT
  Thomas Michel, of NYC - 6 Aug. 1836
DRUMMOND
  John, of NYC, merchant - 17 Feb. 1837
  Stewart, of Albany - 10 July 1833
DRURY
  John, of Oswegatchie, St. Lawrence Co., lately from Eng. - 12 May
    1838
DRYDEN
  William, of Denmark, Lewis Co. - 6 Jan. 1836
DUBAY
  John, of Rochester, Monroe Co. - 4 Apr. 1832
DUBOIS
  Edward, of NYC, native of Switzerland - (sworn in Jefferson Co.)
    26 May 1843
  Francis, of NYC, turner - 27 Apr. 1837
  Francis Blake, of Buffalo, Erie Co. - 8 July 1836
  Frederick Lewis, of NYC - 12 Aug. 1842
DUCHAMPE
  Jean Baptiste, of NYC - 23 Feb. 1836
DUCK
  Daniel, of Aurora, Erie Co., surgeon, late of London, Eng. - 17
    Nov. 1831
DUFFY
  Patrick, of NYC, late of Ire. - 2 May 1827
  Peter, of NYC - 17 Feb. 1830
DUFTOS
  John, of Walton, Lewis Co. - 21 Sept. 1841
DUKE
  Thomas, of NYC - 7 Aug. 1847
DUMASTIER
  Anne, of NYC, single woman, for several years past res. of said
    city - 22 Feb. 1831
DUMVILLE
  Benjamin, of Newburgh, Orange Co. - 13 Feb. 1840
DUNCAN
  William, of NYC, tailor, born in Scotland, res. of NYC since 1811
    when he arrived in NYC from Europe - 15 Oct. 1827
DUNHAM
  Ann (late Ann Nicholas, daughter of Robert Nicholas, of Westmore-
    land), of Oneida Co. - 12 Apr. 1836
DUNLAP
  William, of Watertown, Jefferson Co. - 23 Sept. 1845
DUNLOP
  John, of Watertown, Oneida Co. - 27 Dec. 1834
DUNN
  Charles Edward, of Brownville, Jefferson Co. - 16 Sept. 1837
  Frances, of NYC, single lady, residing at 397 Fourth St. - 10
    Nov. 1841
  John, of Hudson, Columbia Co. - 10 Dec. 1830
  Maria, of NYC - 22 May 1834
  William, of Onondaga Co. - 7 Dec. 1839
  William, of Lorraine, Jefferson Co. - 8 Mar. 1845
DUNOUT
  Antoine, of Western, Oneida Co. - 5 Oct. 1827
DUQUERRO
  Joseph F., of NYC, jeweller, French subject - 19 Feb. 1827
DURANT
  John, of NYC, silversmith - 2 Jan. 1830
  Thomas, of NYC, printing ink manufacturer - 27 Dec. 1827
DURNIN
  Patrick, of Southfield, Richmond Co. - 15 Aug. 1845

DURONDE
  Paul M. Picard, of NYC, merchant tailor - 8 May 1827
DUROSS
  Edward, of Jefferson Co. - 27 May 1833
DURRANT
  William, of Hamilton, Madison Co., formerly res. of Parish of
    Burlingham, Co. of Norfolk, Eng. - 21 Feb. 1846
DUVAL
  Lawrence, of NYC - 28 Aug. 1843
  Malachi, of Jamaica, Queens Co., railroad contractor - 21 Feb.
    1837
DUVILLARD
  John Peter, of NYC - 18 July 1832
DWYER
  Michael, of Riga, Monroe Co., born in Co. of Limerick, Ire., on
    24 Sept. 1809 - 2 Dec. 1844
DYCKS
  Henry G., of Brookhaven, Suffolk Co., native of Portland, Co. of
    Wiltshire, Eng. - 14 Oct. 1844
DYE
  William, of Williamsburgh, Kings Co. - 7 May 1844
EARLE
  Bernard, of NYC, house-carpenter - 4 Oct. 1847
EARLY
  James, of Chili, Monroe Co. - 18 Apr. 1836
  John, of Southampton, Suffolk Co. - 9 Oct. 1833
  Michael, of Southampton, Suffolk Co., native of Ire. - 9 Oct. 1833
EARP
  William, of Rockland Co. - 13 Apr. 1836
EASTER
  John, of Wayne Co. - 25 Sept. 1833
EASTERBROOK
  Nicholas, of Onondaga Co. - 23 Feb. 1835
EASTON
  Ephraim, of Albany - 14 June 1833
  Frederick, of Livingston Co. - 2 Jan. 1844
  Grace (wife of John Easton), of NYC - 5 Sept. 1845
  William, of NYC, late of U.K. - 11 Apr. 1831
  William, of Newtown, Queens Co. - 27 Dec. 1845
EASTWOOD
  Joseph, of Rochester, Monroe Co. - 16 Jan. 1841
EATON
  Edward, of Eaton, Madison Co. - 3 Apr. 1843
EBERHARD
  John Andrew, of Albany - 13 July 1825
ECCLES
  Thomas, of Wayne Co. - 26 Jan. 1831
ECCLESTON
  Edward, of Rochester, Monroe Co., born a British subject; has been
    in U.S. the past 15 years - 13 Feb. 1839
ECKHART
  Caspar, of NYC - 26 Mar. 1845
ECKHOFF
  John Frederick William, of Clarkstown, Rockland Co.; res. of U.S.
    for about 10 years - 1 Nov. 1847
ECLES
  John, of Oswegatchie, St. Lawrence Co. - 24 Oct. 1838
EDDIE
  John, of NYC, grocer - 30 Apr. 1834
EDEN
  Jane, of NYC, late of Loftus, Eng. - 31 Aug. 1826
  Matthew, of NYC, subject of U.K., res. of NYC for between 5 and
    6 years last past; took incipient measures about June 1822- 13
    June 1826

EDMOND
  Joseph, of Le Roy, Jefferson Co. - 27 Feb. 1835
EDUS
  Joseph, of Lyme, Jefferson Co., born at Gourgeou, Dept. of Haute
    Saone, France, in 1810; he removed to N.Y. in 1833 - 4 Nov.
    1841
EDWARDS
  George, of New Hartford, Oneida Co. - 4 Mar. 1834
  George, of New Hartford, Oneida Co. - 25 Feb. 1834
  Henry, of Seneca Falls, Seneca Co. - 27 Mar. 1834
  Thomas, of Rochester, Monroe Co., native of Parish of Edgefield,
    Eng.; emigrated in 1829 - 23 June 1834
  Thomas, of NYC, late of U.K. - 28 Feb. 1835
EGQUEN
  Joseph, of NYC, shipwright - 10 Nov. 1827
EHERTH
  Godfrey, of Croghan, Lewis Co. - 23 Sept. 1843
EHRHARDT
  Dietrich, of Wayne Co. - 28 Sept. 1830
EICHENLAUB
  Michael, of Wayne Co. - 26 Sept. 1833
EISENTRAGER
  Ludwig, of Wayne Co. - 5 Mar. 1846
ELGAR
  James, of Oneida Co. - 15 Oct. 1835
ELIAS
  Christian, of Euphratah, Fulton Co., native of Hessen, Germany;
    came to U.S. in Sept. 1832 - 6 Sept. 1842
ELLIOT
  John, of Buffalo, Erie Co. - 17 June 1833
ELLIOTT
  John, of Burlington, Otsego Co. - 1 Apr. 1834
  John, of NYC - 22 Apr. 1839
  Josiah, of Erie Co., native of Staffordshire, Eng. - 4 Feb. 1845
  Martha (wife of William Elliott), of NYC - 19 Sept. 1845
  Mary Varty, of Buffalo, Erie Co., formerly of Great Salkeld,
    Cumberland Co., Eng. - 28 Aug. 1837
  William, of NYC, mason - 3 May 1826
  William, of NYC, drover - 2 Apr. 1842
ELLIS
  James, of Williamsburgh, Kings Co. - 16 Sept. 1840
  Thomas, of Lockport, Niagara Co. - 14 Sept. 1833
ELLWANGER
  John, of Lansingburgh, Rensselaer Co. - 10 Apr. 1837
ELPHICK
  James, of Vernon, Oneida Co. - 13 Sept. 1839
ELSTON
  David, of Kings Co. - 28 Sept. 1836
ELWELL
  William, of NYC, accountant - 15 June 1835
ELWOOD
  John, of Albion, Oswego Co., native of Witherel, Cumberland Co.,
    U.K. - 12 Dec. 1834
EMERY
  James, of Whitestown, Oneida Co. - 10 Sept. 1832
  William, of Rochester, Monroe Co. - 9 June 1847
ENGLAND
  John, of East Bloomfield, Ontario Co. - 22 Feb. 1841
  John, of Queens Co. - 16 June 1845
ENGLER
  Charles, of NYC, merchant - 16 Feb. 1836
ENGLISHBEE
  Francis, of NYC - 19 Mar. 1844
ENNIS
  Michael, of Verona, Oneida Co., late of Moor, Ire. - 20 May 1825

ENNIS (continued)
   Michael, of NYC - 19 Oct. 1832
   Patrick, of Verona, Oneida Co., late of Clonburn, Ire. - 20 May
     1825
ENOUY/ENONY?
   Joseph, of NYC - 26 May 1835
EPHRAIM
   Hirsch Jacob, of Buffalo, Erie Co. - 5 Dec. 1836
ERARD
   Nicholas, of Onondaga Co. - 27 Apr. 1837
ERHART
   Philip, of Wayne Co. - 28 Sept. 1830
ERNEST
   Christian, of Chicktawaga, Erie Co. - 20 Sept. 1842
ERNST
   Philip, of Wayne Co. - 26 Sept. 1833
ESMERALDO
   Joseph I., of NYC - 19 June 1834
ESPENCHEAD
   John, of Wayne Co. - 26 May 1836
   John, Jr., of Wayne Co. - 26 May 1836
ESTEN
   James, of De Kalb, St. Lawrence Co., late from Ire. - 17 Nov.
     1827
ESCH
   Eve, of Verona, Oneida Co. - 14 Dec. 1835
ESTIFF/ESTEFF
   Bastian, of Lewis Co. - 22 Sept. 1834
EUSTACE
   Joshua, of Rochester, Monroe Co. - 15 Oct. 1842
EUSTIS
   Tobias, of Jefferson Co. - 31 Jan. 1846
EVANS
   Ann, of Utica, Oneida Co. - 20 Sept. 1832
   Edward, of Utica, Oneida Co. - 20 Sept. 1832
   John, of Troy, Rensselaer Co., born in Herefordshire, Eng. - 20
     July 1837
   Mary, of NYC - 21 Sept. 1847
   Owen, of Oneida Co., native of North Wales, G.B. - 17 Nov. 1832
   Richard, of NYC - 10 Dec. 1834
   Robert, of Albany, tailor - 22 Oct. 1828
   Robert, of West Turin, Lewis Co. - 14 Mar. 1845
   Thomas, of Jamaica, Queens Co. - 28 June 1836
EVEREST
   George, of Little Falls, Herkimer Co., late of G.B. - 17 May 1833
EVERS
   Patricia, of NYC, formerly of Co. of Longford, Ire. - 13 Sept.
     1830
EVERSHED
   John, of Brighton, Monroe Co. - 7 Apr. 1836
EVERTON
   John, of Deerfield, Oneida Co. - 21 Dec. 1830
EVITT
   Edward, of NYC - 13 Sept. 1845
EWBANK
   James, of NYC - 25 Aug. 1834
EYRE
   Charles Edmund, of NYC, dyer and cleaner, age 27, late of London,
     Eng. - 27 Feb. 1843
EZER
   John, of Wayne Co. - 28 Sept. 1830

FACH
   John G.T., of Coemans, Albany Co. - 16 June 1836
FAGAN
   Patrick, of Lansingburgh, Rensselaer Co. - 9 Dec. 1847

FAIRWEATHER
  William H., of Flushing, Queens Co., merchant, native of Prov.
    of New Brunswick, colony of U.K. - 24 June 1835
FALLER
  John, of Clay, Onondaga Co. - 10 June 1834
FALLS
  Hugh, of Butternuts, Otsego Co. - 30 Nov. 1840
FALTZ
  George, of Erie Co., age 23 - 30 Nov. 1830
FANLSTICK
  Michael, of Wayne Co. - 26 Sept. 1833
FANNELLY/FLANNELY
  Timothy, of NYC, formerly of Ire. - 16 Dec. 1835
FANNING
  Martin, of Somers, Westchester Co. - 3 May 1836
FARINOLI
  Frederico, of NYC - 10 Aug. 1844
FARNAN
  Eugene, of Brooklyn, Kings Co. - 4 Oct. 1828
FARNI
  Barbara, of Lewis Co. - 31 Aug. 1838
  Joseph, of Watson, Lewis Co. - 9 Sept. 1834
  Pierre, of Lewis Co. - 31 Aug. 1838
FARRAND
  Frederick, of Hudson, Columbia Co. - 11 June 1846
FARRELL
  Thomas, of Brooklyn, Kings Co., native of Ire. - 10 Sept. 1842
  William, of Spafford, Onondaga Co. - 17 Mar. 1836
FARREN
  Richard, of City of Albany - 6 Jan. 1836
FARRIER
  Emanuel, of Dutchess Co. - 7 Apr. 1845
FAUCHE
  Victor, of NYC, merchant - 3 Feb. 1835
FAUDE
  Carl, of Buffalo, Erie Co. - 20 Oct. 1843
FAULKNER
  James, of Brooklyn, formerly of Leith, Scotland - 13 Nov. 1828
FAULSTECK
  George, of Wayne Co. - 28 Sept. 1830
FAUSNER
  Henry, of Brooklyn, Kings Co. - 4 Nov. 1841
FAUST
  Charles, of Canajoharie, Montgomery Co., formerly subject of the
    King of Banam (sic!) - 5 Sept. 1840
FAVARGER
  Charles Louis, of NYC - 13 July 1846
FAWCETT
  John, of NYC, organ-builder - 28 Nov. 1834
  Sarah (wife of John Fawcett, of NYC, organ-builder), res. of the
    12th Ward of NYC - 16 Apr. 1844
FAX
  John G., of Brooklyn, Kings Co., late of U.K. - 20 Mar. 1837
FAZON
  Robert, of NYC - 8 May 1826
FEATHERSTONE
  William, of Sangerfield, Oneida Co. - 12 Sept. 1831
FECKER
  Joseph, of Albany - 15 Feb. 1837
FEDERSPIEL
  John, of Buffalo, Erie Co. - 10 Dec. 1835
FEEKER
  Joseph, of Albany Co. - 19 Sept. 1833
FELLOWS
  Thomas, of NYC - 6 Aug. 1830

FENERTY
  Andrew, of Cambria, Niagara Co. - 14 Oct. 1833
FENNER
  William, of NYC - 15 Jan. 1833
FENTON
  David, of Meredith, Delaware Co., native of Scotland - 1 Aug.
    1832
FERBER
  Peter, of NYC - 13 Apr. 1835
FERGUSON
  Alexander, of NYC, silversmith - 26 July 1847
  Thomas, of Albany, late of Co. of Caven, Ire. - 14 Oct. 1834
  William, of Pitsfield, Chenango Co., late of Ire.; for 13 years
    res. of U.S. - 19 Nov. 1836
FERME/FEMEE
  John, of NYC - 1 Oct. 1834
FERRERO/FERERO
  Adelaide (wife of Stephen Ferrero), of NYC, born in the Roman
    States; first arrived in U.S. in 1832 and again, after absence
    of 6 months, in 1840 - 11 June 1842
  Stephen, of NYC, born in Piedmont; arrived in U.S. in 1832 and
    again, after absence of 6 months, in 1840 - 11 June 1842
FERRERS
  Jane Ann, of NYC - 12 Dec. 1843
FERRIGAN
  John, of NYC, butcher - 29 Sept. 1829
FETERS
  Lewis, of Buffalo, Erie Co. - 4 May 1844
FICKERT
  Joseph Christoph, of Croghan, Lewis Co. - 23 Sept. 1843
FIELD
  Alfred, of NYC, merchant - 12 June 1846
  George, of NYC, late of Eng., lithographer - 26 Apr. 1837
FIGUEIRO/FIGUEIRA
  Fortunato J., of NYC - 30 Apr. 1834
  Paulo Joaquin, of NYC - 30 June 1830
FINK
  Johannes, of Erie Co., native of Schletzstadt, France; came to
    U.S. 1 May 1843 - 30 Aug. 1844
FINLAY
  Cornelia A., of Poughkeepsie, Dutchess Co. - 16 Feb. 1843
  Louisa B., of Poughkeepsie, Dutchess Co. - 16 Feb. 1843
  Mary D,, of Poughkeepsie, Dutchess Co. - 16 Feb. 1843
  Norman M., of Greenport, Columbia Co. - 20 Jan. 1843
  Sarah M., of Poughkeepsie, Dutchess Co. - 16 Feb. 1843
FINLEY
  John, of Lansingburgh, Rensselaer Co. - 3 Apr. 1830
FINN
  Matthias, of Albany, tailor - 28 Oct. 1835
FIRTH
  George, of Glen, Montgomery Co., born in Yorkshire, Eng.; came
    to U.S. in 1842; made declaration of intent in June 1846 - 19
    Oct. 1847
  Thomas, of North Hempstead, Queens Co., late of G.B. - 25 Aug.
    1835
FISHER
  George, of Kirkland, Oneida Co. - 19 Oct. 1840
  Henry, of Ledyard, Cayuga Co., native of Leeds, Yorkshire, Eng. -
    20 Mar. 1834
  John T., of NYC, late of U.K. - 18 Aug. 1834
  Thomas, of Onondaga, Onondaga Co. - 1 May 1844
FISK
  Paul, of Canajoharie, Montgomery Co. - 22 July 1840
FITCHER
  John, of Oneida Co. - 11 Oct. 1834

New York Alien Residents, 1825-1848

FITZPATRICK
  Peter, of Albany Co. - 4 Feb. 1835
FLAMMER
  John G., of NYC, book-crimper - 3 Mar. 1834
FLANNAGAN/FLANAGAN
  Edward, of NYC, grocer - 19 Sept. 1825
  Margaret, of City of Albany, native of Ire. - 11 Oct. 1847
  Mary, of City of Albany, native of Ire. - 15 Oct. 1847
FLEETWOOD
  John, of NYC, brewer - 27 Nov. 1835
FLEMING
  George, of Newburgh, Orange Co. - 12 Apr. 1841
  John, of Seneca Co. - 11 Nov. 1844
  Peter, of NYC, civil engineer; declared intent 23 Aug. 1824 -
    5 Aug. 1825
  Robert, of Albany, late of Granard, Co. of Longford, Ire. - 3
    July 1825
FLEMMING
  John, of Buffalo, Erie Co. - 6 June 1832
FLETCHER
  James H., of NYC - 25 Mar. 1840
  Job, of NYC, locksmith - 29 Aug. 1835
  Joseph, of Onondaga Co., born in G.B. - 26 Nov. 1832
FLICK
  Joseph, of Onondaga Co. - 16 Sept. 1835
FLIEDNER
  Christian, of Queens Co. - 27 Nov. 1847
FLOWERS
  George, of Brooklyn, Kings Co., native of Eng., res. of U.S.
    since 15 June 1832
FLUKER
  William, of Genesee Co. - 5 Feb. 1834
FLYNN
  Patric, of Southampton, Suffolk Co., native of Ire. - 9 Oct. 1833
  Patrick, of Brownville, Jefferson Co. - 4 May 1831
  William, of NYC, late of U.K. - 10 Aug. 1832
FOGARTY
  Denis, of NYC - 29 Mar. 1847
  John, of NYC, late of Co. of Dublin, Ire. - 8 June 1843
  Mary (wife of John Fogarty), of NYC - 11 May 1847
  Patrick, of NYC - 31 May 1844
FOLEY
  Patrick, of Rockland Co., subject of U.K. - 9 May 1839
FOOKS
  William Waldron, of Charlton, Saratoga Co., born in Co. of Dor-
    setshire, U.K. - 27 Apr. 1831
FOOS
  Casper, of Rochester, Monroe Co. - 11 Aug. 1842
FORBES
  David, of Canajoharie, Montgomery Co., native of G.B. - 6 Dec.
    1833
  John, of Lenox, Madison Co. - 24 Dec. 1841
  Peter, of Canajoharie, Montgomery Co., native of G.B. - 6 Dec.
    1833
  Robert, of Junius, Seneca Co. - 19 Jan. 1835
  William, of Montgomery Co. - 2 Nov. 1836
FORD
  Ambrose, of NYC - 4 Dec. 1835
FORNON/FORNUN
  Frederick, of Columbia Co. - 6 Apr. 1844
FORRESTER
  Nathaniel, of Niagara Co. - 14 Jan. 1836
FORSTER
  Frances (wife of Thomas Forster), of NYC - 17 Apr. 1846

FORSYTH
  William, of NYC, carpenter - 10 Oct. 1831
FOSHOUR
  John, of NYC, native of Hesse Cassel - 6 May 1834
FOSTER
  John, of Cortland Co. - 31 Jan. 1848
  Joseph, of Otsego, Otsego Co. - 1 Feb. 1831
  Spencer, of Schoharie Co. - 3 Jan. 1835
  William, of Otsego, Otsego Co. - 1 Feb. 1831
FOUGEROU
  Joseph Simon, of Buffalo, Erie Co. - 9 Dec. 1830
FOWLER
  Joseph, of NYC, merchant - 9 May 1836
FOX
  Andrew, of Chili, Monroe Co. - 14 Nov. 1835
  Edward, of Buffalo, Erie Co., late of Bourton-on-the-Water,
    Gloucestershire, Eng. - 3 Sept. 1831
  Henry, of NYC - 4 May 1837
  Joseph F., of Troy, Rensselaer Co. - declared intention at Jus-
    tices Court in Albany - 5 Sept. 1836
  Mary, of Chili, Monroe Co. - 14 Nov. 1835
FOY
  Patrick, of Beekmantown, Clinton Co., late of Co. of Cavan, Ire. -
    12 July 1837
FOYLE
  John of City of Albany - 18 Jan. 1836
FRANCIS
  Isaac, of NYC, dentist - 29 Dec. 1826
  John, of Whitestown, Oneida Co. - 30 Aug. 1833
  John, Jr., of Whitestown, Oneida Co. - Aug. 1833
  Pierre Keff, of NYC, formerly of Belgium - 19 Apr. 1842
  Rosalie (wife of Pierre K. Francis), of NYC - 10 Apr. 1844
FRANKLIN
  Edward, of Utica, Oneida Co., native of London, Eng. - 5 Apr.
    1832
FRANKS
  Thomas, of Pittstown, Rensselaer Co. - 4 Jan. 1838
FRASER
  William, of NYC - 11 Oct. 1847
FRAWGOTT
  Christian, of Monroe Co. - 22 May 1837
FREDENBURGH/FREDENBERGH/FREDENBERGHER
  Valentine, of Wayne Co. - 26 Sept. 1834
FREDERICK
  Oser Jean, of NYC - 31 Mar. 1841
FREELAND
  James, of NYC - 19 Mar. 1846
FREMEY/FREEMEY
  Francis, of Buffalo, Erie Co. - 10 Dec. 1831
FRENCH
  Jacob, of NYC - 25 Mar. 1834
FRESTED
  Richard, of NYC, engraver - 19 June 1827
FREW
  Hugh, of NYC, shoe dealer - 28 Dec. 1843
FRICKER
  Michael, of Lewis Co. - 16 May 1840
FRIDLINGTON
  James, of Sangerfield, Oneida Co. - 15 Mar. 1831
FRIEDMAN
  Paulus, of Greece, Monroe Co. - 6 Aug. 1846
FRISON
  Jacob Victor, of Bennington, Wyoming Co. - (sworn in Erie Co.)
    24 Sept. 1846

FROMAGET
  Anselm, of Newark, N.J. - (sworn in NYC) 7 Aug. 1838
FROMHOLT
  John, of New Haven, Oswego Co., native of Sweden - 8 June 1836
FROST
  Alfred Thomas, of Albany Co. - 18 Sept. 1846
  James, of NYC, late of U.K. - 23 June 1836
FRUIN
  John, of Greig, Lewis Co. - 25 Oct. 1833
FULLAGAR
  William, of NYC, carpenter, born in Eng.; in 1822 arrived in NYC
    from Europe - 5 June 1826
FULLER
  James Cummings, of Skaneateles, Onondaga Co. - 9 June 1834
FULLERTON
  James, of NYC - 8 Sept. 1847
FURLONG
  Paul, of NYC, porter - 12 Dec. 1825
FURNAIR
  Henry, of Canajoharie, Montgomery Co., native of Germany - 14
    May 1833
FURNER
  Francis, of Wayne Co. - 25 Jan. 1831
FURST
  Martin Izrael, of NYC - 2 Nov. 1837
FURSTENBERGER
  John Jacob, of Le Roy, Jefferson Co. - 18 June 1833
FYHRAMT
  Jacob G., of NYC - 14 Sept. 1836
FYSON
  Robert, of Poughkeepsie, Dutchess Co., late of Cambridgeshire,
    Eng.; took incipient measures in Court of Common Pleas of
    Dutchess Co. - 29 Aug. 1836

GADDIS
  William, of Albany - 27 Oct. 1829
GAEDIN
  Jaques, of NYC - 30 July 1842
GALE
  Edmund E.W., of Albany Co. - 27 Aug. 1845
GALLAGHER
  John, of NYC, shopkeeper - 24 June 1842
GALLERY
  James, of Greece, Monroe Co. - 20 Aug. 1834
GALLIER
  James, of NYC - 1 Oct. 1832
GALLON
  Jane, of NYC - 16 Dec. 1844
GALLWEY
  James, of NYC - 24 Jan. 1838
GAMBLE
  Sarah, of NYC, single woman - 22 Nov. 1847
GANDREY
  William, of NYC - 21 Jan. 1839
GANES
  James, of Lewis Co. - 6 Jan. 1835
GANNING/GUNNING
  Thomas, of NYC - 19 May 1834
GANNON
  Thomas, of Clinton, Dutchess Co. - 31 Oct. 1837
GANS
  Balzee, of Wayne Co. - 5 Oct. 1830
  Philip, of Wayne Co. - 28 Sept. 1830
GARAGHAN
  Thomas, of NYC - 18 Mar. 1847

New York Alien Residents, 1825-1848

GARAZZI
  Anton, of NYC - 22 July 1847
GARDINER
  William, of Onondaga Co. - 5 Oct. 1843
GARDNER
  Edward, of Ontario Co., native of Hereford, Eng.; has resided
    5 years in the U.S. - 22 Nov. 1834
  James J., of Glen, Montgomery Co., born in Scotland - 11 Oct.
    1842
  Richard, of Florence, Oneida Co. - 6 Oct. 1831
  William Henry, of Utica, Oneida Co., lately from Deal, Kent Co.,
    Eng. - 14 Mar. 1831
GARETY
  Thomas, of NYC - 23 Sept. 1836
GARNIERE
  Jean Michel, of Oneida Co. - 25 July 1846
GARNISS
  John, of NYC, intelligence office keeper - 15 Mar. 1826
GARRETT
  John, of Niagara, Niagara Co. - 4 Jan. 1838
  William, of Niagara, Niagara Co. - 4 Jan. 1838
GARVEY
  Edward C.K., of Rossie, St. Lawrence Co. - 11 Mar. 1839
GASCOIGNE
  Charles, of NYC, merchant - 5 Feb. 1828
GASKIN
  Edward, of Sangerfield, Oneida Co. - 12 Sept. 1831
GASCOW
  Raimond. of NYC - 31 Jan. 1827
GASS
  Charles, of Lansingburgh, Rensselaer Co. - 29 Apr. 1844
  Joseph, of Onondaga Co. - 27 Apr. 1837
GASSER
  Benedict, of Erie Co., native of Bern, Switzerland; came to U.S.
    on 1 May 1844
GASZYUSKI
  Titus Felix John Neponvoign, of Orange Co. - 23 Sept. 1846
GATES
  Elizabeth, of Sodus, Wayne Co., British subject - 23 Sept. 1840
  Ellen (wife of Oliver Gates), of NYC - 12 Oct. 1846
  Francis, of Schroeppel, Oswego Co. - 18 Oct. 1845
GAUDRY
  Jenny, of Buffalo, Erie Co., widow, formerly of France - 28 Nov.
    1840
GAUSSARDID
  Juan Antonio, of NYC - 13 Dec. 1844
GAZE
  John C., of NYC, subject of U.K. - 8 July 1839
GEARE
  Benjamin Way, of Brooklyn, Kings Co. - 23 Mar. 1836
GEARN
  George, of Newburgh, Orange Co., formerly of Inverness, Scot-
    land - 18 Feb. 1839
GEE
  Edward A., of NYC, merchant - 15 Nov. 1833
GEESR
  Joseph, of Rochester, Monroe Co. - 8 May 1847
GENET
  Claude, of Williamsburgh, Kings Co., glass-blower - (sworn in
    NYC) 20 Oct. 1846
GENT
  William, of NYC, subject of U.K., res. of U.S. between 19 and 20
    years; took incipient measures in Apr. 1836 - 25 July 1836
GEORGE
  George, of Albany - 2 Dec. 1834

GEORGE (continued)
  James, of Westchester Co. - 1 Nov. 1834
  Jean Nicolas, of Lewis Co. - 31 Aug. 1838
  Robert, of Westchester Co. - 1 Nov. 1834
GEPNER/GOPNER
  Louis/Ludwig, of Erie Co. - 4 Dec. 1834
GERBER
  John, of Watson, Lewis Co. - 9 Sept. 1834
GERLACH/GERLASCH
  Ferdinand, of Alexandria, Jefferson Co. - 5 Sept. 1834
GERMANY
  Philip, of Wayne Co. - 26 Sept. 1834
GERNTON
  Mary (widow of John Gernton), of NYC - 15 Oct. 1847
GERSTNER
  Melchior, of Rochester, Monroe Co. - 7 Sept. 1847
GESCHEIDT
  Charles G., of NYC. - 20 Apr. 1838
  Lewis Anthony, of NYC, physician - 14 Dec. 1836
GIBBON
  Edward Masters, of Buffalo, Erie Co., late of Milton, Co. of
    Kent, Eng. - 13 June 1832
GIBBS
  Henry, of NYC - 5 Aug. 1835
  Richard, of Elbridge, Onondaga Co. - 7 Dec. 1831
GIBLIN
  Patrick, of Galway, Saratoga Co. - 17 Oct. 1842
GIBSON
  David, of Brooklyn, Kings Co. - 10 May 1839
  David, of Lockport, Niagara Co. - 14 Oct. 1846
  James, of NYC, late of U.K. - 22 Sept. 1847
  James, of NYC, baker - 8 Feb. 1848
  John, of Buffalo, Erie Co., British subject, for many years past
    res. of N.Y. - 2 Apr. 1831
  John, of Albany Co., formerly of G.B. 29 Nov. 1834
  John Downie, of City of Albany - 2 July 1836
  William, of Elba, Genesee Co. - 2 Oct. 1839
  William, of Hempstead, Queens Co., British subject; came to U.S.
    on 7 Apr. 1827 - 31 May 1843
  Wood, of NYC - 12 Mar. 1840
GIGNOUX
  Claudius, of NYC, merchant - 22 Apr. 1835
  Francis Regis, of Brooklyn, Kings Co., native of Lyons, France -
    (sworn in NYC) 23 Dec. 1843
GILBERT
  Catharine (wife of Edmund T. Gilbert), of NYC - 16 Dec. 1847
  James, of Glen, Wayne Co. - 23 Feb. 1835
GILBLING
  Ludwig, of Oneida Co. - 9 July 1836
GILBORNE
  Henry, of Root, Montgomery Co. - (sworn in Cherry Valley, Otsego
    Co.) 1 Mar. 1845
GILCHRIST
  Andrew, of Argyle, Washington Co. - 16 Oct. 1843
GILES
  George, of Oswego Co., native of Gloucestershire, Eng. - 5 June
    1834
  Horn, of Westmoreland, Oneida Co., native of Eng. - 27 Aug. 1842
GILFILLAND
  Joseph, of NYC - 11 Oct. 1841
GILL
  James D., of NYC - 11 Sept. 1846
  William, of Brooklyn, Kings Co., born in G.B. - 12 Nov. 1845
GILLALLY/GELLALLY
  John, of NYC - 26 Feb. 1844

GILLEY
    Samuel, of Elbridge, Onondaga Co., born subject of G.B. - 30
        Sept. 1830
GILLIAM
    John, for past 4 years res. of NYC, formerly subject of U.K.;
        took incipient measures 19 Sept. 1836 - 23 Sept. 1836
GILLICK
    Phillip, of NYC - 26 July 1842
GILLIGAN
    John, of Albany, born in Ire. - 25 June 1829
    John, of Sangerfield, Oneida Co. - 16 Mar. 1831
GILLILAND
    John L., of Brooklyn, Kings Co. - 20 May 1830
GILLINGS
    Edward, of Lockport, Niagara Co. - 16 Sept. 1836
GILLISPIE
    John, of NYC, late of U.K. - 23 Feb. 1833
GIRADOT
    Francis Lewis Augustus, of Jamaica, Queens Co. - 5 Feb. 1847
GIRVAN
    Gilbert, of NYC - 14 Feb. 1831
    James, of NYC, tailor - 24 Feb. 1830
GLADWISH
    Hugh, of Greensburgh, Westchester Co. - 16 May 1833
GLASS
    Barbara F., of Rockland Co.; her dec'd husband, John Glass, had
        made application on 21 July 1827 on behalf of himself, his
        wife and their children, Elizabeth, Ann, Barbara and John -
        25 Aug. 1834
    Jane, of Sterling, Cayuga Co. - (sworn in Wayne Co.) 17 Jan. 1845
    Robert, of Jefferson Co. - 24 Feb. 1838
GLEDSTON
    William, of Niagara Co. - 12 Jan. 1836
GLEESON
    Johanna, of Albany Co. - 26 Nov. 1847
GLEN
    Andrew, of Marshall, Oneida Co., native of Parish of Stranolar,
        Co. of Donegal, Ire. - 29 Oct. 1840
GLENNY
    George, of NYC - 4 Mar. 1837
GLOVER
    Townsend, of Fishkill, Dutchess Co. - 12 Aug. 1841
GOADBY
    James, of NYC, grate-maker - 6 Apr. 1830
    William, of NYC, grate-maker - 6 Apr. 1830
GODET
    Thomas Martin Du Bois, of NYC - 11 Aug. 1843
GODFREY
    Kemp, of NYC, late of U.K. - 26 Feb. 1834
GODGUIN
    Emanuel F., of NYC - 13 Nov. 1833
GOETS
    Nicholas, of Buffalo, Erie Co. - 22 Aug. 1831
GOETZMAN
    Philip, of Wayne Co., born in France - 16 May 1844
GOHNEN (or GOHNER?)
    Katrina, of Bushwick, Kings Co., formerly of Rothenburgh, King-
        dom of Wuertemberg - (sworn in NYC) 6 Dec. 1847
GOLDBERG
    Heres Lyon, of NYC - 10 Dec. 1837
GOLDING
    James F., of Albany - 25 July 1838
    John, of NYC - 11 Feb. 1836
GOLDSMITH
    John Louis, of Champion, Jefferson Co. - 3 Sept. 1832

GOLSH
  Alfred, of NYC - 17 Feb. 1842
GOOD
  William, of NYC, grocer - 15 June 1827
GOODCHILD
  Edward, of Wayne Co. - 28 Jan. 1836
  Henry, of Wayne Co. - 1 Feb. 1834
GOODENOUGH
  William, of Rochester, Monroe Co. - 4 Apr. 1844
GOODSMAN
  Elizabeth (wife of Thomas Goodsman, of NYC, carman), of NYC -
    10 Sept. 1844
GOODWIN
  Edwin P., of Utica, Oneida Co., native of Co. Mayo, Ire., age 26;
    came to U.S. in 1842 - 17 Nov. 1843
GORDON
  Archibald, of Richmond Co., British subject - 5 Sept. 1839
  Robert, of Wayne Co. - 20 Jan. 1840
GORMLY
  Owen, of NYC, laborer, born in Ire., res. of NYC since Sept.
    1823 - 11 June 1825
GOSTANGER
  Lorenz, of Lyme, Jefferson Co., born in Germany, subject of the
    Duke of Hohenzollern - 11 July 1843
GOTIER
  Marian, of Rome, Oneida Co. - 26 June 1844
GOW
  Alexander, of Niagara Co. - 2 July 1844
GOWER
  Elizabeth, of Milton, Saratoga Co. - 17 Jan. 1839
  Jesse, of Milton, Saratoga - (sworn in Schenectady Co. Court) -
    17 Jan. 1839
  John, of Milton, Saratoga Co. - 17 Jan. 1839
  Stephen S., of NYC - 21 June 1836
  William, of Newtown, Queens Co., farmer - 3 Oct. 1835
GRAAF
  Arnold, of NYC - 7 Oct. 1847
  Mary (wife of Arnold Graaf, of NYC), of NYC - 12 Oct. 1847
GRACEY
  John, of Chautauque Co., born an English subject - 14 Oct. 1836
GRADY
  Francis, of NYC - 19 Oct. 1832
  James, of NYC - 19 Oct. 1832
GRAEVE
  Werner Francis Herman, of NYC - 5 July 1845
GRAF
  Joseph, of Bennington, Wyoming Co. - 3 Apr. 1847
GRAFT
  Frederick, of Canajoharie, Montgomery Co., from Hanover, subject
    of his late Britannic Majesty; came to U.S. 26 June 1830 - 14
    Jan. 1839
GRAHAM
  Anne, of Cazanovia, Madison Co. - 19 Apr. 1842
  Arthur, of Oswegatchie, St. Lawrence Co., late from Ire. - 12 July
    1831
  Ben, of NYC, merchant, born in Scotland; he took incipient mea-
    sures in the Marine Court in NYC on 3 Oct. 1835 - 15 Apr. 1836
  David, of Argyle, Washington Co. - 10 Mar. 1840
  Elizabeth, of Argyle, Washington Co. - 10 Mar. 1840
  Francis, of NYC, gentleman - 12 Dec. 1829
  James, of Jefferson Co., born in town of Bellyhupham, Ire. - 3
    Aug. 1835
  Jane, of NYC, widow - 19 June 1843
  John, of Williamsburgh, Kings Co. - 11 July 1831
  John, of Brooklyn, Kings Co. - (sworn in NYC) 14 May 1846

New York Alien Residents, 1825-1848

GRAHAM (continued)
  Margaret, of NYC - 12 Jan. 1848
  William, of Phelps, Ontario Co. - 24 Feb. 1834
GRAHAME
  Robert, of Brooklyn, Kings Co. - 3 Sept. 1846
GRAM
  Johann W., of Buffalo, Erie Co. - 27 Dec. 1844
GRANGE
  William, of Oneida Co., native of Eng., res. of N.Y. since 1830 -
    22 Apr. 1833
GRANGER
  John, of Williamsburgh, Kings Co., citizen of U.K.; res. of the
    village of Williamsburgh for 2 years and of NYC for 12 years
    before; declared intention 29 Aug. 1844 - 20 Sept. 1844
GRANT
  John, of NYC - 13 Jan. 1835
  Robert, of NYC - 8 Oct. 1847
GRAVES
  Alexander, of NYC - 23 Aug. 1834
  Charles, of Chazy, Clinton Co. - 28 Jan. 1840
  Henry, of Minden, Montgomery Co. - 1 Nov. 1834
  John, of Wayne Co. - 23 May 1832
  John, Jr., of Wayne Co. - 23 May 1832
GRAY
  George, of Skaneateles, Onondaga Co. - 3 Sept. 1833
  John James, of NYC - 16 May 1826
  Robert, of Oxford, Chenango Co., born in Co. of Tyrone, Ire.; in
    1816 departed from Ire. and that summer arrived at Otsego Co.;
    in 1829 removed to Oxford - 25 Feb. 1832
  Zachariah, of Cayuga Co., native of Huntingdonshire, Eng. - 18
    Oct. 1834
GRAYSTON
  John, of Williamsburgh, Kings Co., carpenter - 6 Nov. 1847
GREADY
  John, of NYC, drover, born in Ire. - 25 July 1827
GREASLEY
  Thomas Taft, of NYC - 12 Mar. 1834
GREBBS
  Michael, of Canajoharie, Montgomery Co. - 31 Aug. 1841
GREEN
  Elizabeth, of NYC - 22 Apr. 1846
  Elizabeth (wife of Patrick Green), of NYC - 27 July 1846
  Elizabeth T. (late Elizabeth Walker), of NYC - 6 Mar. 1844
  Jesse, of NYC, haircloth- manufacturer - 21 May 1834
  William, of Brighton, Monroe Co., born 14 Jan. 1799 in Eng.; he
    emigrated to U.S. in Apr. 1830 and landed at NYC in May 1830 -
    26 Mar. 1834
  William, of Onondaga Co. - 30 Nov. 1838
GREENFIELD
  Robert, of Jefferson Co. - 18 Sept. 1835
GREENWOOD
  John, of Chenango Co. - 9 June 1835
GREER
  James, of Plattsburgh, Clinton Co. - 25 Jan. 1832
GREGG
  John, of Brooklyn, Kings Co. - 13 July 1843
GREGORY
  John, of NYC - 17 Sept. 1833
GREN
  Charles Alm, of City of Albany - 10 Mar. 1836
GRENTRINGEN
  Francis Joseph, of Irondequoit, Monroe Co. - Nov. 1846
GRESS
  Joseph, of NYC, French subject; declared intent in Marine Court
    on 5 Nov. 1839 - 23 June 1840

New York Alien Residents, 1825-1848

GRESSARD
  Jean David, of Mexico, Oswego Co. - 2 Feb. 1831
GRIEBER
  Johan Baptist Nicolaus, of Onondaga Co. - 5 June 1843
GRIFFIN
  John, of NYC - 5 Feb. 1842
  Richard, of Poughkeepsie, Dutchess Co., formerly of Ire. - 5 Oct.
    1842
GRIFFITHS
  Edward, of Greenburgh, Westchester Co., subject of G.B. - 31 Oct.
    1845
  John, of NYC, late of Bangor in G.B. - 8 Feb. 1826
GRIGOR
  David, of Hammond, St. Lawrence Co. - 8 June 1827
GRIMARD
  Peter, of Albany - 20 July 1831
GRIMES
  John, of Lockport, Niagara Co. - 8 Jan. 1836
GRIMSHAW
  Samuel, of NYC, merchant - 25 Apr. 1835
GRISSON
  Gotthelf, of Albany - 18 Dec. 1833
  Samuel, of NYC, merchant, native of Hamburgh, Germany - 25 Oct.
    1838
GROFF
  John George, of Lockport, Niagara Co. - 19 Oct. 1840
GROGAN
  Mary, of Albany Co. - 15 June 1847
GROMAUD (or GROMAND?)
  Nicholas, of Mexico, Oswego Co. - 2 Feb. 1831
GROSELANDE
  Augustus, of NYC, native of Switzerland, res. of U.S. for four
    years past - 12 July 1847
GROTTKE
  Godfried, of Buffalo, Erie Co. - 20 Oct. 1843
GROVE
  Henry D., now of White Creek, Washington Co., who intends to re-
    side in Hoosic, Rensselaer Co. - 28 Feb. 1831
  Samuel, of Brooklyn, Kings Co. - 14 Feb. 1837
GROVES
  Samuel, of NYC - 4 Nov. 1845
GRUNENTHAL/GRUNNENTHAL
  William Theodore, of NYC, merchant - 27 Feb. 1835
GUENTHER
  Frederick Biedermann, of City of Albany, late of Germany - 15 Aug.
    1836
GUERIN
  Francis, of NYC - 8 Aug. 1825
GUIGON
  Augustus, of Shankaken, Ulster Co., tanner, native of France -
    23 July 1835
GUINAN
  Terry, of Hudson, Columbia Co. - 1 Apr. 1839
GUINACHIO/GENOCHIO
  Andra/Andro, of NYC, native of Sardinia - 19 Nov. 1833
GUINTHER
  George, of Deerfield, Oneida Co., late of Prussia - 31 Oct. 1844
GUMBELL
  Joseph M., of Buffalo, Erie Co. - 12 Nov. 1834
GUNN
  Jacob, of Niagara Co. - 15 Feb. 1836
GUNTE
  Adam, of NYC - 5 Apr. 1837
GUPPY
  Samuel, of NYC - 22 Jan. 1834

GUPPY (continued)
  William, of Onondaga Co. - 9 Sept. 1836
GURNEE
  Elizabeth (wife of William F. Gurnee), of Haverstraw, Rockland
    Co. - 2 Feb. 1842
GUY
  Michael, of Verona, Oneida Co., late of Killoughey, Ire. - 20
    May 1825

HAACK
  Louisa Cornelia (wife of John Wolfgang Haack), of Buffalo, Erie
    Co. - 14 Oct. 1847
HAAG
  Nicolaus, of Rochester, Monroe Co. - 8 Nov. 1838
HAAS
  Ulrich, of Wayne Co. - 26 Sept. 1834
HADAWAY
  Thomas H., of NYC - 27 Aug. 1838
HADDOCK
  Thomas, of NYC - 21 Feb. 1844
HADFIELD
  Eliza Ann (wife of Robert Hadfield), of Erie Co. - 23 Oct. 1843
  Robert, of Erie Co. - 23 Oct. 1843
HADLEY
  John, of Wayne Co. - 22 May 1832
HAGGERT
  James, of Madison Co. - 16 Feb. 1835
HAGGERTY
  Darby, of NYC - 5 Aug. 1829
  Margaret, of Richmond Co. - 6 Jan. 1845
  Timothy, of Erie Co. - 7 Nov. 1846
HAIN
  Charles, of Sand Lake, Rensselaer Co. - 8 Jan. 1834
HAIR
  James, of Rochester, Monroe Co. - 15 Jan. 1836
HALEY
  Bridget (widow of John Haley), of NYC - 1 Oct. 1846
HALL
  Ann, of Burlington, Otsego Co. - 14 Oct. 1834
  Daniel, of Newtown, Queens Co. - 28 Jan. 1837
  Edward, of Burlington, Otsego Co. - 14 Oct. 1834
  Elizabeth, of Rochester, Monroe Co. - 4 Oct. 1837
  Isaac, of Newtown, Queens Co. - 27 Jan. 1837
  Joseph, of NYC - 28 Mar. 1833
  Joseph, of Kings Co. - 14 Sept. 1837
  Peter, of Herkimer Co. - 4 Mar. 1833
  Sarah, of Richland, Oswego Co. - 13 July 1845
  William, of Newtown, Queens Co., late of U.K. - 26 Feb. 1833
  William F., of Brooklyn, Kings Co. - 11 Oct. 1833
HALLE
  Abraham H., of Columbia Co. - 21 Nov. 1827
  Louis Francois, of NYC, jeweller - 28 Sept. 1829
HALLIARD
  Thomas, of Brooklyn - 27 Jan. 1829
HALLIGAN
  James, of Westfield, Richmond Co. - 6 June 1845
HALLWORTH
  Thomas, of NYC - 30 Apr. 1846
HALPIN
  John, of Dutchess Co., late of Dublin, Ire. - 19 Feb. 1834
HALSEY
  David, of Castleton, Richmond Co. - 17 Apr. 1845
HALSTROM
  Peter, of Wayne Co. - 25 Jan. 1831

HAMBLIN
   Thomas S., of NYC, tragedian, res. of said city for more than 2
      years - 2 Apr. 1835
HAMELL
   Hugh, of Poughkeepsie, Dutchess Co. - 23 Jan. 1836
HAMER
   John, of New Hartford, Oneida Co., formerly of Radnorshire in
      Wales - 11 Apr. 1845
HAMIL
   Mary, of Troy, Rensselaer Co., subject of G.B. - 26 Feb. 1845
   Patrick, of Troy, Rensselaer Co., born at Louth, Co. of Louth,
      Ire., age now 34; emigrated from Liverpool; arrived at NYC in
      1840 - 21 Jan. 1845
HAMILL
   John, of NYC, formerly of Ire. - 16 Mar. 1843
HAMLIN
   Robert, of Onondaga Co. - 26 Aug. 1840
HAMILTON
   James, of Easton, Washington Co. - 20 Sept. 1830
   James, of NYC - 16 Dec. 1834
   John M., of Buffalo, Erie Co. - 28 Sept. 1835
   Robert, of Harpersfield, Delaware Co., late of Co. of Monaghan,
      Ire. - 8 June 1832
HAMLET/HAMLEET
   John, of Jamaica, Queens Co., late of G.B. - 13 Apr. 1835
HAMMOND
   Robert, of Erie Co. - 29 Mar. 1837
HAMPSHIRE
   John, of Lockport, Niagara Co. - 8 Feb. 1845
HANBOLD
   Ernest Ferdinand, of NYC - 27 Apr. 1847
HANCE
   John F., of NYC, subject of U.K. - 24 Mar. 1831
HANCOCK
   Robert, of Williamsburgh, Kings Co. - 30 June 1846
HAND
   Christopher, of Newburgh, Orange Co. - 12 June 1841
HANDS
   Henry, of NYC - 1 Oct. 1841
HANDYSIDES
   Reuben, of Warsaw, Genesee Co. - 19 Oct. 1832
HANKY
   Frederick, of Monroe Co. - 18 Oct. 1837
HANLEY
   William, of Oneida Co., native of London, Eng. - 13 Oct. 1834
HANLON
   Dennis, of Verona, Oneida Co., late of Killoughey, Ire. - 19 May
      1825
   Esther, of Verona, Oneida Co., late of Killoughey, Ire. - 19 May
      1825
HANNA
   James, of NYC, porter - 10 July 1838
   Samuel, of Kinderhook, Columbia Co. - 19 Feb. 1831
   Thomas, of Newburgh, Orange Co. - 19 Mar. 1846
HANNEGAN
   Edward, of NYC, cartman - 5 Jan. 1829
HANSARD
   John, of Albany - 10 Mar. 1837
HANSEL
   Jacob, of Erie Co. - 30 Apr. 1836
   Jacob, of Erie Co. - 23 May 1836
HANSELMAN
   Michael, of Buffalo, Erie Co. - 7 Dec. 1831
HANSEN
   Niels Christian Holger Engelbret, of Catskill, Greene Co., subject
      of Denmark - 16 May 1835

HANSON
  Jonathan, of NYC - 5 July 1837
HARDIE
  James, of Syracuse, Onondaga Co. - 30 Sept. 1845
HARDMAN
  Thomas, of NYC - 8 Mar. 1847
HARDY
  Barnabas, of City of Albany - 3 Mar. 1836
  John, of Western, Oneida Co., native of Eng. - 4 Mar. 1831
  Thomas, of NYC, formerly resident of Birmingham, Eng. - 20 June
    1836
  William, of Albany - 16 June 1837
HARGREAVES
  James, of Schenectady, Schenectady Co. - 29 Oct. 1842
HARLEY
  Elizabeth, of Monroe Co. - 29 Feb. 1840
HARMON
  Philip, of NYC, merchant, born in Bavaria, res. of NYC since
    1818, when he arrived there from Europe - 18 Nov. 1825
HARNWELL
  Adam, of Canandaigua, Ontario Co. - 21 Aug. 1833
HAROLD
  John, of NYC, importer of watches - 22 June 1835
HARRIS
  Charles, of NYC, watchmaker - 31 May 1826
  Dennis, of NYC, sugar refiner - 26 Sept. 1844
  George, of New Cornwall, Orange Co., whitesmith - 23 Apr. 1835
  Joseph, of NYC - 23 Feb. 1847
  Noah Morris, of Allegheny Co. - 27 Feb. 1833
  Thomas E., of Orangetown, Rockland Co. - 30 Sept. 1846
  William, of Oneida Co., native of Stanwick, Northamptonshire,
    Eng. - 11 June 1835
  William, of NYC - 20 May 1847
HARRISON
  David, of Oneida Co. - 19 Feb. 1833
  George, of NYC - 10 Mar. 1834
  Henry George, of Buffalo, Erie Co. - 4 Mar. 1835
  John, of NYC, residing at 19 Courtlandt St., grocer - 16 Jan.
    1841
  Joseph, of Smithville, Chenango Co., farmer, from Dromskill, Co.
    of Monaghan, Ire. - 8 Nov. 1830
  Joseph, of NYC, hatter - 8 Mar. 1834
  Lawrence, of Albany Co. - 28 June 1847
  Richard, of Williamsburgh, Kings Co. - 13 May 1847
  Robert, of Lansingburgh, Rensselaer Co. - 11 May 1841
  Thomas, of Brooklyn, Kings Co. - 21 Jan. 1845
HART/HEART
  Jean, of Chautauque Co. - 8 June 1837
HARTLEY
  Hannah (wife of Joseph Hartley), of NYC - 17 Apr. 1846
HARTMAN/HARTMANN
  Margaret (wife of Frederick Hartmann), of NYC - 1 Dec. 1845
HARTT
  John Thompson, of NYC, dyer - 6 Mar. 1826
HATRZO
  Philipp, of NYC, shoemaker - 8 May 1845
HARVEY
  James, of Onondaga Co. - 28 Sept. 1835
HARWOOD
  Thomas, of Mohawk, Montgomery Co., British subject, res. of N.Y.
    for past 6 years - 8 Apr. 1840
  William, of NYC - 13 Sept. 1833
HASKELL
  John, of Buffalo, Erie Co. - 28 Sept. 1835

HASLEHURST
  Samuel, of Oneida Co. - 23 Sept. 1835
HATLIFF
  David, of Trenton, Oneida Co. - 8 Apr. 1831
HATON
  John B., of Croghan, Lewis Co. - 23 Sept. 1841
HAUCK
  Siegfried, of Lewis Co. - 21 Sept. 1830
HAUSR
  Jacob, of Rochester, Monroe Co. - 9 Aug. 1847
HAVELL
  Robert, of Brooklyn, Kings Co., born in U.K. - 22 May 1841
HAVERCORN
  Michael, of Buffalo, Erie Co. - 6 June 1831
HAWES
  Siday, of City of Albany, late of Norfolk, Eng. - 18 Oct. 1832
HAWKE
  Robert, of Monroe Co. - 21 Mar. 1844
HAWKES
  John, of NYC - 24 July 1843
HAWKESWORTH
  James, of NYC, lately of Barbadoes - 19 Nov. 1834
HAWKINS
  David, of Rochester, Monroe Co. - 22 Sept. 1836
  Francis, of Rochester, Monroe Co. - 11 Oct. 1836
  George, of Rochester, Monroe Co., late of Eng. - 6 Dec. 1831
  John, of Ithaca, Tompkins Co., native of London, Eng. - 11 Sept.
    1832
  John, of New Rochelle, Westchester Co. - 14 June 1836
HAWKSLEY
  Joseph F., of NYC - 1 Mar. 1843
HAWLEY
  Henry, of Brooklyn, Kings Co. - 26 Feb. 1839
HAWWORTH
  Thomas, of Poughkeepsie, Dutchess Co., late of Eng. - 26 Oct.
    1835
HAWS
  John W., of Brownville, Jefferson Co. - 31 July 1845
HAWSE
  John, of Batavia, Genesee Co., citizen of U.K. - 12 June 1839
HAY
  James, of NYC - 17 May 1833
  Thomas, of Castleton, Richmond Co. - 16 July 1836
HAYDEN
  James, of Kings Co. - 9 Jan. 1837
HAYDON
  John, of Onondaga Co. - 2 Dec. 1836
HAYES
  Hiram, of Kinderhook, Columbia Co., native of Eng. - 11 Apr.
    1833
  Joseph, of Troy, Rensselaer Co. - 30 Mar. 1844
  Lawrence, of Watertown, Jefferson Co. - 18 Feb. 1840
  Margaret, of Brooklyn, Kings Co. - 19 Aug. 1847
HAYLER
  Hugh, of Onondaga Co. - 23 Aug. 1837
HAYNE
  Ellen (wife of John Hayne, of NYC), of NYC - 23 Feb. 1843
HAYNES
  Francis, of Brooklyn, Kings Co., millwright - (sworn in NYC) 19
    Jan. 1848
HAYS
  James, of Eastchester, Westchester Co., laborer - 8 July 1834
HAYTER
  Philip, of NYC, baker - 4 Aug. 1826

HAZELWOOD
  Richard, of Antwerp, Jefferson Co. - 29 Feb. 1832
HEAD
  Thomas, of Kingston, Ulster Co. - 10 June 1834
HEALY
  Andrew, of Wayne Co. - 29 Jan. 1834
HEAPS
  John, of Ghent, Columbia Co. - 22 Nov. 1831
HEATH
  William, of Albany - 18 Sept. 1846
HEBERLE
  Peter, of Irondequoit, Monroe Co. - 19 Sept. 1843
HECKLE
  John, of NYC - 19 June 1838
  Robert, of NYC - 30 May 1838
HECKSCHER
  Charles August, of NYC, merchant, born in Hamburgh, Germany; on
    10 Apr. 1829, then aged upwards of 21, made declaration of in-
    tent - 10 Apr. 1830
HEDDON
  Thomas, of Stafford, Genesee Co. - 24 Mar. 1834
  Thomas, Jr., of Stafford, Genesee Co. - 24 Mar. 1834
HEDGES
  James, of NYC, late of U.K. - 20 July 1836
HEEATT
  Joseph D., of Hudson, Columbia Co. - 2 May 1833
HEENAN
  Timothy, of Watervliet, Albany Co.; migrated from Dublin, Ire.,
    and arrived at town of Whitehall, N.Y., in 1832 - 27 Mar. 1838
HEFFERNAN
  John, of Rochester, Monroe Co. - 5 Oct. 1840
  William, of Southampton, Suffolk Co. - 10 May 1845
HEFFORD
  John, of Buffalo, Erie Co., subject of G.B. - 13 Mar. 1843
  Thomas, of Buffalo, Erie Co., British subject - 13 Mar. 1843
HEID
  Michael, of Wayne Co. - 28 Sept. 1830
HEIM
  Joseph, of NYC, late of Germany - 21 Dec. 1825
HEINEMAN
  Frederick, of Erie Co., native of Langenbergheim in Grand Duke-
    dom of Hessen Darmstadt; came to U.S. 24 Oct. 1843 - 30 Aug.
    1844
HEINRICH
  Maria Sophia, of Deerfield, Oneida Co., late of Prussia - 23
    Sept. 1844
HEIS
  Philip, of Wayne Co. - 26 Sept. 1834
HEISER
  Frederick, of Canajoharie, Montgomery Co. - 24 Feb. 1838
  Godfrey, of Albany - 8 Oct. 1832
HELLA
  Augustus, of Ephrata, Fulton Co., formerly of Hesse Castle, in
    Germany ; came to U.S. in July 1835 - 14 Jan. 1839
HELLINGER
  Jacob, of Brighton, Monroe Co. - 8 Aug. 1838
HELLORAN
  Mathew, of Lyme, Jefferson Co. - 8 Dec. 1842
HELLRIEGLE
  Conrad, of Wayne Co. - 26 Sept. 1834
HEMINGS
  Isaac, of Onondaga, Onondaga Co. - 6 Nov. 1845
HENDERSON
  Catharine, of NYC - 25 July 1844
  Thomas, of NYC - 12 Mar. 1827

New York Alien Residents, 1825-1848

HENDERSON (continued)
    William, of NYC - 12 May 1843
    William, of Eagle, Allegheny Co. - 27 Feb. 1843
HENICKE
    Frederick Augustus, of NYC - 14 Mar. 1835
HENNIKER
    Robert, of Hartwick, Otsego Co., late of Westwell. Kent Co.,
        Eng. - 7 Feb. 1838
HENRIQUES
    Abigail (wife of Joseph Henriques), of NYC - 20 Apr. 1836
    David, of NYC, late of Island of Jamaica - 8 Feb. 1827
    Joseph, of NYC, late of Island of Jamaica - 30 Mar. 1826
    Moses, of NYC, late of Island of Jamaica - 6 Apr. 1826
    Sarah, of NYC, widow - 21 Apr. 1836
    Sarah, of NYC - 12 Apr. 1837
HENREY
    James, of Oswego, Oswego Co. - 8 Feb. 1840
HENRY
    Mary, of NYC - 14 Jan. 1830
    Thomas, of Albany - 26 July 1832
HEPTONSTALL
    William, of Depuyster, St. Lawrence Co., late of Yorkshire,
        Eng. - 18 Jan. 1831
HERBENER
    Henry, of Onondaga Co. - 3 Oct. 1839
HERITAGE
    Richard, of Seneca Co. - 20 Feb. 1834
HERMAN
    Adam, of Lima, Livingston Co. - 5 Nov. 1839
HERMON
    Auden, of Bennington, Wyoming Co. - 3 Apr. 1847
HERNANDEZ
    Charles F., of NYC, late of Havana - 19 Dec. 1842
HERRING
    Honora Victorine, of NYC, subject of U.K. - 15 Mar. 1841
    James, of Gates, Monroe Co. - 10 Nov. 1846
HERTLE
    Peter, of Rochester, Monroe Co. - 26 Oct. 1840
HERZIEG
    Benedict, of Little Falls, Herkimer Co. - 14 Sept. 1831
HESS
    Anthony, of Buffalo, Erie Co. - 28 Mar. 1844
HETHERINGTON
    George, of Salina, Onondaga Co. - 2 Dec. 1833
HEUWLETT
    Samuel, of Spafford, Onondaga Co. - 16 May 1832
HEYDIENGER
    John, of NYC, marble-cutter; made declaration of intent on 13
        Aug. 1844 - 12 Apr. 1845
HEYDINGER
    John, of NYC - 23 May 1846
HEYNE
    Frederick, of NYC - 13 Nov. 1847
HEYWOOD
    Joseph, of Geneva, Ontario Co. - 18 Aug. 1831
HEZSELDINE
    William, of Madison, Madison Co. - 26 Mar. 1838
HIATT
    John, of Henrietta, Monroe Co. - 1 Mar. 1840
HICKEY
    John, of Flatbush, Kings Co., formerly of Ire. - 3 May 1836
HICKS
    John, of Greenwich, Fairfield Co., Conn. - (sworn in NYC) 14
        Feb. 1828

52

HIERSH
  John, of Buffalo, Erie Co. - 6 June 1831
HIGHET
  John, of NYC, turner - 17 May 1826
HILL
  Benjamin, of Rochester, Monroe Co. - 6 Jan. 1844
  John, of NYC, engraver - 22 Mar. 1833
  John, of Watervliet, Albany Co. - 16 Apr. 1834
HILTON
  Edward, of NYC, grocer - 20 Dec. 1832
HINGSTON
  Mary, of NYC, widow - 12 Dec. 1837
HINRICKS
  Charles, of NYC - 12 May 1841
HINSHELWOOD
  Sarah Ross, of Cooperstown, Otsego Co. - 4 Nov. 1836
HIRSCH/HIRCHY
  Christian, of Watson, Lewis Co. - 9 Sept. 1834
  Simon, of Watson, Lewis Co. - 2 July 1834
HIRST
  Arthur, of Brooklyn, merchant - 5 Oct. 1831
HITCHINS
  Francis, of Hosick, Rensselaer Co. - 23 Dec. 1835
HOBLEY
  Charles, of NYC - 5 Apr. 1843
  Jesse, of NYC - 5 Apr. 1843
  Thomas, of NYC - 5 Apr. 1843
HOCK
  Jacob, of NYC - 7 Dec. 1846
HODGE
  James, of Albany Co. - 17 May 1847
HODGKINSON
  Joseph, of Livingston Co. - 7 Nov. 1846
HODGSDON
  George, of NYC, accountant, native of Bermuda - 9 Apr. 1834
HODGSON
  John, of Rochester, Monroe Co. - 4 Dec. 1846
HODSON
  Joseph, of Southfield, Richmond Co. - 13 Aug. 1847
HOEFFLER
  Andrew, of Rochester, Monroe Co. - 10 June 1840
HOGAN
  Robert, of NYC, physician, late of U.K., 4 years a res. of N.Y.
    State - 22 Oct. 1830
HOGG
  Andrew, of NYC, stone-cutter, formerly of the U.K., res. of N.Y.
    since 15 Apr. last past - 18 June 1830
  James, of Brooklyn, Kings Co. - (sworn in NYC) 22 Nov. 1845
  Thomas, of Queensbury, Warren Co. - 1 Jan. 1846
HOGGS
  Charles, of Albany Co. - 6 Dec. 1847
HOGUET
  Anthony, of NYC, merchant - 9 June 1836
HOLDEN
  William, of Onondaga Co. - 30 Nov. 1837
HOLLANDE
  Peter F.F., of NYC, merchant, late of France - 2 July 1835
HOLLER
  Catharine (born Catharine Biehn, wife of Lorenz Holler), of NYC -
    21 Nov. 1844
HOLME
  John, of Lansingburgh, Rensselaer Co. - 2 Mar. 1830
HOLMES
  Ann, of NYC - 21 Jan. 1840
  George, of Chenango, Broome Co., age 36 - 9 Dec. 1833

HOLMES (continued)
  Joseph, of Niagara Co. - 10 Feb. 1836
HOLROYD
  Mark, of Chenango Co. - 16 Apr. 1840
  Stephen, of Chenango Co. - 16 Apr. 1840
  William, of Cortland Co. - 23 Mar. 1840
HOLST
  Marias, of Pittsford, Monroe Co. - 13 June 1840
HONEY
  Robert, of NYC - 21 Nov. 1834
HOOPER
  John, of NYC, musical-instrument- maker - 7 Sept. 1826
HOOVER
  Fidel, of Rochester, Monroe Co.; came to U.S. in 1832 - 5 Oct.
    1835
HOPE
  Matthew, of NYC, grocer, late of the U.K. - 8 May 1823
HOPKINS
  John, of Flatbush, Kings Co. - 24 Aug. 1845
  John D., of Brooklyn, Kings Co. - 21 Mar. 1836
  Thomas, of Saugerties, Ulster Co. - 6 May 1834
HOPPER
  William, of Onondaga Co., born in G.B. - 28 Nov. 1832
  William, of Onondaga Co. - 9 Oct. 1834
HORNBY
  Edward Orsen, of Canandaigua, Ontario Co., born in London, Eng. -
    25 Nov. 1839
  John, of NYC, soap-boiler - 26 Aug. 1828
HORNE
  Charles J, of Amity, Allegheny Co., age 25 and upwards; arrived in
    U.S. within past 4 years - 13 Mar. 1830
  Jeffery, of Amity, Allegheny Co. - 12 Aug. 1844
HORSLEY
  John H., of Phelps, Ontario Co. - 15 Mar. 1839
HORSPOLE
  Edman, of Niagara Co., late of U.K. - 22 Oct. 1833
HORTON
  Daniel, of NYC - 14 Oct. 1838
HOSKIN
  Catharine (widow of Peter Hoskin, late of NYC), of NYC - 30
    Sept. 1844
HOSMER
  John, of NYC, carpenter - 17 Mar. 1827
HOSTER
  Jacob, of Wayne Co. - 26 Sept. 1835
HOUGH
  James, of NYC - 21 Mar. 1837
HOUGHTON
  James, of Rochester, Monroe Co. - 22 Dec. 1832
HOWCUTT
  John, of Buffalo, Erie Co., British subject - 16 Jan. 1837
HOWELL
  Thomas, of NYC - 19 Feb. 1836
  Walter S., of Mendon, Monroe Co. - 8 Feb. 1837
  William, of NYC - 10 Dec. 1834
HOYT
  Catharine, of Rochester, Monroe Co. - 20 June 1835
HUBBARD
  Edward, of Sangerfield, Oneida Co. - 15 Mar. 1831
HUDDART
  Richard Townsend, of NYC - 17 May 1836
HUDDLESTON
  David, of Chautauque Co., late of Downe, Ire. - 23 Feb. 1838
HUDSON
  Mary Anne, of Ithaca, Tompkins Co.; arrived 12 Dec. 1833 in NYC -

New York Alien Residents, 1825-1848

HUDSON (continued)
  Mary Anne (continued) - 27 Dec. 1844
  William, of Oswegatchie, St. Lawrence Co., late from Eng. - 15
    Sept. 1827
  William, of Schodack, Rensselaer Co., born in Eng. - 2 Mar. 1830
HUE
  Anthony, of NYC, native of France - 22 Aug. 1831
HUEY
  James, of Crawford, Orange Co. - 2 Feb. 1834
HUFF
  Philipp, of Callicow, Sullivan Co. - 13 June 1843
HUGHES
  James, of Brooklyn, Kings Co., laborer - 25 July 1835
  John, of New Brighton, Richmond Co. - 7 Feb. 1837
  John, of West Turin, Lewis Co., British subject - 1 May 1839
  John, of NYC - 8 May 1847
  Michael, of NYC, shoemaker - 27 June 1826
  Patrick, of NYC, carpenter - 14 June 1826
  Patrick, of Troy, Rensselaer Co., native of Gortmaron, Co. of
    Tyrone, Ire. - 21 Jan. 1828
  Thomas, of NYC, stone-cutter; took incipient measures in Marine
    Court on 17 Aug. 1835 - 18 Apr. 1837
  William, of Rensselaer Co. - 30 Mar. 1837
HUGHS
  William, of NYC, formerly of Corvalley, Co. of Monaghan, Ire. -
    7 Nov. 1825
HULME
  William, of Hudson, Columbia Co. - 9 Jan. 1844
HUMBLE
  James D., of NYC - 17 Aug. 1842
HUME
  James, of Burlington, Otsego Co., late of the Parish of Huneham,
    Roxburyshire, Scotland - 13 Oct. 1832
  John, of New Lisbon, Otsego Co. - 8 Nov. 1833
  Robert, of Burlington, Otsego Co. - 27 Apr. 1835
  Thomas, of Burlington, Otsego Co. - 18 Sept. 1834
  Walter, of Wayne Co. - 23 May 1837
  William, of Burlington, Otsego Co. - 8 Nov. 1833
HUNT
  Benjamin, of Queens Co., res. there 38 years last past - 25 Feb.
    1831
  George, of Onondaga Co. - 3 Mar. 1836
  James, of Mount Pleasant, Westchester Co. - 28 May 1839
  Thomas W., of Royalton, Niagara Co. - 23 June 1842
HUNTER
  Patrick, of Geneva, Ontario Co., for some years res. of the U.S. - ·
    23 July 1836
  William, of Rochester, Monroe Co. - 3 Jan. 1847
HUPE
  Narcisse, of Albany Co. - 7 May 1847
HURDSMAN
  Thomas, of Seneca, Ontario Co. - 27 Apr. 1835
HURST/HIRST
  Akid, of Rochester, Monroe Co. - 20 June 1835
HURLEY
  Philip, of Lockport, Niagara Co. - 11 Sept. 1834
HUSKER
  William, of Wayne Co. - 28 Jan. 1841
HUSTER
  Amelia (wife of Henry Huster), of NYC - 18 Oct. 1847
HUSTLER
  Janet, of Westmoreland, Oneida Co. - 15 Sept. 1840
  John, of Whitestown, Oneida Co., native of Eng. - 27 Oct. 1834
HUSTON
  Robert, of NYC - 1 Apr. 1844

HUTCHINGS/HUTCHINS
  Abraham/Abram, of Niagara Co. - 2 Sept. 1835
HUTCHINSON
  Thomas, of Lancaster, Erie Co. - 8 Feb. 1834
HUXTABLE
  John, of Hartland, Niagara Co., late of Devonshire, Eng. - 11
    Feb. 1835
HYLAND
  John, of Verona, Oneida Co., late of Clunsast, Ire. - 20 May 1825
  Patrick, of Verona, Oneida Co., late of Clunsast, Ire. - 20 May
    1825
  Thomas, of Verona, Oneida Co., late of Clunsast, Ire. - 20 May
    1825
  Thomas, Jr., of Verona, Oneida Co., late of Clunsast, Ire. - 20
    May 1825
  William, of Verona, Oneida Co., late of Clunsast, Ire. - 20 May
    1825
HYNES
  John, of Rochester, Monroe Co. - 20 Feb. 1839
IBBOTSON
  Robert, of Kings Co. - 14 Oct. 1836
ILLENDEN
  Richard, of Genesee Co. - 5 Feb. 1834
ILLMAN
  Thomas, of NYC, engraver , late of U.K. - 28 Jan. 1833
IMRIE
  John, of Andes, Delaware Co., native of Scotland - 29 Aug. 1833
INCEURE
  Augustus, of Albany, native of Frankfurt on the Mayne, subject
    of Austria - 19 Aug. 1841
INGLIS
  George, of NYC - 27 May 1833
INSTONE
  Thomas, of Bushwick, Kings Co., carpenter - 14 Sept. 1846
IRELAND
  William M., of NYC, physician, subject of U.K. - 22 May 1828
  William M., of NYC, physician - 26 May 1834
IRVIN
  James, of Onondaga Co., British subject - 16 Mar. 1839
IRVINE/ERVIN
  Christopher, of Leyden, Lewis Co. - 10 June 1834
IRWIN
  Edward, of Bethany, Genesee Co. - 20 Oct. 1840
  James, of Ulster, Ulster Co., res. of N.Y. State since 1816 -
    5 June 1832
ISAAC
  Lyon, of NYC, straw manufacturer - 26 Aug. 1845
IVERS
  John, of NYC, plaisterer - 4 Feb. 1829
IVESON
  John, of North Hempstead, Queens Co., native of Haslington, Co.
    Lancaster, Eng. - 15 Oct. 1828
IWANOWSKI
  Alexander, of Watervliet, Albany Co., late of Poland; declared
    intention 18 Nov. 1837 in Albany - 29 Jan. 1839
JACK
  John, of NYC, late of U.K. - 7 Feb. 1844
JACKSON
  Ann, of Williamsburgh, Kings Co., late of U.K.; declared intent
    on 3 May 1843 - 8 May 1843
  Benjamin, of NYC, merchant - 7 Mar. 1831
  Edward, of Brockport, Monroe Co. - 12 July 1847
  George, of Washington Ave. in Brooklyn, Kings Co., broker - 19
    Sept. 1843

JACKSON (continued)
  John, of NYC - March 1838
  John C., of NYC, merchant, in Water St. - 7 Sept. 1840
  Sarah, of NYC, native of U.K. - 1 May 1833
  Thomas, of Westfield, Richmond Co. - 19 Apr. 1846
  William, of Brooklyn, Kings Co. - 29 June 1843
JACLARD
  Sebastien, of NYC, wigmaker - 28 Jan. 1834
JACLET
  Jean Baptiste, of Hastings, Oswego Co. - 2 Feb. 1831
JACOB
  Jane, of Poughkeepsie, Dutchess Co. - 28 Nov. 1845
JACOBS
  Harriet (widow of William Jacobs, late of the Isle of Wight,
    farmer), of NYC, formerly of the Isle of Wight - 4 Aug. 1830
  Moses, of NYC - 26 Sept. 1837
JACQUOT
  Nicholas, of Lyme, Jefferson Co. - 25 Feb. 1835
JAMES
  Anthony, of NYC - 25 Apr. 1833
  George Giles, of NYC - 23 Jan. 1834
  James, of Saugerties, Ulster Co. - 31 Mar. 1834
  Joseph Christopher, of Onondaga Co., native of G.B. - 12 Feb.
    1833
JAMESON
  James, of Lockport, Niagara Co. - 6 Jan. 1836
JAMISON
  Elizabeth (wife of Marmaduke Jamison, of NYC), of NYC - 9 Feb.
    1837
JANE
  Anthony, of Wayne Co. - 24 Jan. 1839
JANIN
  Antoine Benoit, of Southfield, Richmond Co. - 30 May 1844
JAQUES
  Dinah, of Wayne Co. - 25 Sept. 1838
JARMAN
  John, of Buffalo, Erie Co. - 26 Mar. 1831
JAY
  James, of Onondaga Co. - 10 Dec. 1832
  Joseph, of Onondaga Co. - 13 Dec. 1832
JEAN
  Jean Christophe Grand, of Le Roy, Jefferson Co. - 3 Dec. 1833
JEANERET
  Robert Jas., of Albany, late of U.K. - 25 Oct. 1841
JEFFERSON
  Thomas, of Oswego, Oswego Co. - 23 Dec. 1836
JEFFREY
  James K., of Westmoreland, Oneida Co. - 26 Aug. 1833
JEHLEN
  Andrew, of Rochester, Monroe Co. - 5 Apr. 1847
JENKINS
  Thomas, of Brooklyn, Kings Co., carpenter; for 4 years last past
    res. of Brooklyn - 14 Apr. 1826
JENNINGS
  Edward, of Rochester, Monroe Co. - 11 Oct. 1838
  John, of Lyme, Jefferson Co. - 31 May 1841
  Joseph, of Amsterdam, Montgomery Co. - 1 Dec. 1835
JERICO
  John, of NYC - 10 Apr. 1837
JERROME
  Joseph, of Champlain, Clinton Co. - 5 July 1830
JESSOP
  Henry, of NYC - 5 Oct. 1838
JIPHAINE
  Peter Victor, of Tonawanda, Erie Co. - 4 Mar. 1839

New York Alien Residents, 1825-1848

JOESBURRY/JOESBERRY
  Joseph, of Catskill, Greene Co. - 20 June 1845
JOHN
  Elias, of NYC - 2 Sept. 1840
JOHNSON
  Francis, of Clayton, Jefferson Co. - 10 July 1847
  George, of NYC, haircloth manufacturer - 21 May 1834
  James, of Utica, Oneida Co., native of Ire. - 5 Feb. 1833
  James B., of NYC - 9 Apr. 1845
  James S., of Benton, Yates Co. - 9 Oct. 1835
  John, of Brooklyn, Kings Co. - 26 May 1832
  John, of NYC - 10 Nov. 1834
  Samuel, of NYC - 5 May 1837
  William, of Orange Co. - 24 Aug. 1840
JOHNSTON
  Archibald, of Denmark, Lewis Co. - 6 Jan. 1836
  Charles, of NYC - 23 Apr. 1835
  Eleanor (widow of James Johnston, late of NYC), of NYC - 26
    Dec. 1843
  John, of Westfield, Chautauque Co., British subject - 24 June
    1828
  Mary, of Franklinville, Cattaraugus Co. - 11 Feb. 1839
  Robert, of NYC - 15 Sept. 1843
  Samuel S., of Williamsburgh, Kings Co. - 30 Dec. 1826
  William, of NYC - 30 June 1846
JOHNSTONE
  Jane (wife of Oliver Johnstone, of NYC), of NYC, subject of
    U.K. - 25 Aug. 1843
JOICE
  Richard, of Oswego, Oswego Co. - 6 Oct. 1841
  William, of NYC, stone-cutter, native of Ire. - 30 Jan. 1841
JOLLY
  Mary Elizabeth, of NYC, formerly of Belgium - 13 Nov. 1837
JOLY
  John A., of NYC, late of Geneva, Switzerland - 9 Oct. 1833
JONES
  Catharine, of Onondaga Co. - 31 Aug. 1838
  Daniel L., of NYC - 11 Mar. 1836
  David, of NYC - 25 Apr. 1837
  Edward, of Sullivan, Madison Co. - 17 Mar. 1831
  Frederick, of NYC - 2 Feb. 1846
  George, of Canajoharie, Montgomery Co., British subject; came
    to U.S. on 1 June 1831 - 26 Feb. 1839
  George, of NYC - 6 Sept. 1841
  George Leonard, of Albany - 7 Mar. 1840
  Henry, of Marcellus, Onondaga Co. - 24 Dec. 1847
  James, of Providence, R.I., now res. of NYC - 16 Dec. 1836
  James, of NYC, res. of Williamsburgh, Kings Co. - 21 May 1838
  John, of NYC - 28 Sept. 1837
  John, of Albany - 25 Oct. 1841
  Joseph H., of Constantia, Oneida Co., native of Wales; came to
    U.S. in July 1841 - 15 Dec. 1843
  Margaret (widow of Jonas Jones), of NYC, for some years res. of
    the U.S. - 20 May 1845
  Mary Ann, of NYC, single woman, for some years res. of the U.S. -
    20 May 1845
  Rowland, of Turin, Lewis Co. - 3 Jan. 1837
  Simon, of Utica, Oneida Co. - 27 Apr. 1835
  Thomas E., of Winfield, Herkimer Co. - 29 Dec. 1836
  William, of NYC - 1 June 1833
  William, of Rockland Co., engineer, late of Shropshire, Eng. -
    24 May 1834
  William, of Brooklyn, Kings Co. - 6 Mar. 1841
  William, of Camillus, Onondaga Co. - 15 Dec. 1842
  William John, of Ithaca, Tompkins Co., late of London, Eng. -

JONES (continued)
  William John (continued) - 7 Mar. 1833
JORDAN
  Edward, of Columbia Co. - 27 Apr. 1847
  Thomas, of NYC, merchant - 20 Oct. 1836
JOSEPH
  Emily, of NYC - 13 Apr. 1837
  Francis, of Hudson, Columbia Co. - 5 Aug. 1841
  Philip, of Rensselaer Co. - 28 Nov. 1836
JOST
  John, of Poughkeepsie, Dutchess Co. - 2 Oct. 1840
JUDGE
  James, of Schroeppel, Oswego Co., native of Kent, Eng. - 18 Oct.
    1845
  Thomas, of Oswego Co., native of Kent, Eng. - 18 Oct. 1845
JULIUS
  George Henri, of Pleasant Valley, Dutchess Co. - 3 Apr. 1837
JUNG
  Conrad, of Wayne Co. - 26 Sept. 1834
  Edmund F., of Liberty, Sullivan Co., late of Prussia - 26 Aug.
    1845
  Kissemer/Kissimer, of Wayne Co. - 26 Sept. 1834
JUNIOR
  Sarah (wife of David Junior), of Williamsburgh, Kings Co. -
    (sworn in NYC) 25 Oct. 1847

KAHN
  Charles, of NYC, merchant, late of Stockholm, Sweden - 20 Sept.
    1832
KAHOE
  John, of Parishville, St. Lawrence Co. - 22 June 1825
KALBFLEISCH
  Conrad, residing at 165 Second St., NYC, tailor - 16 Nov. 1836
  Martin, of NYC, painter - 27 June 1831
KALES
  John, of Chenango Co. - 4 Jan. 1832
KAMPER
  William Heinrich/William Henry, of NYC - 17 Jan. 1843
KANTZ
  Jacob, of Monroe Co. - 26 Oct. 1836
KARNEY
  James, of Orleans Co. - 2 July 1839
KARR
  John, of Schenectady, Schenectady Co. - 8 Nov. 1841
  William, of Watertown, Jefferson Co. - 2 Apr. 1839
KAY
  James, of Erie Co. - 14 Apr. 1836
KAYSER
  John Christian, of Croghan, Lewis Co. - 23 Sept. 1843
KEANE
  James, of NYC - 23 Oct. 1847
KEARNEY/KERNEY
  Mary, of Castleton, Richmond Co., British subject - (sworn in
    NYC) 14 Feb. 1845
KEEFER
  Antonio, of Lewis Co. - 3 Mar. 1834
  Antone, of Turin, Lewis Co. - 3 Jan. 1837
KEEGAN
  Peter, of Albany - 20 Mar. 1844
KEEL
  George, of Waterloo, Seneca Co., British subject - 16 Dec. 1844
  Joel, of Onondaga, Onondaga Co., late of G.B. - 6 Oct. 1834
KEELING
  Isaac, of Cherry Valley, Otsego Co.; he arrived in NYC on 2 June
    1822 directly from town of Rocester, Co. of Staffordshire,
    Eng. - 13 Feb. 1826

New York Alien Residents, 1825-1848

KEENEN
  Peter, of Plattsburgh, Clinton Co. - 24 Jan. 1832
KEENZY
  Frederick, of Rochester, Monroe Co. - 3 Sept. 1839
KEERS
  James, of Rochester, Monroe Co. - 7 Feb. 1839
KEGAN
  James, of NYC - 9 May 1832
KEIMBURGER
  Theobold, of Erie Co., native of Lahr, Dukedom of Baden; arrived
    in U.S. 1 May 1843 - 30 Aug. 1844
KELLETT
  Joseph Patrick, of Brooklyn, Kings Co. - (sworn in NYC) 10 Oct.
    1844
KELLEY
  Bernard, of Verona, Oneida Co. - 15 June 1825
KELLY
  Daniel, of Erie Co., lately arrived in U.S. - 25 Jan. 1836
  James, of Cayuga Co., res. of N.Y. for past 5 years; came to
    U.S. from Donegal, Ire. - 7 Feb. 1841
  John, of City of Albany - 6 Jan. 1836
  Samuel R., of Williamsburgh, Kings Co., British subject; he de-
    clared intentions 15 July last - 19 Dec. 1844
KEMP
  James, of Meredith, Delaware Co - 22 Jan. 1839
KEMPSTER
  John, of Madison Co., native of G.B. - 17 July 1834
KENAN/KENEN
  Michael, of Kings Co. - 24 Dec. 1834
KENDELL
  Robert, of Erie Co. - 3 Dec. 1834
KENNEDY
  John, of Verona, Oneida Co., late of Tarlton, Ire. - 20 May 1825
  Lena, of Oswegatchie, St. Lawrence Co. - 27 Jan. 1834
  Mary, of Verona, Oneida Co. - 15 June 1825
  Thomas, of Poughkeepsie, Dutchess Co. - 31 Mar. 1845
KENNY
  John, of Hebron, Washington Co. - 8 Dec. 1831
KENT
  James, of Wilson, Niagara Co., subject of G.B. - 5 Mar. 1838
  Mary, of NYC - 25 June 1834
KENWORTHY
  William, of NYC, carpenter - 9 Sept. 1826
KENYON
  James, of Buffalo, Erie Co. - 20 June 1834
KERLEY
  Owen, of Onondaga Co. - 13 Mar. 1838
KERR
  Catharine (widow of James Kerr), of NYC - 2 July 1846
  Hugh, of NYC, carpenter - 28 July 1834
  John, of St. Lawrence Co., late of Ire. - 5 Dec. 1825
  William, of NYC, shoemaker - 24 Dec. 1828
KERSHAW
  John, of Manlius, Onondaga Co. - Feb. 1831
KERWIG
  Philip, of Jamaica, Queens Co., age 62, born in City of Stral-
    berg, Westphalia, Prussia - 2 Aug. 1845
KESLER
  Jacques, of Rochester, Monroe Co. - 9 Apr. 1836
  Martin, of Oswegatchie, St. Lawrence Co. - 6 Sept. 1834
KESSLER
  George, of Kinderhook, Columbia Co., born in France - 11 July
    1839
KETCHUM
  Mary Ann, of Black Rock, Erie Co., late of Eng. - 29 Nov. 1847

New York Alien Residents, 1825-1848

KETTERER
  Henry, of Gorham, Ontario Co., age 46, native of Dept. of the
    Lower Rhine, France, res. of the U.S. for about 5 years - 20
    Aug. 1833
KEVINNY
  Patrick, of Troy, Rensselaer Co., born in Co. of Roscommon, Ire.;
    left Ire. in May 1831 and came to Troy that year; declared his
    intent in Oct. 1833 - Mar. 1836
KEY
  Leonard Ash, of NYC, formerly of Yorkshire, Eng. - 9 Mar. 1841
KEYES
  Thomas Michael, of Jefferson Co. - 25 May 1847
KEYS
  Thomas, of Saugerties, Ulster Co. - 7 Dec. 1837
KEYSER
  Masset, of Utica, Oneida Co. - 22 Oct. 1839
KIECKHOEFER
  Adolphus T., of NYC, formerly of Hamburgh, Germany - 8 Mar. 1837
KIEFER
  Andrew, of Rochester, Monroe Co. - 12 Oct. 1837
  Jean, of Lewis Co. - 31 Aug. 1838
  John Adam, of Rochester, Monroe Co. - 12 Oct. 1837
  Joseph, of Watson, Lewis Co. - 16 Oct. 1833
KIEMEL
  Henry Edward, of NYC - 13 May 1834
KIERS
  Robert, of Brooklyn, Kings Co., carpet-weaver - 3 Jan. 1845
KIERULFF
  Jacob Elias, of Wayne Co. - 9 Sept. 1833
  Niels Andreas Vibe, of Wayne Co. - 9 Sept. 1833
KILBY
  William, of Brooklyn, Kings Co., painter and glazier - 27 Apr. 1829
KILGOUR
  Robert, of NYC, native of U.K. - 19 Nov. 1833
KILLINGTON
  Edward, of NYC - 11 July 1836
KIMBER
  James, of Onondaga Co. - 29 Aug. 1834
  Frederick, of Onondaga Co. - 5 Mar. 1834
KINCAID
  James, of Niagara Co. - 3 May 1836
KINCH
  Rebecca (wife of William Kinch, brewer), of NYC - 30 July 1844
KINCHELLA
  Ann (wife of John Kinchella), of NYC - 22 May 1844
  John, Jr. (alias Kingsley), of NYC - 25 May 1844
  Mary Ann (daughter of John and Ann Kinchella), of NYC - 22 May
    1844
KING
  Alexander, of Erie Co. - 8 Mar. 1836
  John, of Pittsford, Monroe Co., born in town of Abylaise (Abbey-
    leix), Queens Co., Ire., on 15 Apr. 1801; came to N.Y. State
    by way of Whitehall, N.Y., in July 1825 and since then resided
    in Pittsford - 9 Apr. 1831
  Richard, of Phelps, Ontario Co. - 19 May 1847
  Sally, of Genesee Co. - 5 Feb. 1834
  William, of New Windsor, Orange Co., late of U.K. - 20 Jan. 1837
KINGDON
  Henry, of Stafford, Genesee Co. - 15 Mar. 1841
KINGHORN
  Henry, of NYC - 7 Nov. 1846
KINGSWORTH
  Thomas, of Palmyra, Wayne Co. - 23 Mar. 1844
KINKART
  James, of NYC - 16 Mar. 1843

KINNARD
  Charles, of Somers, Westchester Co., late of G.B. - 8 July 1835
KINNEY
  Patrick, of Southampton, Suffolk Co. - 10 May 1845
  Peter, of Lowville, Lewis Co. - 23 Apr. 1836
KINSKY
  George, of Erie Co. - 3 Mar. 1835
KINTZ
  Philip, of Lancaster, Erie Co. - 8 Oct. 1833
KIPP
  Fatinuet (or Fatineut?), of Brooklyn, Kings Co. - 8 Dec. 1847
KIRBILLER/KERBILLER/KERBELLER
  Jean/John, of Le Roy, Jefferson Co. - 12 Oct. 1836
KIRBY
  William, of Oswegatchie, St. Lawrence Co., late from Eng. - 18
    July 1828
KIRK
  Mary, of NYC - 13 July 1844
  Mary, residing at 140 East Broadway, NYC - 10 Apr. 1847
KIRKLAND
  John, of Broadalbin, Montgomery Co. - 30 Sept. 1837
KIRKPATRICK
  Henry, of Saratoga, Saratoga Co. - 1 Sept. 1842
  Hugh, of NYC, weaver - 7 Mar. 1833
KISSOCK
  William, of Franklinville, Cattaraugus Co. - 11 Feb. 1839
KITCHEN
  Matthew, of Wayne Co. - 22 May 1832
KITCHING
  George, of NYC, malster - 20 May 1831
KLANE
  Jacob, of Onondaga Co. - 8 Sept. 1837
KLEIN
  Ernest, of Erie Co., native of Lieblos in Hessen; arrived in U.S.
    on 22 Aug. 1844 - 30 Aug. 1844
KLENDGEN
  John D., of NYC, formerly of Hamburgh, Germany - 25 Nov. 1832
KLEPSER
  John George, of Buffalo, Erie Co., late of Kingdom of Wuertem-
    berg - 23 Jan. 1837
KLIEBENSTEIN
  Frederick, of Sand Lake, Rensselaer Co. - 8 Jan. 1834
KNIGHT
  Enoch, of Wayne Co. - 30 Sept. 1830
  James F., of NYC, engineer - 18 Dec. 1827
  Richard, of Phelps, Ontario Co. - 11 Jan. 1842
  William S. Q., of Genesee Co. - 3 Feb. 1842
KNOCK
  Richard, of Newtown, Queens Co., farmer - 1 July 1834
KNOTT
  Benjamin, of Utica, Oneida Co., native of Ire. - 7 Dec. 1827
KNOX
  John, of Wilson, Niagara Co. - 14 Sept. 1836
  Robert, of Onondaga Co. - 14 Nov. 1836
KOBBE
  William A., of NYC, native of Idstein, Duchy of Nassau, Germany -
    16 Mar. 1836
KOCHLEY
  Joseph, of Lewis Co. - 21 Sept. 1830
KOHLER
  Marcel, of West Turin, Lewis Co. - 24 Sept. 1847
  Michael, of Le Roy, Jefferson Co., native of Hohensoller Her-
    hinger (Hechingen?), Germany - 13 July 1833
KONDOLF
  Henrie, of Gates, Monroe Co. - 19 June 1840

KONZLAER
  Thomas, of Rochester, Monroe Co. - 9 Apr. 1836
KROVITS
  Charles I., of NYC, formerly of Hungary - 26 Nov. 1836
KUNDERT
  Matthias, of NYC - 15 Mar. 1836
KUNKLEMANN
  Jacob Charles, of NYC, merchant - 20 July 1837
KUNZ
  George, of Wayne Co. - 26 Sept. 1834
KURRLE
  Michael I., of NYC - 15 Mar. 1840
KUTZ
  Erasmus A., of NYC, mathematical instrument maker - 31 May 1826

LABRUSSE
  Philippe, of Albany - 3 Dec. 1833
LACALIN
  Onesippe, of NYC - 12 Oct. 1844
LACHAISE
  James Armand, of NYC - 15 Nov. 1833
LACLAIR
  Alexander, of Champion, Jefferson Co. - 17 Aug. 1846
LADD
  William F., of NYC - 22 Apr. 1844
LADEN
  Michael, of Manlius, Onondaga Co. - 24 Mar. 1832
LADENBURGH
  Peter, of Lewis Co. - 19 Sept. 1843
LADLEY
  George Henry, of NYC - 17 Feb. 1844
LAFARE
  John, of Antwerp, Jefferson Co., formerly of G.B. - 9 Nov. 1847
LAFFERTY
  William, of Albany - 6 Apr. 1833
LAFORCE
  Jacob, of Rochester, Monroe Co. - 20 May 1847
LAGOIRE
  John Battis, of Flatbush, Kings Co. - 28 Nov. 1843
LA GRANGE
  Isaac, of Watervliet, Albany Co. - 1 Dec. 1836
  Isaac, of Guilderland, Albany Co. - 17 Mar. 1835
  Marie Anne Jouny, widow, of NYC - 6 Jan. 1834
LAHR
  George, of NYC - 6 Jan. 1845
LAIDLER
  William, of New Lisbon, Otsego Co. - 29 Apr. 1835
LAING
  William, of Kings Co, late a marine - (sworn in NYC) 3 July
    1844
LAKE
  Edward, of Buffalo, Erie Co. - 13 Mar. 1837
LAKER
  Benjamin, of Albany Co. - 14 Jan. 1848
LALLIER
  Nicholas, of Lewis Co. - 31 Aug. 1838
LALOR
  Martin, of NYC, pump-maker - 16 Oct. 1843
LAMB
  Henry, of Buffalo, Erie Co. - 7 July 1831
  John, of Buffalo, Erie Co. - 6 July 1831
  William, of Rochester, Monroe Co. - 8 Mar. 1844
LAMBE
  Thomas Fountaine, of Erie Co. - 3 Mar. 1825
LAMBERT
  Charles A., of NYC - 15 Oct. 1838

LAMBERT (continued)
  John, of NYC, milkman - 26 Sept. 1826
  Marie Josephine, of NYC - 24 June 1847
  Pierre, of NYC - 24 June 1847
LAMIBEER
  William, of NYC, mason - 22 Sept. 1838
LAMIRAL/LAMAREL
  John, of NYC - 6 June 1835
LAMONT
  John, of Munro, Orange Co. - 27 Feb. 1832
LANCASTER
  William Walter, of Wayne Co. - 29 Jan. 1834
LANDER
  John Calvert, of Onondaga Co. - 29 Dec. 1846
LANDERS
  Edward, of NYC, native of Ire.; arrived in NYC 24 Sept. last
    past - 7 Oct. 1829
  Michael D., of NYC, native of Ire.; arrived in NYC about a year
    ago - 7 Oct. 1829
LANE
  George Arminque, of NYC, born in Eng.; arrived in NYC in August
    1833 - 1 June 1836
LANG
  Valentine, of Lewis Co. - 21 Sept. 1830
  William, of Sheldon, Wyoming Co. - 30 Mar. 1846
LANGDON
  John Davy, of Albany, gentleman - 17 Mar. 1831
L'ANGLOIS
  Marie, single woman, res. of NYC for several years past - 22 Dec.
    1829
  Reine, of NYC, single woman - 22 Dec. 1829
LANSLEY
  Thomas, of Albany Co. - 28 Jan. 1835
LANTHERER
  Felix, of Rochester, Monroe Co. - 17 Aug. 1847
LANTZ
  John, of Le Roy, Jefferson Co., born in Dept. of the Lower Rhine
    in France in 1788; removed to N.Y. in 1831 - 29 Feb. 1840
LAPORTE
  Joseph, of Plattsburgh, Clinton Co., late of Montreal, Lower
    Canada - 7 Feb. 1843
LARABARDIER
  Joseph, of Onondaga Co. - 8 Sept. 1838
LARKIN
  Honnour (wife of John Larkin, of NYC), of NYC, for some years a
    res. of the U.S. - 18 Apr. 1845
  John, of Fordham, Westchester Co. - 27 May, 1847
LARRY
  Cornelius, of Ogdensburgh, St. Lawrence Co. - 26 Dec. 1834
LARSEN
  Christian, of NYC, machinist - 29 Aug. 1844
LATAPIE
  Bertrand, of NYC - 23 Oct. 1847
LAUER
  Elizabeth, widow, of Utica, Oneida Co. - 8 Aug. 1844
LAUGHLIN
  James, of Palmyra, Wayne Co. - 28 Sept. 1837
  Jane, of Palmyra, Wayne Co. - 27 Sept. 1837
  John, of NYC, born Co. of Derry, Ire.; sailed from Londonderry
    and arrived in NYC in 1810 - 24 Jan. 1828
LAVERICK
  Nathan, of Niagara Co. - 6 Jan. 1836
  William, of Sennett, Cayuga Co. - 29 May 1838
LAWES
  John, of Green Point, Kings Co. - 30 June 1843

LAWLESS
  Peter, of Albany - 13 Nov. 1839
LAWRENCE
  Sophia, of NYC - 3 Jan. 1848
  Stephen, of Ontario Co. - 26 Nov. 1839
LAWSON
  Alexander, of Buffalo, Erie Co. - 22 Dec. 1845
  Peter, of Buffalo, Erie Co., late of Denmark - 22 Sept. 1835
  Peter, of Williamsburgh, Kings Co., native of Denmark - (sworn
    in NYC) 19 Feb. 1844
  William, of Brooklyn, Kings Co., merchant, residing in Johnson
    St. - 25 Apr. 1844
  William, of NYC, turner - 29 June 1843
LAWTON
  Ellen, of Athens, Greene Co. - 11 Apr. 1844
  Mary, of Athens, Greene Co. - 11 Apr. 1844
LEACH
  Isaac, of NYC, weaver - 4 Apr. 1827
LEARY
  Andrew, of NYC, late of U.K. - 5 Jan. 1826
LEATHER
  Thomas, of Onondaga Co. - 11 June 1845
LEAVY
  Matthew, of NYC, merchant - 4 Mar. 1833
LE BARBIER
  Adolphus, of NYC, native of France - 28 July 1834
LECLERC
  Fortune, of NYC, merchant - 5 Oct. 1835
LE CLERE
  Augustus, of NYC - 26 July 1836
  Frederick, of Mexico, Oswego Co. - 2 Feb. 1831
  Louis Isidore, of NYC, merchant - 2 Feb. 1835
LE COUTEULX
  Antoinette, of Buffalo, Erie Co. (wife of Alphonse Le Couteulx,
    of Buffalo), late of Rouen, France - 27 Nov. 1840
  Charlotte Laurie Marie (wife of William B. Le Couteulx, of Buf-
    falo), of Buffalo, Erie Co., late of France - 28 Nov. 1840
LEDERER
  Isaac, of Columbia Co. - 17 Feb. 1844
LEDERMAN
  Anna, of NYC, late of Germany - 21 Mar. 1845
LEE
  Edmund, of Lockport, Niagara Co. - 7 Jan. 1833
  Isabella (wife of Gideon Lee), of NYC - 20 Oct. 1835
  John, of NYC - 9 Mar. 1842
  Levi, of Onondaga Co. - 6 Dec. 1832
  Richard, of Albany - 5 July 1837
  Richard Hargreave, of Buffalo, Erie Co. - 17 Mar. 1830
  William, Sr., of NYC - 2 Oct. 1845
LEECH
  Samuel, of NYC, accountant - 13 Apr. 1829
LEES
  James, of Buffalo, Erie Co., late of town and county of Notting-
    ham, Eng. - 10 Dec. 1831
LEFEVRE
  Lefioit, of Sharon, Schoharie Co. - 18 Aug. 1843
LE HINE
  Murty, of Adams, Jefferson Co., late of Parish of Balavaurne, Co.
    of Cork, Ire. - 1 June 1830
LEHERBERG
  Lazarus, of Columbia Co. - 17 Feb. 1844
LEHRBERG
  Kaufman, of Columbia Co. - 28 Feb. 1844
LEICHTNAM
  François, of Cambria, Niagara Co., born at Breidanbach, Dept. of

New York Alien Residents, 1825-1848

LEICHTNAM (continued)
    Francois (continued) Moselle, France - 5 Sept. 1843
LEIDLEY
    James, of Buffalo, Erie Co. - 16 Dec. 1842
LEININGER
    Adam, of Monroe Co., late of Germany - 26 Oct. 1835
LEITCH
    John, of Cornwall, Orange Co., born in Argyleshire, Scotland -
        27 May 1828
LEMAIRE
    Christopher, of NYC, shoemaker, lately of village of Bremont,
        Dept. of Meurthe, France - 1 Nov. 1833
LEMMON
    David, of Troy, Rensselaer Co., native of Bellagigger, Ire. - 13
        Feb. 1827
    Thomas, of Troy, Rensselaer Co., native of Bellamacrally, Ire. -
        29 Mar. 1829
    William, of Troy, Rensselaer Co., late of Ballamacrolly, Ire. -
        13 Feb. 1827
LEMONIA
    Vetile, of Jefferson Co., formerly of Prov. of Upper Canada -
        21 Mar. 1842
LE MOYNE
    Adolphe, of NYC - 20 Aug. 1831
LEONARD
    John, of Onondaga Co. - 6 Mar. 1834
LESLIE
    Joseph, of Onondaga Co. - 29 Feb. 1836
LE SUEUR
    Pierre, of NYC - 31 Mar. 1841
LETTSOM
    William P., of Buffalo, Erie Co. - 8 July 1836
LEVENGSTON
    Salomon M., of NYC, merchant - 10 Aug. 1827
LEVY
    Sarah, of NYC, widow - 15 May 1834
LEWIN
    Henry, of NYC - 26 Dec. 1833
LEWIS
    Benjamin G., of Flatbush, Kings Co., mason, formerly of London,
        Eng. - 1 June 1839
    Evan, of NYC, hatter - 12 Apr. 1826
    George, of Salina, Onondaga Co. - 4 Mar. 1844
    John, of NYC, blacksmith - 20 Mar. 1839
    John, of Skaneateles, Onondaga Co. - 6 July 1847
    Joseph, of NYC, gunsmith - 6 July 1836
    Thomas, of NYC - 29 Mar. 1832
    Thomas, of Wayne Co. - 22 Sept. 1835
LIAS
    Dominique, of NYC - 24 Apr. 1845
LIDGERWOOD
    James, of Watervliet, Albany Co., mason - 21 Feb. 1829
    John, of NYC - 25 Apr. 1828
LIEBER
    Andrew, of Canajoharie, Montgomery Co., native of Germany - 14
        Aug. 1834
LIMMER
    William Lionel, of Flushing, Queens Co., house-carpenter, born
        in Eng. - 12 Nov. 1839
LINCK
    Lewis, of Lewis Co. - 21 Sept. 1830
LINDLEY
    George, of Brooklyn, Kings Co., gardener - (sworn in NYC) 22 Jan.
        1847
    Thomas, of Hastings, Westchester Co., now in NYC, machinist -18

66

LINDLEY (continued)
  Thomas (continued) May 1846
LINDSAY
  James, of Fairfield, Herkimer Co. - 2 Feb. 1836
  John, of Fairfield, Herkimer Co., late of Glasgow, Co. of La-
    nark, Scotland; for last 5 years res. of Oneida Co. and Her-
    kimer Co.; for past 3 years res. of Newport but now res. of
    Fairfield - 2 Feb. 1836
  Robert, of NYC, native of Ire. - 14 Aug. 1828
LINES
  Edward, of Onondaga Co. - 26 Feb. 1839
LINSENER
  John D., of Manlius, Montgomery Co. - 18 May 1838
LINTON
  James, of Rome, Oneida Co. - 5 Sept. 1835
LIPSEY
  John, of NYC - 5 Nov. 1846
LISTER
  Samuel, of NYC, merchant - 12 June 1829
LITTLE
  Charles, of Brooklyn, Kings Co. - 21 Feb. 1831
LIVINGSTON
  James, of NYC - 4 June 1845
  William, of NYC - 30 June 1834
LLOYD
  Daniel, of Saugerties, Ulster Co., res. of U.S. for about one
    year and 5 months - 31 Jan. 1832
  Susan, of Buffalo, Erie Co., formerly of G.B. - 25 Sept. 1845
LOCKHART
  Alexander, of NYC - 2 Feb. 1844
LOCKLAND
  Alexander, of La Grange, Dutchess Co. - 14 Mar. 1836
LODGE
  John, of Sag Harbour in Southampton, Suffolk Co. - 31 May 1845
  Joseph, of Kings Co. - 9 Dec. 1833
LOGAN
  David, of Rochester, Monroe Co. - 7 Feb. 1839
  Henry, of Milton, Saratoga Co., native of U.K. - 24 Oct. 1840
  Jane, of NYC - 17 Apr. 1844
LOHMANN
  John P., of Cairo, Greene Co., saddler and harness-maker - 21
    Feb. 1835
LOMAS
  William, of Mamaroneck, Westchester Co., cotton manufacturer - 7
    Apr. 1828
LONG
  Frederick, of Erie Co. - 8 Dec. 1835
  Frederick, of Erie Co., lately come to the U.S. - 16 Mar. 1836
  George Henry, of Wayne Co. - 26 Sept. 1833
  John, Sr., of NYC, wheelwright and blacksmith - 26 Jan. 1848
  William, of Buffalo, Erie Co. - 2 Feb. 1848
LONGFIELD
  William, of NYC - 25 Feb. 1833
LONGHI
  Teresa (wife of Moses G. Longhi, a naturalized citizen), of NYC -
    26 Aug. 1842
LONGMAN
  Robert, of NYC - 24 Oct. 1835
LONGMUIR/LONGMIER
  Gabriel, of Rochester, Monroe Co., brewer - 8 Apr. 1835
  John, of Rochester, Monroe Co., brewer - 8 Apr. 1835
LOSON
  Nicholas, of Watson, Lewis Co. - 25 June 1840
LOUBAT
  Alpheus, of NYC - 28 Oct. 1843

LOUDEN
 James, Jr., of Vienna, Oneida Co., farmer - 28 Sept. 1836
 Joseph, of Vienna, Oneida Co., native of Eng. - 13 Feb. 1838
LOUGHRY
 James, of Newburgh, Orange Co. - 19 Nov. 1835
LOUIS/LEWIS
 Etienne, of NYC, cabinetmaker, native of France - 1 Sept. 1835
LOUTT
 Francis Morland, of Williamsburgh, Long Island - (sworn in NYC)
  9 Mar. 1847
LOVIAT
 Jean Francois, of NYC - 5 June 1834
 Joseph, of NYC - 7 Sept. 1834
 Victoire Virginie, of NYC - 5 June 1834
 Victoire Virginie, of NYC - 7 Sept. 1834
LOWDEN
 Jane (widow of Charles Lowden, late of NYC), of NYC - 25 Aug.
  1845
LOWE
 George S.E., of NYC, late of U.K., clerk - 27 Dec. 1826
 Joseph, of NYC - 23 Aug. 1836
 Joshua, of NYC, engraver - 26 Apr. 1834
 William, of Erie Co., lately arrived in U.S. - 30 Aug. 1836
LOWREY
 William, of NYC, engineer - 14 Mar. 1835
LUCAS
 Frances (wife of William Lucas, of NYC) - 30 Apr. 1846
 William, of NYC - 8 May 1846
LUCHRINGER
 John Jacob, of Onondaga Co. - 29 Apr. 1840
LUCKOCK/LUCKCOCK
 William, of Erie Co. - 9 Apr. 1835
LUDLOW
 Archibald, of City and Co. of Albany - 22 June 1836
LUKE
 John, of NYC, professor of music - 26 Mar. 1836
LUMISDEN
 James, of Hartford, Conn., born in Parish of Lasswed (Lasswade),
  Co. of Edinburgh, Scotland - 17 Jan. 1839(sworn in Hartford;
  he had taken incipient measures there on 28 Aug. 1838 in the
  County Court); for some reason his naturalization is recorded
  in New York
LUSH
 Richard, Sr., of Rye, Westchester Co. - 1 Aug. 1838
LUX
 George, of Wayne Co. - 26 Sept. 1833
 Henry, of NYC - 22 Mar. 1838
LUYSTER
 Mary (wife of John Luyster, Jr.), of La Grange, Dutchess Co.,
  native of Eng. - 19 Apr. 1830
LYNCH
 Bernard, of NYC - 3 Apr. 1837
 Charles, of Troy, Rensselaer Co. - 19 Feb. 1835
 Fanny (wife of William Lynch), of NYC - 29 July 1846
 John, of Rochester, Monroe Co. - 14 Jan. 1848
 Michael, of NYC, dry-goods merchant - 15 July 1835
 Patrick, of NYC, blacksmith, formerly of Ire. - 21 June 1826
 Thomas, of NYC, laborer, formerly of Kent Co., Eng. - 16 Mar. 1227

Mc ADAM
 James G., of Delhi, Delaware Co. - 21 Dec. 1835
Mc AFFEE
 Archibald, of Brownville, Jefferson Co. - 31 May 1839
Mc ALLIS
 James, of NYC, manufacturer - 19 Feb. 1827

Mc ALOON
  James, of Plattsburgh, Clinton Co. - 1 Oct. 1834
Mc ARDLE
  Francis, of Brooklyn, Kings Co. - 2 Dec. 1825
Mc ARTHUR
  Alexander, of Troy, Rensselaer Co. - 30 July 1844
  James, of NYC - 17 Mar. 1845
Mc AUSLEN/MACAUSLEN
  Peter, of Kortright, Delaware Co., native of Scotland - 22 Mar.
    1832
Mc AVOY
  Patrick, of Onondaga Co. - 4 Oct. 1836
Mc BARRON
  Thomas, of NYC - 22 Aug. 1845
Mc BRIDE
  Robert, of Livingston Co. - 27 May 1833
Mc BURNEY
  Isabella, of NYC, widow - 18 Mar. 1843
Mc CABE
  Andrew, of Wayne Co., born in Ire. - 14 June 1838
  Elizabeth (wife of Hugh Mc Cabe, of NYC), of NYC - 27 May 1845
  James, of Scarsdale, Westchester Co., farmer - 18 May 1832
  John, of Knox, Albany Co., formerly of Co. of Caven, Ire. - 6
    Nov. 1840
  John, of Ticonderoga, Essex Co.; took incipient measures 30 Sept.
    1840 - 27 Oct. 1841
Mc CALL
  Andrew, of NYC, weaver, subject of U.K. - 12 Nov. 1840
  Terence, of Albany - 27 Oct. 1829
Mc CANAN
  Peter, of Albany - 24 Apr. 1834
Mc CANN
  John, of NYC - 24 June 1847
  Thomas, of Newburgh, Orange Co. - 28 Feb. 1833
Mc CARTHEY
  Charles, of NYC, mason - 2 Dec. 1836
Mc CARTHY
  John, of NYC - 31 July 1833
  Timothy, of Oswego, Oswego Co. - 11 Dec. 1843
Mc CARTIN
  Barnard, of NYC, tailor - 4 Oct. 1826
Mc CARTY
  Dennis, of Massena, St. Lawrence Co. - 18 Dec. 1833
  Dennis, of Macedon, Wayne Co. - 12 Oct. 1841
  John, of Adams, Jefferson Co., native of Co. of Cork, Ire., res.
    of N.Y. from 1830 - 16 July 1834
  Michael, of NYC - 25 Apr. 1834
Mc CARY
  John W., of Lysander, Onondaga Co. - 4 Nov. 1842
Mc CLASKY
  Owen, of Albany - 30 June 1829
Mc CLURE
  David, of NYC - 17 Apr. 1845
Mc CLUSKEY
  Barney, of NYC - 14 June 1834
  Patrick, of NYC, grocer, born in Ire.; res. of NYC for 7 years
    last past - 8 May 1824
Mc COMB
  James, of NYC - 18 Nov. 1831
Mc COMBE
  Elizabeth, of Utica, Oneida Co., late of U.K. - 5 Sept. 1835
Mc CONNEL
  Alexander, of Troy, Rensselaer Co., native of Bela McCoul, Co.
    of Donegal, Ire. - 19 Oct. 1830

Mc CONNELL
  Daniel, of Allegheny Co., native of Ire. - 27 Oct. 1831
  John, of Canandaigua, Ontario Co., native of Scotland - 14 June
    1830
Mc CONOCHIE
  Alexander, of NYC, late of Scotland - 31 Jan. 1828
Mc CORMACK
  James, of Chester, Orange Co. - 12 June 1846
Mc COURT/Mc CORT
  Peter, of NYC, tinsmith - 30 Nov. 1827
Mc COWLIFFE
  Margaret (widow of John Mc Cowliffe, late of NYC, speculator),
    of NYC - 8 Aug. 1840
Mc COY
  John, of NYC, dyer - 23 May 1828
Mc CRACKEN
  John, of NYC - 24 Sept. 1832
Mc CREA
  Isaac, of Williamsburgh, Kings Co., native of Ire. - 5 Aug. 1844
Mc CULLOCH
  Alexander, Jr., of Buffalo, Erie Co. - 21 June 1833
Mc DERMOT
  John, of Buffalo, Erie Co. - 23 Mar. 1831
Mc DERMOTT
  James, of Wayne Co. - 24 Jan. 1831
  Michael, of NYC, grocer - 17 Nov. 1830
Mc DONAL
  Matthew, of NYC, cartman, native of Ire. - 5 May 1825
Mc DONALD
  Francis, of NYC - 31 Oct. 1845
  James, of NYC - 25 Aug. 1836
  James, of Stapleton, Richmond Co. - 2 Aug. 1844
  John S., of Brooklyn, Kings Co. - 1 Oct. 1827
  Patrick, of Castleton, Richmond Co. - 3 June 1844
  William, of Albany Co. - 24 Jan. 1835
Mc DONALL
  James. of Erie Co. - 3 Dec. 1834
Mc DONOUGH
  Henry, of NYC, student at law, born in Eng.; took incipient mea-
    sures in Marine Court in NYC on 11 Apr. 1834 - 15 Apr. 1836
  James, of Utica, Oneida Co. - 3 Aug. 1827
Mc DOUGAL
  John, of Champion, Jefferson Co. - 3 Sept. 1832
Mc DOUGALD
  Dugald, of Niagara Co., native of Scotland - 7 Jan. 1834
Mc EACHAM/Mc EACHERN
  Robert, of NYC - 30 Aug. 1832
Mc ELHINNEY
  John, of Brooklyn, Kings Co. - 14 Dec. 1839
Mc ELROY
  James, of NYC, formerly of Ire., for the last 10 months res. of
    NYC - 28 Dec. 1825
Mc ENERNEY
  Edward, of Troy, Rensselaer Co. - 18 Apr. 1837
Mc EVILA
  David, of City of Albany, subject of U.K. - 28 Apr. 1837
Mc EWAN
  John, of Montgomery Co. - 21 Dec. 1830
Mc EWEN
  Thomas, of Canajoharie, Montgomery Co., subject of G.B. - 11 May
    1831
Mc EWIN
  David, of Canajoharie, Montgomery Co. - 17 June 1842
  James, of Canajoharie, Montgomery Co. - 17 June 1842

New York Alien Residents, 1825-1848

Mc FADDEN
  Mary, of NYC, widow - 10 Sept. 1845
MC FARLAN
  Robert, of Cleaveland, Oswego Co., native of Scotland - 7 July
    1834
Mc FARLANE
  George, of Catskill, Greene Co., laborer - 8 Aug. 1838
  John, of NYC, res. there since 1804, born in Scotland - 16 Dec.
    1826
  John, of Allegheny Co. - 1 Jan. 1833
  William, res. of NYC since Nov. 1822 when he arrived there from
    Province of Lower Canada, born in Scotland - 27 Dec. 1826
MACFARLENE/Mc FARLENE
  John, of Easton, Washington Co. - 24 Oct. 1835
Mc FERREN
  Robert, of Albany Co. - 25 Oct. 1847
MACGAVIN
  William, of Brooklyn, Kings Co. - 8 June 1831
Mc GEE
  Edward, of Rochester, Monroe Co. - 9 Mar. 1844
  James, of NYC - 15 Oct. 1847
  Mathew, of NYC - 29 Mar. 1847
Mc GEORGE
  John, of Kings Co. - 4 Apr. 1836
  Thomas, of Brooklyn, Kings Co. - 15 June 1836
Mc GILVARY
  Dougal, of Batavia, Genesee Co. - 1 Feb. 1831
Mc GINNIS
  Daniel, of NYC, gardener, native of Ire. - 5 Oct. 1825
Mc GIRR
  Patrick, of City of Albany, laborer - 9 June 1828
Mc GIVNEY
  John, of Steuben Co., native of Ire., age 40, res. of U.S. for
    15 years - 29 Apr. 1833
Mc GIVRAL/Mc GIVREN
  Patrick, of Oswegatchie, St. Lawrence Co. - 28 Dec. 1835
Mc GLAUGHLIN
  James, of Brooklyn, Kings Co., laborer - 4 Aug. 1825
Mc GOEY
  John, of Oswegatchie, St. Lawrence Co., late from Ire. - 24 Mar.
    1829
Mc GOWAN
  Bartholomew, of NYC, laborer - 23 May 1825
Mc GRADE
  Hugh, of Williamsburgh, Kings Co. - (Dec. 1845
MACGREGOR/Mc GREGOR
  Fanny, of Kingston, Ulster Co. - 5 Feb. 1835
  Fanny, of Staten Island - 12 July 1841
  James, of NYC, gentleman - 25 May 1831
Mc GROGAN
  Hugh, of Albany - 16 Dec. 1835
Mc GROTH
  Margaret, of NYC - 22 Oct. 1847
Mc GUCKIAN
  Edward, of NYC, labourer - 21 Sept. 1842
Mc GUINNESS
  Matthew, of Vernon, Oneida Co. - 13 Dec. 1836
Mc GUIRE
  Peter, of NYC, labourer - 21 June 1827
Mc GURK
  Thomas, of Lockport, Niagara Co. - 10 Nov. 1845
Mc ILVEEN
  John, of NYC, goods merchant, born in Ire. - 20 May 1846
Mc ILWAIN
  James, of NYC, bootmaker - 30 June 1829

71

Mc INTOSH
  Daniel, of NYC, dyer - 2 Jan. 1830
  Margaret, of Otsego Co. - 21 Dec. 1832
  Robert, of Kings Co. - 20 Feb. 1833
MAC INTYRE
  Duncan, of Canajoharie, Montgomery, res. there since Nov. 1829 -
    6 June 1833
Mc INTYRE
  Edward, of Waterloo, Seneca Co. - 21 Dec. 1844
Mc KAY
  Ann, of Rochester, Monroe Co. - 11 Aug. 1842
Mc KECKNIE
  Robert, of Palmyra, Wayne Co. - 27 Jan. 1838
Mc KEE
  Joseph, of NYC - 4 Oct. 1845
MAKEE
  John, of Cairo, Greene Co. - 10 Apr. 1839
Mc KENNA
  James, of Manlius, Onondaga Co. - 24 Dec. 1836
Mc KENZIE
  Donald, of Chautauque Co. - 11 Oct. 1833
  Peter, of Camden, Oneida Co., born in Co. of Ayr, Scotland - 4
    Dec. 1832
MACKEY
  John, of Tompkins Co., formerly of Ire. - 19 May 1836
Mc KIM
  John, of Niagara Co. - 3 May 1836
Mc KINLEY
  Thomas F., of Flatbush, Kings Co. - 23 Feb. 1833
Mc KINNEY
  Patrick, of NYC - 10 Mar. 1835
MACKINTOSH
  Thomas, of NYC - 29 Sept. 1832
Mc KINZIE
  George, of Minden, Montgomery Co. - 23 Sept. 1840
Mc KITTRICK
  John, of Greenpoint, Columbia Co. - 10 Oct. 1846
  William, of Columbia Co. - 4 June 1847
Mc KOWNE
  Peter, of Rochester, Monroe Co. - 5 Oct. 1840
Mc LAREN
  John, of Onondaga Co. - 20 Apr. 1840
Mc LAUGHLIN
  James, of Greenfield, Saratoga Co. - 11 Dec. 1838
  John, of Kings Co. - 13 June 1836
  John, of Albany - 23 Feb. 1839
  Michael, of Newport, Herkimer Co., native of Ire. - 6 Dec. 1827
  Patrick, of New Port, Herkimer Co., subject of U.K. - 7 July 1827
  Patrick, of Troy, Rensselaer Co., born in Parish of Killronan,
    Co. of Roscommon (Kilronan is in Co. of Galway!), Ire., res.
    of Troy since Nov. 1835 - Mar. 1836
  Robert, of Brooklyn, Kings Co., laborer - 23 Nov. 1825
  Samuel, of Brooklyn, laborer - 23 Nov. 1825
  William, of Brooklyn, Kings Co., born in Ire.; came to U.S. in
    May 1841 - 29 May 1845
MACLEAN
  Henry Clinton, of Buffalo, Erie Co. - 14 Sept. 1835
Mc LEICH/Mc LACH
  James, of Fulton Co. -13 Feb. 1847
Mc LELAND
  John, of Wayne Co. - 26 Jan. 1832
MACLIN
  Andrew, of NYC - 4 Aug. 1836
Mc LOUGHLIN
  William, of NYC - 10 Apr. 1840

Mc MAHAN
  John, of Albany - 27 May 1844
Mc MAHON
  Edward, of Rochester, Monroe Co. - 17 Dec. 1836
Mc MANUS
  Bridget (widow of Patrick Mc Manus), of NYC - 12 Feb. 1847
  Sarah, of NYC, formerly of London, Eng. - 27 Oct. 1842
Mc MASTER
  William, of Orleans Co. - 30 Sept. 1842
Mc MASTERS
  William, of Buffalo, Erie Co. - 6 Mar. 1834
Mc MEEKAN
  James, of Buffalo, Erie Co., late of Co. of Antrim, Ire. - 15
    Mar. 1836
Mc MEEKIN
  David, of Albany Co. - 29 July 1847
Mc MENNOMY
  Edward, of NYC, late of Ire. - 27 Jan. 1826
  Francis, of NYC, late of Ire. - 27 Jan. 1826
Mc MILLAN
  Thomas, of New Scotland, Albany Co. - 10 May 1845
Mc MULLAN
  James, of NYC, weaver, late of U.K. - 14 Mar. 1825
Mac MULLEN
  Daniel, of Brooklyn, Kings Co., boatman - 25 July 1827
Mc MULLIN
  John P., of Mendon, Montgomery Co. - 12 Nov. 1839
Mc MURRAY
  Woodrow, of Livingston Co. - 27 May 1833
Mc NAMARA
  Thomas, of Onondaga Co. - 25 Nov. 1833
Mc NIFF
  Philip, of NYC, native of Ire. - 17 Mar. 1828
Mc PHAIL
  John, of City of Albany - 6 Apr. 1836
Mc PHERSON
  Daniel, of Monroe Co. - 1 Nov. 1841
  Duncan, of Le Roy, Genesee Co., born in Parish of Logan, Inver-
    nessshire, Scotland, in Jan. 1781; emigrated to State of N.Y.
    in Aug. or Sept. 1812 and has resided there ever since - 12
    Oct. 1830
  Peter, of NYC - 26 July 1847
Mc PLINN
  Richard, of Albany - 12 May 1832
Mc QUEAN
  Thomas P., of Montgomery Co. - 20 Apr. 1839
Mc QUILLON
  John, of Watertown, Jefferson Co. - 24 Dec. 1832
MAC RAE
  Duncan, of NYC, merchant - 31 May 1836
Mc STRAFFICK
  William, of Brooklyn, Kings Co. - 20 Mar. 1829
MACULLY
  James F., of NYC, teacher - 13 Mar. 1839
Mc VITY
  Thomas, Jr., of Saratoga Co.; came to U.S. on 10 or 11 Nov.
    1841 - 14 Mar. 1846
Mc WILLIAMS
  John, of Plattsburgh, Clinton Co. - 10 Nov. 1832
MACKIN
  John, of Onondaga Co. - 11 Mar. 1831
  Owen, of Onondaga Co. - 16 Mar. 1831
MADDEN
  Charles Armstrong, of NYC - 19 Feb. 1833

MADDOCK
  Edward, of Vienna, Oneida Co. - 12 Oct. 1825
MADGE
  John, of Casenovia, Madison Co. - 3 Sept. 1846
MAFFIT
  William, of North Hempstead, Queens Co. - 8 Oct. 1834
MAGINNIS
  Michael, of Williamsburgh, Kings Co., baker - (sworn in NYC) 7
    Oct. 1847
MAHARG
  James, of Albany - 10 June 1846
MAHER
  Phillip, of Lowville, Lewis Co. - 18 May 1835
MAIER
  Xavier, of NYC - 8 Jan. 1845
MAIRECOLAS
  Joseph, of NYC, shoemaker, late of the Dept. of Meurthe, France -
    1 Nov. 1833
MAIRESSE
  Charles, of NYC - 26 Mar. 1844
MAITLAND
  John, of Brooklyn, Kings Co. - 28 Apr. 1835
MALIUS
  John, of Elbridge, Onondaga Co. - 8 Dec. 1831
MALONE
  Sylvester, of NYC, for some years res. of N.Y. - 13 Feb. 1845
  Thomas, of Henrietta, Monroe Co. - 5 Apr. 1837
MALLET
  Janin, of NYC, carpenter - 18 Oct. 1833
MALLON
  Hugh, of Brooklyn, Kings Co. - 27 Sept. 1828
MALTMAN
  James, of NYC, stone-cutter - 5 Aug. 1826
  William, res. of NYC for 14 years last past - 8 Feb. 1830
MANGER
  Charles, of NYC, carpenter, formerly of Island of Guernsey - 31
    Mar. 1831
  Daniel, of NYC, house-painter, formerly of Island of Guernsey -
    31 Mar. 1831
MANIORT
  John, of NYC - 12 Nov. 1833
MANNEL
  Joseph, of Albany, native of Nottinghamshire, Eng. - 6 July 1835
MANNING
  Thomas, of Potsdam, St. Lawrence Co. - 3 Jan. 1828
MANNINGTON
  Alfred, of Vienna, Oneida Co. - 13 Apr. 1831
  Alfred, of Vienna, Oneida Co. - 4 Apr. 1836
MARCHAY
  John Matthias, of NYC, late of Denmark - 29 Mar. 1832
MANSBENDEL
  Susan (widow of James Mansbendel), of Morehouseville, Hamilton
    Co. - (sworn in NYC) 2 June 1845
MANSON
  Daniel, of NYC, baker - 4 July 1842
MARBACH
  Caspar, of Erie Co., native of Gaechlingen, Switzerland; arrived
    in U.S. 16 June 1844 - 30 Aug. 1844
MARCHAND
  Joachim, of Tonawanda, Erie Co. - 3 June 1847
MARIE
  Donnin/Donin Louis, of Flatbush, Kings Co. - 6 July 1843
  Martin, of NYC, farmer, late of Dept. of Upper Saone, France -
    1 Nov. 1833

New York Alien Residents, 1825-1848

MARIET
  Sussane, of Mexico, Oswego Co. - 2 Feb. 1831
MARION
  Amedee Jean, of NYC, merchant, lately of France - 17 Dec. 1832
MARIUTTE
  Achille, of NYC, merchant, French citizen - 23 Nov. 1832
MARQUIS
  Alexander, of Plattsburgh, Clinton Co. - 24 Sept. 1838
MARSCH
  Charles, of NYC - 15 Oct. 1838
MARSELE
  Julius, of Martinsburgh, Lewis Co. - 1 Mar. 1838
MARSH
  James, of NYC - 18 Nov. 1839
MARSHALL
  Alexander, of NYC - 27 Aug. 1846
  Charles, of NYC, res. of U.S. since 16 Oct. 1817, formerly of
    the U.K.; took incipient measures on 16 Oct. 1817 in Marine
    Court - 31 Aug. 1825
  Frances Mary, res. for more than 4 years of Greenbush, Rensse-
    laer Co. - 18 Feb. 1830
  James Dudley, of Oneida Co. - 9 June 1835
  John Worrel, of Brooklyn, Kings Co. - 12 June 1827
MARTIN
  Andrew, of Kings Co., late of U.K. - 20 Feb. 1837
  Dorcas (widow of Alexander Martin), of NYC, born in U.K. - 4
    Apr. 1844
  Francis, of Croghan, Lewis Co. - 23 Sept. 1841
  George, of Otsego Co. - 23 Feb. 1836
  John, of NYC - 29 Apr. 1845
  Patrick, of Newport, Herkimer Co. - (sworn at Albany) 3 Apr.
    1827
  Peter, of Greenbush, Rensselaer Co. - 6 Jan. 1836
  Robert, of NYC - 7 Dec. 1835
  Samuel, of NYC - 25 Apr. 1832
  Thomas, of NYC - 27 Sept. 1843
MARTINEZ
  Sylvano Augusto, presumably of NYC - 19 Aug. 1844
MARVIDEL/MARVEDELL
  Ferdinand, of NYC - 23 Oct. 1834
MASETH
  Joseph, of Utica, Oneida Co. - 20 Sept. 1831
MASTERS,
  Stephen Bunnet, of Brooklyn, Kings Co. - 25 Apr. 1828
MASTERTON
  William E., of NYC - 30 Apr. 1846
MATFIELD
  Gustavus A., of NYC, late of Hamburg, Germany - 15 June 1837
MATHES
  George, of Barre, Orleans Co. - 26 Jan. 1847
MATHEWS
  Charles, of Catlin, Chenung Co. - 30 Nov. 1847
  James, of NYC, merchant - 1 May 1844
MATHEY
  Aime, of NYC, watchmaker - 21 Apr. 1831
MATHIEU
  Andre, of Albany - 3 Dec. 1833
MATHIS
  Christian, of Queens Co. - 15 Dec. 1847
MATHIVET
  Pierre, of Watertown, Jefferson Co. - 27 Sept. 1832
MATHY
  Francois, of Western, Oneida Co. - 3 Aug. 1827
MATILE
  Edward, of NYC - 10 Mar. 1846

75

MATILE (continued)
  Louise Sophie (wife of Edward Matile), of NYC - 10 Mar. 1846
MATIOVICH
  Antonio, of NYC - 30 Jan. 1839
MATTINSON
  John, of Barre, Orleans Co., subject of G.B. - 21 June 1841
MAUVAIS/MAUVIES
  Zenon, of NYC, French subject - 23 Apr. 1835
MAVER
  Morris, of Sing Sing, Westchester Co., carpenter - 22 Feb. 1840
MAW
  Robert John, of NYC - 25 Mar. 1844
MAWSON
  Lewis, of NYC, subject of U.K. - 14 Feb. 1837
MAXTED
  Edmund, of Albany - 4 Dec. 1835
  Thomas, of Onondaga Co., British subject - 12 Feb. 1833
  William, of Onondaga Co., British subject - 12 Feb. 1833
MAXWELL
  Archibald, of Manlius, Onondaga Co. - 28 Nov. 1833
  Thomas, of Onondaga Co. - 30 Aug. 1828
MAY
  Charles, of Little Falls, Herkimer Co. - 1 May 1845
  John Shults, of Canajoharie, Montgomery Co. - 31 Aug. 1841
  Westfall, of Chatham, Columbia Co. - 1 Oct. 1845
MAYER
  John, of NYC, merchant, native of G.B. - 20 Mar. 1844
  John, of Williamsburgh, Kings Co. - 28 Jan. 1846
MAYFIELD
  John G., of East Chester, Westchester Co. - 21 Apr. 1840
MAYHEW
  John, of NYC - 18 Dec. 1835
MECHIN
  Rene, of NYC - 30 Jan. 1835
MEIERR
  Peter, of Williamsburgh, Kings Co. - 11 Aug. 1845
MEL
  John, of NYC, merchant - 25 Feb. 1833
  John, Sr., of NYC, gentleman - 7 Oct. 1833
MELLY
  Andrew Anthony, of NYC - 29 Nov. 1833
MELVILLE
  Alexander, of NYC - 7 Aug. 1841
MEMBERY
  George, of Hounsfield, Jefferson Co., age 26, born in Eng.; emi-
    grated to NYC in July 1830 - 19 Aug. 1830
MEMBERRY
  Amos, since 16 Oct. 1832 a res. of Hounsfield, Jefferson Co.,
    native of the Parish of Chard, Somerset Co., Eng., where he
    was born on 4 Dec. 1775; migrated to NYC on 4 Oct. 1832 - 23
    Nov. 1832
MENNIE/MINNE
  James, of Denmark, Lewis Co. - 6 Jan. 1836
MERCURRIE
  Margaret, of NYC - 19 Jan. 1848
MERKLE
  John, of Canajoharie, Montgomery Co. - 31 Aug. 1841
MERRILL
  Hugh, of Phelps, Ontario Co. - 19 Feb. 1842
MERRIMAN
  Isaac, of Whitestown, Oneida Co. - 10 Sept. 1832
  Robert, of Whitestown, Oneida Co. - 10 Sept. 1832
MERRITT
  Robert, of Manlius, Onondaga Co., lately come from Eng. - 31 Mar.
    1831

MERRITT (continued)
  William F., of Rochester, Monroe Co. - 10 Dec. 1842
MESMER
  Casper, of Lancaster, Erie Co. - 5 Jan. 1843
MESNEIL
  Nicholas, of NYC, machinist - 18 Oct. 1833
MESSENGER
  Harry, of NYC, subject of U.K. - 6 Oct. 1832
  John, of NYC, brewer - 2 Aug. 1825
METCALF
  James, of Kings Co., butcher - 27 June 1844
  John, of Chittenango, Madison Co. - 27 June 1837
METS
  Julius, of NYC - 25 Apr. 1831
METSCHEW
  Michael, of NYC, late of Germany - 17 Feb. 1835
METZ
  Christian, of Buffalo, Erie Co. - 3 July 1843 '
  Michael, of Deerfield, Oneida Co. - 15 Mar. 1836
METZLER
  John H., of NYC, shoemaker - 6 Jan. 1826
MEUZER
  Michael, of Wayne Co. - 28 Sept. 1830
MEYER
  Ann Charlotte (wife of Lewis H. Meyer, of NYC, merchant), of
    NYC, who came to NYC on 6 June 1839 - 4 Dec. 1840
  Laurens, of Rochester, Monroe Co. - 12 Oct. 1837
  Leonhard, of Lewis Co. - 21 Sept. 1830
  Lewis H., of NYC, merchant, who came to U.S. last on 9 June
    1836; he was born at Bremen, Germany, and brought to the U.S.
    at the age of about 1 and was kept here until about the age
    of 13, when he was sent to Europe to complete his education -
    4 Dec. 1840
  Martain, of Lewis Co. - 7 Oct. 1830
MIDDLETON
  David, of West Troy, Albany Co. - 17 July 1843
  Robert, of Granville, Washington Co. - 21 Feb. 1844
  Thomas, of NYC - 24 Nov. 1845
MILBURN
  John, of NYC - 11 Oct. 1847
MILFORD
  Edward, of NYC, hotel-keeper - 25 Apr. 1836
MILL
  David, of NYC - 29 Oct. 1840
MILLAR
  John, of NYC, hatter, native of Eng., res. of N.Y. since 1830 -
    26 Dec. 1833
  John, of Brookhaven, Suffolk Co. - 17 Oct. 1843
  John J., of NYC, hatter - 19 Oct. 1835
  Robert, of Troy, Rensselaer Co.; declared intention 1 Nov.
    1834 - 8 Mar. 1837
MILLER
  Alexander, of Albany Co. - 1 Jan. 1836
  Archibald, of Buffalo, Erie Co., grocer, age now 33, born in
    town of Hallowel, Co. of Prince Edward, Midland District,
    Upper Canada, res. of Buffalo for about 7 years last past -
    22 Mar. 1831
  Edward, of NYC - 19 July 1845
  Elizabeth, of Otsego Co. - 11 Jan. 1833
  Franz, of NYC, physician - 13 Jan. 1844
  George Act., of NYC - 13 Nov. 1847
  George Frederick W. (also called Frederick W. Miller), of Frank-
    fort, Herkimer Co., for 12 years past res. of N.Y. State -
    6 Mar. 1846
  Hugh, of Oswegatchie, St. Lawrence Co., from Ire. 20 Aug. 1827

MILLER (continued)
  Jacob, of Jamaica, Queens Co. - 24 Mar. 1847
  James, of Denmark, Lewis Co., formerly of Perthshire, Scotland -
    26 Sept. 1826
  John, of Kings Co. - 1 Nov. 1837
  Ludwig Frederick Warick (sometimes called Lewis Frederick Mil-
    ler), of Deerfield, Oneida Co., native of Wittenburgh, Ger-
    many - 19 Aug. 1839
  Mary Margaret, of Otsego Co. - 11 Jan. 1833
  Nicholas, of Buffalo, Erie Co. - 22 Aug. 1831
  Thomas, of Truxton, Cortland Co. - 17 Nov. 1847
  William, of NYC, butcher, native of U.K.; took incipient mea-
    sures 2 May 1828 - 24 Jan. 1831
MILLETT
  Thomas Mathew, of NYC - 30 May 1845
MILLIGAN
  Ann (wife of Robert Milligan), of Canajoharie, Montgomery Co.,
    native of Mullebreck, Co. of Down, Ire. - 27 Dec. 1844
  Lawrence, of Orange Co. - 10 Mar. 1834
MILLINGTON
  John W., of Rensselaer Co., native of Eng. - 17 May 1831
MILLWARD/MILLARD
  James, of NYC, silk dealer - 2 Nov. 1846
MILNE
  Alexander, of Haverstraw, Rockland Co. - 30 Sept. 1845
MILON
  Pierre J.S., of NYC - 17 Feb. 1838
MILOR
  Sarah, of NYC - 3 Oct. 1836
MINGES/MINGS
  Catharine, of Rochester, Monroe Co. - 5 Nov. 1847
MITCHELL
  Agnes, for several years res. of Brooklyn, Kings Co. - 25 Oct.
    1845
  John, of Brooklyn, Kings Co. - 11 Mar. 1835
  Margaret, of Brooklyn, Kings Co., res. there for several years -
    25 Oct. 1845
  Mary, for several years res. of Brooklyn, Kings Co. - (sworn in
    NYC) 25 Oct. 1845
MITTLEBERGER
  Francis, of Wayne Co. - 17 Jan. 1832
Moat
  Horatio Shepheard, of NYC - 22 July 1833
MOERSCHEL
  William, of Erie Co., native of Ronnebergh, Grand Dukedom of
    Hessen Darmstadt; came to U.S. 22 Aug. 1844 - 30 Aug. 1844
MOLONAY
  Michael, of Lockport, Niagara Co. - 14 Oct. 1833
MOLONY
  John, of Amsterdam, Montgomery Co. - 9 Oct. 1840
  Richard, of Onondaga Co. - 22 June 1830
MONK
  Joseph, of NYC, florist - 16 Sept. 1846
MONKS
  John, of Cold Spring, Putnam Co. - 12 Aug. 1846
MONNIER
  Francis X., of Greenwich, Washington Co., born in France - 6
    Aug. 1840
MONTALVO
  Ramon, of NYC - 11 Oct. 1847
MONTEATH
  Thomas L. Stuart, of Ontario Co., late of G.B. - 23 Aug. 1832
MONTEETH
  Robert, of Watertown, Jefferson Co. - 19 Apr. 1841

MONTGOMERY
  Alexander, of St. Lawrence Co., late of Ire. - 11 Feb. 1826
  John, of Waterloo, Seneca Co.- (sworn in Monroe Co.) 23 July
    1836
  William, of Rochester, Monroe Co., born in Co. of Lanark, Scot-
    land; emigrated to N.Y. in Aug. 1832 and has ever since been
    a res. of Monroe Co. - 15 June 1836
MONTI
  Jose Antoni, of NYC - 6 Jan. 1836
MOODY
  William, of Rye, Westchester Co. - 4 July 1831
MOONEY
  Arthur, of Troy, Rensselaer Co. - 20 Mar. 1841
  William, of Onondaga Co. - 5 Apr. 1836
MOORE
  George, of NYC, tobacco manufacturer - 22 Dec. 1827
  James, of NYC - 26 Nov. 1831
  James, of Troy, Rensselaer Co. - 14 Feb. 1838
  Joseph, of NYC - 12 Aug. 1834
  Lindley Murray, of Flushing, Queens Co., teacher - 2 June 1827
  Lodge, of Fort Edward, Washington Co., late of U.K. - 9 May 1832
  Louisa Catharine, of NYC - 30 Apr. 1836
  Lucinda, of NYC - 6 Apr. 1841
  Patrick, of NYC, grocer, native of Ire. - 7 Mar. 1828
  Roger Francis, of NYC - 13 June 1831
MOORHEAD
  Charles, of Troy, Rensselaer Co., native of Ulster, Ire. - 10
    July 1837
  Robinson, of Buffalo, Erie Co. - 15 Mar. 1830
MORAN
  Daniel, of Brooklyn, Kings Co., marketman - (sworn in NYC) 26
    Mar. 1844
  Patrick, of NYC, gardener - 4 Jan. 1828
  Patrick, of Troy, Rensselaer Co. - 11 June 1836
  Thomas, of Troy, Rensselaer Co. - 11 June 1836
  Thomas, of Rochester, Monroe Co. - 11 Aug. 1847
MORANGE
  Benjamin, of NYC, manufacturer - 26 Feb. 1827
MORE
  John, of NYC, late of the Netherlands - 16 Apr. 1829
MORGAN
  Bernard, of Stapleton, Richmond Co. - 28 Oct. 1839
  James, of Brighton, Monroe Co., born in Gloucestershire, Eng;
    arrived in N.Y. State in July 1830 - 6 Oct. 1831
  Joseph P., of NYC - 21 Apr. 1834
  Patrick, of Liberty, Sullivan Co., late of Ire. - 27 Aug. 1845
MORGANE
  Victor, of NYC, French subject - 16 Sept. 1842
MORING
  Charles Henry F., of NYC - 22 Sept. 1841
  Henry F., of NYC - 16 Sept. 1845
MORLEY
  Luke, of Wayne Co. - 27 Sept. 1831
MORLOT
  Charles, of NYC, late of France - 22 June 1836
MORRIS
  Ephraim, of Hector, Tompkins Co. - 12 July 1834
  George, of Onondaja, Onondaga Co. - 28 Sept. 1839
  John, of Troy, Rensselaer Co. - 4 Mar. 1837
  Reuben, of Onondaga Co. - 29 Sept. 1835
  William, of NYC - 17 Aug. 1835
MORRISON
  Lewis, living at 428 Houston St., NYC - 13 Jan. 1846
  Moses, of NYC, late of U.K. - 2 May 1844

MORROGH
  Mary (wife of John Morrogh), of NYC - 19 Nov. 1844
MORROUGH
  James, of NYC - 11 Oct. 1834
  John, of NYC - 11 Oct. 1834
MORROW
  John, of Saratoga Co., born in Co. of Antrim, Ire., age 26 - 27
    Mar. 1844
MORTIMER
  John, Sr., of Kings Co. - 9 Sept. 1836
MORTON
  John, of NYC, storekeeper - 16 Apr. 1827
  Robert, of Livingston Co., native of Scotland - 8 July 1846
MORTRIER
  Barthelemis, of Williamsburgh, Kings Co., glass-cutter - 27 Oct.
    1846
MOSQUERON
  David Aubusten, of Hartwick, Otsego Co. - 6 Aug. 1834
MOSS
  Philip, of Greenbush, Rensselaer Co. - 23 Dec. 1836
  Thomas, of Albany - 16 Feb. 1832
MOTT
  Louisa D. (wife of Valentine Mott), of NYC - 28 Aug. 1844
MOULD
  James, of Rockland, Sullivan Co. - 1 Feb. 1839
  John, of Albany Co. - 18 Oct. 1847
MOULTON
  Stephen, of NYC - 5 Oct. 1834
MOUNCEY
  Isaac, of Frankfort, Herkimer Co. - 4 Jan. 1836
MOUNT
  Lawrence, of NYC - 30 Apr. 1832
MOUSSARD
  Evrard Samson Hippolite, of Hempstead, Queens Co. - 28 Dec. 1833
MOWAT
  John, of Syracuse, Onondaga Co. - 7 Oct. 1842
MOYSES
  Samuel, of Kings Co. - 31 Jan. 1826
MOZER
  Felicité (widow of Laurent Mozer, late of NYC), of NYC - 26 May
    1845
MUELLER
  Francis Anton, of Rochester, Monroe Co. - 6 Aug. 1839
MULDAWZ
  Moritz, of NYC - 13 May 1836
MULHERAN
  Margaret, of Kings Co. - 29 Sept. 1835
MULHOLLAND
  Patrick, of Poughkeepsie, Dutchess Co., late of Downs, Ire. -
    4 Feb. 1834
MULLANY
  James, of Oneida Co., native of Ire. - 14 Mar. 1840
MULLEN
  Cecilia, of Brooklyn, Kings Co. - 20 Oct. 1826
  John, of Albany Co. - 26 Apr. 1847
  Michael, of Auburn, Cayuga Co. - 16 Sept. 1844
MULLER
  Charles C., of NYC, merchant, late of Saxony - 8 Dec. 1846
  Peter D., of NYC - 20 June 1842
MULLIGAN
  John, of NYC - 12 Apr. 1847
MULLIN
  Eliza, of NYC, single woman - (July 1846
MULLOY/MALLOY
  Mary (wife of Michael), of NYC - 22 Apr. 1845

New York Alien Residents, 1825-1848

MULLOY/MALLOY (continued)
  Michael, of NYC - 22 Apr. 1845
MULQUEEN
  Solomon, of Albany, formerly of Ire. - 29 June 1841
MUMFORD
  John, of Brooklyn, Kings Co. - 26 May 1846
MUMMERY
  Thomas, of Lorraine, Jefferson Co. - 6 Nov. 1830
MURDOCK
  Andrew, of Albany Co. - 30 Oct. 1847
  David, of Catskill, Greene Co. - 22 Feb. 1844
  Elizabeth, of NYC, formerly of U.K. - 24 June 1836
MURGATROYD
  Thomas, of Gibbonville, Albany Co. - 28 Feb. 1831
MURMON
  Daniel, of Buffalo, Erie Co. - 10 Dec. 1831
MURPHY
  Dennis, of NYC, carpenter - 31 Jan. 1848
  Hugh, of Kings Co. - 20 June 1827
  Jane, of NYC - 23 July 1847
  John, of Watervliet, Albany Co., farmer - 17 Mar. 1828
  John, of Onondaga Co. - 24 Feb. 1834
  Patrick, of Watervliet, Albany Co., farmer - 17 Mar. 1828
  Thomas, of NYC, broker, res. for several years in NYC - 11 May
    1830
MURRAY
  Alexander, of Ontario Co., late from G.B. - 20 Nov. 1834
  Alexander, of Erie Co. - 1 May 1846
  Daniel, of Oswego, Oswego Co., born in Co. of Cork, Ire. - 5
    Dec. 1840
  Elizabeth (wife of James Murray of Rochester and daughter of
    Edward Mc Gee), of Rochester, Monroe Co. - 3 Apr. 1844
  James, of Buffalo, Erie Co. - 2 Dec. 1843
  James, of Monroe Co. - 13 Dec. 1847
  John, of NYC, carpenter, late of U.K. - 7 Apr. 1827
  John, of Kings Co., British subject - 28 Aug. 1840
  John Robert, of Erie Co., late of Liverpool, Eng. - 23 Aug. 1831
  Patrick, of Greenbush, Rensselaer Co. - 30 Oct. 1830
  Thomas, of Buffalo, Erie Co., born in Co. of Roscommon, Ire. -
    11 Oct. 1847
  Timothy, of Buffalo, Erie Co., born in Co. of Roscommon, Ire. -
    11 Oct. 1847
  William, of Lewis Co. - 11 Oct. 1830
MURRY
  Thomas, of Onondaga Co. - 4 May 1840
MURTAGH
  Thomas B., of NYC - 25 June 1832
MURTAUGH
  Thomas, of Albany Co. - 27 Mar. 1846
MYER
  Joseph, of Rochester, Monroe Co. - 3 Sept. 1839
  Michael, of Columbia Co. - 16 May 1832
NALTON
  Thomas, of Oneida Co. - 28 Apr. 1832
NAPIER
  John A., of Watertown, Jefferson Co., born in Ire. - 28 Jan.
    1843
NATH
  Jacob, of Le Ray, Jefferson Co. - 31 Dec. 1840
NATION
  James, of Albany - 11 Feb. 1839
NEBRBASS
  Wendell, of Buffalo, Erie Co. - 6 July 1846
NEDEN
  James, of Lockport, Niagara Co. - 13 Sept. 1836

NEEJER
  Henry, of Oneida Co. - 20 May 1839
NEEVES
  James, of NYC, res. of N.Y. for more than 11 years - 11 Mar.
    1833
NEGUS
  Thomas, of NYC - 24 June 1840
NELSON
  George, of Rochester, Monroe Co. - 1 Mar. 1847
  James, of Rensselaer Co. - 3 Nov. 1834
NERI
  Peter, of NYC, gardener - 20 Mar. 1828
NESBIT/NISBIT
  Alexander, of Albany Co. - 27 Jan. 1835
  George Rae, of Albany Co. - 27 Jan. 1835
  James, of Plattsburgh, Clinton Co. - 7 Sept. 1839
  Joseph, of Plattsburgh, Clinton Co. - 7 Sept. 1839
NESBITT
  Henry, of NYC - 15 May 1832
NETER
  George Michael, of Lewis Co. - 21 Sept. 1830
NEUESENCHWANDER
  Jacob, of West Turin, Lewis Co. - June 1843
NEVE
  Elizabeth (widow of William Neve), of NYC - 7 Sept. 1836
NEVILLE
  Charles Cecil, of Monroe Co. - 6 Jan. 1840
NEW
  James L., of Bushwick, Kings Co. - 14 Sept. 1846
  Thomas, of Ogden, Monroe Co., born in Co. of Berkshire, Eng.,
    on 10 Dec. 1809; arrived in U.S. on 5 Apr. 1836; declared
    intent on 30 Dec. 1842 - 6 Apr. 1843
NEWBURY/NEWBERRY
  Leonard, of Lockport, Niagara Co. - 20 Jan. 1834
NEWCOMBE
  Jane Charlotte, of NYC - 17 Feb. 1845
NEWELL
  James C., of Kings Co. - 21 Apr. 1832
  William, of Albany - 14 Apr. 1846
NEWHOUSE
  Elizabeth (widow of Jacob Newhouse), of NYC - 27 Jan. 1847
NEWITT
  William, of Sangerfield, Oneida Co. - 23 Mar. 1844
NEWLANDS
  James B., of Troy, Rensselaer Co. - 16 Mar. 1836
NEWMAN
  Eleanor, of NYC - 21 Jan. 1845
  James, of Hempstead, Long Island - 28 Jan. 1847
  John, of NYC - 28 June 1838
  Thomas, of City of Albany - 26 Dec. 1836
NEWPORT
  Richard, of Onondaga Co. - 1 Apr. 1846
NEWSON
  Robert, of NYC - 6 Mar. 1837
  William, of NYC, British subject; witness was William Frazer,
    of NYC, stone-cutter - 18 Aug. 1825
NEWSTADT
  Samuel J., of NYC - 5 May 1840
NEWTON
  James, of Floyd, Oneida Co. - 24 Mar. 1830
NICHOLAS
  Robert, of Oneida Co. - 27 Feb. 1834
  Robert H., of Whitestown, Onondaga Co. - 16 Dec. 1837
NICHOLS/NICHOLES
  William, of Wayne Co. - 28 Jan. 1834

New York Alien Residents, 1825-1848

NICHOLSON
  Joseph, of Richfield, Otsego Co., citizen of Eng., whence he
    came to the U.S. after the time he was of full age; for 5 years
    he has been a blacksmith in Richfield; he owns a shop and a
    house there - 28 Feb. 1831
  William, of Hudson, Columbia Co. - 26 Dec. 1836
  William Nelmes, of NYC - 30 July 1840
NIEWERDE
  Gerhard Heinrick, of Rochester, Monroe Co. - 29 Sept. 1846
NIPPER
  William, of Onondaga Co., late of U.K. - 8 July 1830
NIX
  Edward, of NYC - 15 Sept. 1836
NOE
  John F. W., of Buffalo, Erie Co. - 3 July 1843
NOEL
  Nicholas, of NYC, merchant, born in town of St. Quirin, Dept.
    of the Meurthe, France - 1 Sept. 1836
NOLAN
  James, of NYC - 16 Oct. 1837
NOLLOTH
  William Hornsby, of Utica, Oneida Co. - 30 May 1840
NOLLY
  John, of Orange Co., late of U.K. - 6 Apr. 1836
NORMAN
  Abraham, of Wayne Co. - 28 Apr. 1835
NORRIE
  Adam, of NYC, merchant - 27 Sept. 1833
NORRIS
  James, of Troy, Rensselaer Co., born in Co. of Buckingham, Eng.;
    came to U.S. in Apr. 1829 - 10 Aug. 1831
  Jesse, of Onondaga, Onondaga Co. - 2 Apr. 1839
NORTON
  Thomas, of Erie Co., native of G.B. - 19 Jan. 1842
NORWOOD
  David, of Albany - 14 Sept. 1830
NOTT
  William J., of Lyons, Wayne Co. - 6 June 1836
NOURCE
  William Henry, of Williamsburgh, Kings Co. - 13 May 1847
NOWLAN
  Andrew, of Flatbush, Kings Co. - 10 Mar. 1841

OAKES
  Henry, of Canaan, Columbia Co., shoemaker - 11 Nov. 1826
OAKLEY
  George, of Brooklyn, Kings Co. - 12 June 1846
OBERTON
  Alexander, of Lowville, Lewis Co., born in Prov. of Lower Canada -
    28 June 1841
ORORN
  James, of Oswego, Oswego Co. - 3 Apr. 1837
O'BRIEN
  Bridget, of NYC - 12 July 1844
  Hannah, of NYC - 25 Mar. 1844
  Patrick, of Plattsburgh, Clinton Co. - 14 May 1839
  Patrick, of NYC - 16 Jan. 1845
O'BRINE
  Thomas, of Ravenswood, Newtown, Queens Co. - 2 June 1837
O'BRYAN
  Henry, of Lockport, Niagara Co. - 13 Nov. 1835
O'CONNOR
  Patrick, of Utica, Oneida Co., formerly subject of U.K. - 18
    Feb. 1828
O'DONNELL
  Henry, of NYC, born in G.B. - 8 Aug. 1836

New York Alien Residents, 1825-1848

O'DONNELL (continued)
  Rose (wife of Jeremiah O'Donnell), of NYC - 5 Feb. 1847
OGLE
  George, of Onondaga Co., born in G.B. - 26 Nov. 1832
O'HARE
  Michael, of NYC, fruiterer - 16 Apr. 1832
  Thomas, of Galway, Saratoga Co. - 24 Sept. 1841
OHLEIIER
  George, of Wayne Co. - 26 Sept. 1833
OLDRING
  Henry, of NYC, tanner, born subject of U.K. - 10 Nov. 1829
O'LEARY
  Dennis, of Grafton, Rensselaer Co. - 7 Mar. 1842
OLIVER
  James, of Brooklyn, Kings Co. - (sworn in NYC) 6 Sept. 1845
O'MEARA
  Francis, of NYC - 11 Sept. 1845
O'NEAL
  Patrick, of Troy, Rensselaer Co. - 24 Mar. 1845
O'NEIL
  Cormack, of the Sixth Ward in Brooklyn, Kings Co. - 29 May 1847
O'NIEL
  Michael, of Ticonderoga, Essex Co.; took incipient measures 30
    Sept. 1840 - 26 Oct. 1841
ONIONS
  Edward Boden, of Albany - 11 Oct. 1832
OPERSOLD
  John, of Rochester, Monroe Co. - 20 June 1835
ORCHARD
  Benjamin, of Jefferson Co. - 8 Oct. 1832
ORDRONAUX
  Elizabeth, of NYC, widow - 27 May 1843
O'REILY
  Bernard, of Monroe Co. - 5 July 1844
  Patrick, of Albany - 3 Mar. 1837
O'REILLY/O'RIELLY
  James, of Westmoreland, Oneida Co. - 20 May 1837
ORME
  Charles, of Canandaigua, Ontario Co., late of London, Eng. - 31
    Jan. 1838
ORMESTON
  Alexander, of Rockland Co. - 27 Jan. 1837
O'ROURK
  Owen, of Troy, Rensselaer Co., native of Beltenbat (Belturbet),
    Co. of Cavan, Ire. - 13 Mar. 1828
ORR
  Catharine, of Albany - 4 Sept. 1838
  David, of NYC, carpenter - 25 Feb. 1833
  Edward, of NYC - 27 Feb. 1840
  William, of Sullivan, Madison Co. - 17 Mar. 1831
ORRIS
  Robert, of Buffalo, Erie Co. - 25 Sept. 1835
  Robert W., of Buffalo, Erie Co. - 24 Sept. 1835
OSBORN
  Francis, of Rose, Wayne Co. - 24 Sept. 1845
OSBRAY
  Elizabeth, of Brooklyn, Kings Co., widow - 9 Apr. 1833
OSGODBY
  Jacob H., of Rochester, Monroe Co., native of Eng., res. of U.S.
    and N.Y. State since June 1828 - 6 Dec. 1833
OST
  Phillip, of Verona, Oneida Co. - 19 Nov. 1844
O'SULLIVAN
  Edmund, of Albany - 9 May 1826
  Thomas, of Seneca Falls, Seneca Co. - 12 Apr. 1834

New York Alien Residents, 1825-1848

OTTERSON
  Henry, of Watervliet, Albany Co., born citizen of U.K.; on 7
    July 1826 emigrated to U.S. - 14 Jan. 1830
  Henry, of Watervliet, Albany Co., native of U.K.; emigrated to
    U.S. on 7 July 1826 - 30 Oct. 1830
OTTO
  Christian, of NYC - 19 Feb. 1836
  Henry, of NYC, late of Bremen, Germany - 1 Sept. 1840
OTTOWAY
  John, of Oneida Co. - 7 Feb. 1837
OUGHTON
  Robert, of NYC, carpenter - 16 Dec. 1826
OUTHWAITE
  John, of Buffalo, Erie Co. - 30 Aug. 1831
OVINGTON
  Catharine C. (wife of James Ovington), of NYC - 10 July 1844
OWEN
  James, of NYC, merchant, subject of G.B. - 5 Feb. 1844
OWENS
  John, of Scarsdale, Westchester Co. - 3 Dec. 1832
  John T., of Utica, Oneida Co. - 15 Oct. 1833
  Owen, of Oneida Co., formerly of Merionethshire, Wales - 15 Mar.
    1831
OXNER
  Joseph, of West Turin, Lewis Co. - 24 Sept. 1847

PACKHAM
  Eldridge, of Pittsford, Monroe Co., born in Mayfield, Co. of
    Sussex, Eng., on 19 Aug. 1784; arrived in U.S. 27 June 1841 -
    4 Mar. 1845
PAGE
  Charles Reade, of NYC, sadler and trunk-maker - 10 Feb. 1836
  Michael, Sr., of Oswegatchie, late from Lower Canada - 12 July
    1831
  Thomas, of NYC, wheelwright - 24 Feb. 1845
PAGELL
  John, of Blooming Grove, Orange Co. - 22 Sept. 1845
PAGES
  John, of NYC, baker - 1 Nov. 1833
PAIGE
  Robert George, of NYC, professor of music, late of G.B. - 19
    Sept. 1837
PAINE
  George, of Onondaga Co. - 27 Nov. 1839
  Richard, Sr., of Syracuse, Onondaga Co. - 10 Feb. 1847
  William, of Stafford, Genesee Co. - 30 Sept. 1839
PAINTER
  Catherine (wife of William Painter, of NYC, engineer), of NYC -
    24 Mar. 1845
  George, of NYC - 16 June 1836
PALACHE
  Alexander, of NYC, formerly of London, Eng., gentleman - 17 Jan.
    1832
  Mordecai, of NYC, formerly of Kingston, Jamaica, gentleman - 24
    Jan. 1832
PALLISTER
  John, of Wayne Co. - 26 Jan. 1831
  Thomas, of Wayne Co. - 24 Jan. 1831
PALMER
  Charles, of NYC - 21 Dec. 1837
  Edward, of NYC, chair-maker - 10 Aug. 1827
  Mary (widow of William Palmer), of NYC - 8 Feb. 1848
  Thomas, of Winfield, Herkimer Co. - 2 Nov. 1838
PAPE
  Wilhelmine (wife of Charles Pape), of NYC - 7 June 1845

New York Alien Residents, 1825-1848

PAPMORE
  Richard, of Stafford, Genesee Co. - 10 June 1834
PAPPENHAUSEN
  Conrad, of Brooklyn, Kings Co., late of Hamburg, Germany; came
    to the U.S. about 4 years ago - 30 Mar. 1847
PAPPI
  John, of NYC, painter and glazier - 17 July 1835
PANON
  Marius, of NYC, merchant, French subject - 17 Sept. 1831
PARK
  John, of Rochester, Monroe Co. - 14 Aug. 1835
PARKE
  James, of Little Falls, Herkimer Co., late of G.B. - 26 Mar.
    1833
PARKER
  Edward, of Brighton, Monroe Co. - 4 Oct. 1830
  Francis, of Niagara Co. - 7 Jan. 1835
  Francis, of Chautauque Co. - 15 Feb. 1837
  John, of Clay, Onondaga Co. - 6 Oct. 1834
  William, of Clay, Onondaga Co. - 6 Oct. 1834
  William, of Alden, Erie Co. - 7 Oct. 1834
  William, of Castleton, Richmond Co.; age 28 on Mar. last; he
    arrived in Castleton from Eng. on 28 Mar. 1832 - 17 Apr. 1839
PARKS
  David, of Somers, Westchester Co. - 27 May 1841
PARR
  John, of NYC - 11 Nov. 1834
  Thomas, of Elba, Genesee Co. - 25 Nov. 1842
  William, of Oakfield, Genesee Co. - 10 Oct. 1843
PARRY
  Hannah, of Onondaga Co. - 31 Oct. 1835
  Howell, of Kings Co. - 29 Sept. 1841
  John, of Pompey, Onondaga Co. - 9 Apr. 1831
  Joseph, of Hudson, Columbia Co. - 6 Oct. 1832
  Joseph, of Onondaga Co. - 31 Oct. 1835
  William, of NYC - 19 Oct. 1833
PARSONS
  Arthur W., of NYC, merchant, late of Manchester, Eng. - 9 Apr.
    1841
PARTLOW
  John, of Wayne Co. - 26 Sept. 1840
PARTON
  John, of Bushwick, Kings Co., late of G.B. - 27 May 1826
PASCO
  Richard, of Poughkeepsie, Dutchess Co. - 2 Nov. 1840
PASCOE
  Grace, of NYC, late of Devonport, Co. of Devon, Eng. - 28 May
    1845
  John, of Montgomery Co. - (sworn in Otsego Co.) 25 Nov. 1842
  Nicholas Jasper, of NYC, chair-maker, late of Devonport, Co. of
    Devon, Eng. - 27 Sept. 1836
PATTERSON
  Daniel, of Phelps, Ontario Co. - 24 Feb. 1834
  James, of Albany - 15 May 1835
  James, of Cambridge, Washington Co. - 30 Mar. 1837
  Jane, of Geneva, Ontario Co., native of U.K. - 18 Nov. 1835
  John, of Brooklyn, Kings Co., late of Ire. - 22 Mar. 1824
  Joseph, of Galen, Wayne Co. - 5 Sept. 1837
  Robert, of Brooklyn, Kings Co., formerly of Ire. - 9 Dec. 1841
  Robert, of NYC - 7 Aug. 1845
  William, of Brooklyn, Kings Co., labourer, native of Ire. - 9
    May 1825
  William, of Rochester, Monroe Co., subject of G.B. - 30 Oct.
    1847

New York Alien Residents, 1825-1848

PATTO
  Henry, of NYC - 5 Sept. 1828
PATTON
  Elizabeth (widow of James Patton), of Castleton, Richmond Co. -
    27 Feb. 1843
  John, of New Scotland, Albany Co. - 1 Apr. 1833
  Robert, of New Scotland, Albany Co. - 1 Apr. 1833
  William, of New Scotland, Albany Co. - 1 Apr. 1833
PATTULLO
  David, of NYC - 26 Aug. 1843
PAUL
  Francis Wilson, of Ontario Co. - 3 June 1835
  Valentine, of West Turin, Lewis Co. - 6 May 1836
PAULI
  George, of Erie Co. - 23 June 1838
PAXEDDA
  Pasquale, of NYC - 18 Jan. 1834
PAYEN
  Anne (née Marchandean, wife of Jules René Payen), of NYC, late
    of France - 24 Sept. 1840
  Jules René, of NYC, French subject - 24 Sept. 1840
PAYFER
  Francis X., of NYC - 1 Nov. 1844
PEACOCK
  Philip, of Buffalo, Erie Co. - 14 Feb. 1833
  Thomas, of NYC - 20 Mar. 1845
PEARCE
  Amos, of Poughkeepsie, Dutchess Co. - 7 Jan. 1846
  Charles, of NYC, formerly of London, Eng. - 28 May 1839
  George, residing at 413 Broadway, NYC - 18 Nov. 1837
PEARCY
  John, of Brooklyn, Kings Co., late of G.B. - 18 Apr. 1826
PEARSON
  Christopher, of Buffalo, Erie Co. - 14 Mar. 1831
  George, of Kingston, Ulster Co., late of Co. of Durham, Eng. -
    20 June 1843
  John S., of Kings Co. - 13 Mar. 1837
PEEBLES
  James, of Alexandria, Jefferson Co. - 13 July 1839
PEELE
  Thomas, of Buffalo, Erie Co. - 7 Mar. 1835
PEHL
  William, of NYC - 2 Jan. 1847
PELLING
  James, of Bushwick, Kings Co., farmer - 22 Dec. 1830
PENNOCK
  Matthew, of Oneida Co., native of Eng. - 16 May 1844
PENTECOST
  Charles, of Frankfort, Herkimer Co., late of Nailsea, Somer-
    setshire, Eng. - 2 June 1832
PENTON
  William, of Utica, Oneida Co., native of Ire. - 30 Oct. 1827
PEPPER
  Thomas, of Allegheny Co. - 26 June 1832
  William, Jr., of Vernon, Oneida Co. - 18 Apr. 1836
  William, Sr., of Oneida Co. - 27 Aug. 1835
PERRIN
  Arthur, of Brooklyn, Kings Co. - 23 Oct. 1846
  Elizabeth (wife of Arthur Perrin), of Brooklyn, Kings Co. - 8
    Jan. 1845
PERROT
  Ferdinand, of Le Roy, Jefferson Co., native of Co. of Bern,
    Switzerland, born in 1788; emigrated to N.Y. State in 1825 -
    2 Nov. 1835

PERROT (continued)
  Ferdinand, Jr., of Le Roy, Jefferson Co., born in Co. of Bern,
    Switzerland in 1814; emigrated to N.Y. State in 1825 - 2 Nov.
    1835
PERRY
  George, of Montgomery, Orange Co. - 30 Dec. 1835
PERRYMAN
  William, of Williamsburgh, Kings Co.- (sworn in NYC) 24 May 1847
PERSCH
  Daniel, of Buffalo, Erie Co. - 10 Dec. 1835
PESTER
  William, of City of Albany - 6 May 1836
PETERMAN
  Andrew, of Niagara Co. - 15 Apr. 1836
PETERS
  Charles, of Sharon, Schoharie Co. - (sworn in Albany) 19 Mar.
    1845
  Jane (widow of Joseph Priestly Peters), of NYC - 5 Aug. 1843
  John, of Brooklyn, Kings Co. - 18 Apr. 1837
PETIT
  Jacque Philipe, of No. 81 Oliver St., NYC - 28 July 1847
  Pierre, of NYC - 12 Mar. 1836
PETRIE
  James, of NYC - 23 Oct. 1845
  William W., of NYC - 8 Jan. 1836
PETTIT
  Thomas, of Onondaga Co. - 29 Nov. 1836
PFEFFEL
  Peter C., of NYC, citizen of Frankfurt am Main - 4 Sept. 1840
PHELAN
  Timothy, of NYC - 29 Nov. 1826
PHEPPS
  Thomas, of Mendon, Monroe Co. - 29 Dec. 1836
PHILBERT
  Louis Augustus, of Fowler, St. Lawrence Co., formerly of France;
    came to U.S. about middle of June 1833 - 21 Sept. 1837
PHIPPEN
  Henry, of NYC, late of France - 18 July 1843
PHILLIPS
  Lyon, of NYC - 17 Sept. 1837
  Robert, of Lockport, Niagara Co. - 10 Sept. 1836
PHILLIPSON
  John, of Murray, Orleans Co. - 21 Sept. 1836
PIAGET
  Henry Francis, of Kings Co., born Canton of Vaud, Switzerland -
    11 Oct. 1836
PICKERSGILL
  Charles Frederick, of NYC - 27 Oct. 1847
  Hannah Louisa, of NYC - 27 Oct. 1847
  John, of Brooklyn, Kings Co., merchant, late of Eng. - 9 Jan.
    1845
PICKERT
  Lodowick, of Sand Lake, Rensselaer Co. - 1 Apr. 1842
  Michael, of Sand Lake, Rensselaer Co. - 1 Apr. 1842
PICKTON
  John, of Albany - 3 Mar. 1838
PIDDOCK
  Robert, of Lorraine, Jefferson Co. - 6 Nov. 1830
PIERIN
  Abraham, of Rochester, Monroe Co. - 3 Sept. 1839
PIGOTT
  Peter, of Flatbush, Kings Co. - 3 June 1847
PILBROW
  Edward, of NYC, engraver, late of U.K. - 17 June 1833

New York Alien Residents, 1825-1848

PILLOW
  William Hy., of Genesee Co. - 24 Jan. 1834
PIMLEY
  Edward, of Hudson, Columbia Co. - 11 Feb. 1832
  George, of Hudson, Columbia Co. - 9 Feb. 1832
PINFOLD
  Zephaniah, of Otsego Co. - 26 Dec. 1831
PINK
  William, of Williamsburgh, Kings Co., gentleman - 15 Nov. 1847
PITT
  James, of Caneada, Allegheny Co. - 31 May 1844
  John, of Allegheny Co. - 27 Dec. 1833
  Lazarus, of Allegheny Co., native of Dorsetshire, Eng., res. of
    the U.S. from 1 June 1833 - 26 June 1833
  Samuel, of Dorsetshire, Eng., res. of U.S. from 8 June 1830 -
    26 June 1833
  William, of Allegheny Co. - 26 June 1832
PITTAM
  Thomas, of Onondaga Co. - 1 Sept. 1836
PITTS
  Robert, of Brookhaven, Suffolk Co. - 16 Oct. 1845
PLACATHES
  Nicholas, of NYC - 28 Sept. 1839
PLASKETT
  Sarah (widow of William Plaskett) - 15 Apr. 1837
PLATT
  Samuel, of Lockport, Niagara Co. - 7 Jan. 1833
PLAYSTEAD
  John, of Yates Co., native of Eng. - Sept. 1822
PLUCHE
  Charles, of Jefferson Co. - 12 Feb. 1842
  Lewis C., of Jefferson Co. - 12 Feb. 1842
PLUMMER
  Charles, of West Turin, Lewis Co. - 17 Apr. 1843
  William, of Deerfield, Oneida Co., native of Eng. - 4 June 1833
POCCOCK
  Elizabeth, of Utica, Oneida Co., native of Co. of Sligo, Ire.;
    emigrated to N.Y. more than 40 years ago - 8 June 1844
POLLOCK
  James, of Wayne Co. - 27 May 1831
  Thomas, of Williamsburgh, Kings Co. - (sworn in NYC) 2 Nov. 1846
POLMAN
  Charles William, of NYC - 14 Oct. 1847
POLO
  Casimiro, of NYC, native of Havana, Cuba - 22 Dec. 1837
POOL
  Charles, of NYC, mathematical instrument maker and optician - 11
    May 1829
  Hannah S., of NYC - 8 Apr. 1847
POOLEY
  Edward, of Wayne Co. - 26 Jan. 1832
POPE
  Charles, of NYC, carpenter - 19 Oct. 1832
  Charles, Jr., of NYC, carpenter - 19 Oct. 1832
POQUILLON
  Francis Victor, of Erie Co. - 3 June 1840
PORTER
  Archibald, of Watertown, Jefferson Co. - 25 Oct. 1836
  George, of Watertown, Jefferson Co., born in Ire. - 22 June 1844
  Robert, of Watertown, Jefferson Co., born in Ire. - 21 May 1841
  Thomas William, of NYC - 26 Dec. 1833
  William Henry, of Portage, Allegheny Co. - 22 June 1844
PORTHOUSE
  Joseph, of Richland, Oswego Co., native of G.B. - 18 Feb. 1835

POSTETER
  Martin, of Lewis Co. - 21 Sept. 1830
POTTER
  Charles, of Brooklyn, Kings Co., born British subject - 9 Nov.
    1847
POTTINGER
  William, of Williamsburgh, Kings Co. - (sworn in NYC) 31 Jan.
    1848
POTTS
  James, of Watertown, Jefferson Co., born in village of Chambely,
    Lower Canada, on 3 Dec. 1903; emigrated to the U.S. in Dec.
    1837 - 1 Dec. 1842
  William J., of Brooklyn, Kings Co. - 6 Jan. 1838
POU
  Justo, of NYC, druggist - 14 Apr. 1836
POULOT/POUSOT
  George, of NYC, cabinetmaker - 11 Dec. 1833
POULTON
  George, of Oneida Co., native of Worcestershire, Eng. - 18 May
    1835
POUND
  Benjamin Franklin, of Wayne Co. - 28 Mar. 1845
POWELL
  Edward, of Troy, Rensselaer Co. - 21 Sept. 1836
  Horatio, of Onondaga Co. - 29 May 1839
  Robert Ward, of NYC, merchant tailor - 19 Sept. 1838
  Thomas, of Milton, Saratoga Co. - 29 Feb. 1836
POWER
  Catharine (wife of John Power), of NYC - 2 Apr. 1846
  John, now of Buffalo, Erie Co., late of Ire. - 9 Apr. 1836
POWERS
  Ann, of NYC - 14 Sept. 1847
POWERS/POWIS
  Richard, of NYC - 1 Nov. 1834
PRATER
  William, of Deerfield, Oneida Co. - 9 Aug. 1836
PRESTON
  George, of Pomfret, Chautauque Co. - 29 Mar. 1842
PRICE
  David, of Oneida Co., native of Berriew, Montgomeryshire, Wales -
    18 Feb. 1840
  Joseph, of Cherry Valley, Otsego Co. - 15 June 1830
  Owen, of Oneida Co., native of Glanwiddelan, Montgomeryshire,
    Wales - 18 Feb. 1840
PRIDMORE
  Thomas, of Parma, Monroe Co. - 16 Oct. 1844
PRISCOTT
  Henry, of Chenango Co. - 16 Jan. 1846
PRITCHARD
  Elizabeth (widow of Henry Pritchard), of NYC - 3 Nov. 1846
PROCTOR
  Christopher, of Albany - 31 Dec. 1835
  Isaac, of Newtown, Queens Co., born in U.K. - (sworn in Kings Co,
    29 Dec. 1846
  Matthew, of Minisink, Orange Co. - 27 Jan. 1844
PROLE/PROLES
  Alexander, of Stafford, Genesee Co. - 3 Feb. 1835
PROSEQUINE
  Jean Baptiste, of NYC - 25 Sept. 1840
PROST
  Joseph, of Rochester, Monroe Co. - 29 Mar. 1837
PROUDFOOT
  James, of Canajoharie, Montgomery Co., born in G.B. - 22 Feb.
    1832

PROUGEE
  Jean Pierre, of Rochester, Monroe Co. - 19 Jan. 1833
PROUT
  Eliza, of NYC - 14 Dec. 1842
PRYCE
  Thomas, of Oneida Co., native of Llanfair, Montgomeryshire,
    Wales - 18 Feb. 1840
PRYER
  Joseph, of Wayne Co. - 28 Jan. 1836
PUFFETT
  Charles, of Onondaga Co. - 4 Mar. 1839
PUGH
  David, of West Turin, Lewis Co. - 11 Feb. 1836
PUICOMB
  Robert, of Pembroke, Genesee Co., late of U.K. - 14 Oct. 1835
PUNCHARD
  Richard, of NYC, carpenter - 1 May 1847
PUPIN
  Marius, of Hartwick, Otsego Co. - 2 Dec. 1833
PURCELL
  Michael, of NYC, late of U.K. - 25 Oct. 1832

QUAIL
  Daniel, of Madison Co. - 14 Mar. 1844
QUIGLEY
  James, of Brooklyn, Kings Co., milkman - 29 Nov. 1828
  Joseph, of Mount Hope, Orange Co. - 4 Apr. 1835
  Margaret, of Brooklyn, Kings Co., widow - 16 Oct. 1843
QUILLER
  William, of NYC - 8 Mar. 1832
QUILLIARD
  Claude Sylvain, of Delaware Co., formerly of France - 5 Feb.
    1828
QUIN
  Anna, of NYC - 22 Apr. 1845
  Michael, of NYC, late of U.K. - 5 June 1832
QUINN
  Thomas, of Verona, Oneida Co., late of Clunsast, Ire. - 20 May
    1825
QUINLIN/QUINLAIN
  Timothy, of Java, Wyoming Co. - 15 Dec. 1841
QUIRK
  Thomas, of Brooklyn, Kings Co., carpenter - 3 Jan. 1845

RABEAU
  Richard Ernst, of NYC - 4 Nov. 1843
RACEY
  Benjamin, of NYC, brewer, late of U.K.; migrated to U.S. in the
    autumn of 1822 - 1 Aug. 1826
RADAWAY
  Edward, of Elbridge, Onondaga Co. - 19 Sept. 1832
  Richard, of Elbridge, Onondaga Co. - 19 Sept. 1832
RADCLIFF
  Charles, of Buffalo, Erie Co. - 16 Dec. 1842
  John, of NYC - 18 Nov. 1847
RADER
  Regina (wife of Maximilian Rader), of NYC - 18 Oct. 1847
RADLEY
  George, of Genesee Co. - 2 Sept. 1834
  Richard, of Albany Co. - 27 Oct. 1838
RAE
  William, of Mamaroneck, Westchester Co., farmer - 29 Feb. 1832
RAFFERTY
  John, of NYC, formerly of town of Lisagone (Lisnagowan), Co. of
    Cavan, Ire. - 7 Nov. 1825
  Peter, of NYC, mason, born in Ire. - 4 Apr. 1825

New York Alien Residents, 1825-1848

RAINEY
  James, of Wayne Co. - 30 Jan. 1834
RALFF
  William, of Allegheny Co. - 7 Aug. 1832
RALPH
  Edward, of Buffalo, Erie Co. - 24 Dec. 1832
  Mary, of Buffalo, Erie Co. - 24 Dec. 1832
RANKIN
  George Nicholas/Nicholes, of NYC, gentleman - 22 July 1834
RANKINE
  John, of Canandaigua, Ontario Co. - 20 Aug. 1835
RANNO
  John, of Lewis Co. - 20 Sept. 1831
RAPETTE
  Michele, of NYC - 5 Aug. 1842
RATTEN
  James Edward, of Scottsville, Monroe Co., born Co. of Kent, Eng.;
    emigrated to N.Y. State in Aug. 1835 and has been res. of
    Monroe Co. ever since - 28 Mar. 1836
RAWLINS
  Thomas C. of NYC - 3 June 1837
RAWORTH
  Morris, of NYC - 22 Oct. 1839
RAY
  Charles, of Macedon, Wayne Co. - 12 Oct. 1841
  John Baptiste, of NYC, French subject; has been res. of N.Y.
    State for 5 years - 28 Nov. 1833
  William, of Onondaga Co. - 17 Nov. 1838
RAYNOR
  James K., of NYC, gentleman - 2 Aug. 1825
RAZER
  Christopher, of Rochester, Monroe Co. - 3 Mar. 1840
READ
  John, of Buffalo, Erie Co. - 19 Nov. 1842
READER
  John, of Sangerfield, Oneida Co. - 12 Sept. 1831
READING
  Richard, of Buffalo, Erie Co., late of Wittington, Oxfordshire,
    Eng. - 22 Aug. 1831
REATS
  John Henry, of Clarkstown, Rockland Co. - 29 Oct. 1839
  Mary (wife of John Henry Reats), of Clarkstown, Rockland Co. -
    31 July 1840
REBHUN
  Apollonia (wife of Jacob Rebhun), of NYC - 10 Feb. 1848
RECHENBERG
  Charles F.W., of Onondaga Co. - 17 July 1843
REDDIN
  William S., of NYC - 20 May 1836
REDDY
  Owen, of NYC, mason, born in Ire.; has resided in NYC since June
    1824, when he arrived from Europe - 13 Dec. 1825
REDINGER
  Francis, of Lewis Co. - 21 Sept. 1830
REDMAN
  John, of NYC; took incipient measures in 1840; last March he
    purchased a lot of land in Fourth St. - 17 Apr. 1845
REDPATH
  James, of NYC - 17 Mar. 1840
REDWOOD
  Langford, of NYC, heretofore of London, Eng. - 16 June 1831
  Langford W.L., of Flushing, Queens Co., gentleman - 18 May 1844
REEBER
  Maria Elizabeth (née Maria Elizabeth Biehn, wife of John Reeber),
    of NYC - 22 Nov. 1844

92

New York Alien Residents, 1825-1848

REED
  Christopher, of Kirkland, Oneida Co. - 11 July 1836
  Elizabeth, of Peekskill, Westchester Co., residing in St. James
    St., near the corner of Center St. (widow of Richard Reed, late
    of Cortland, Westchester Co., stone-mason) - 17 Feb. 1842
  John, of Albany - 29 Aug. 1833
REEDER
  Henry, of Geneva, Ontario Co., subject of U.K.; took incipient
    measures 5 Nov. 1840 - 23 Dec. 1841
REES
  Thomas, of Clayton, Jefferson Co., British subject - 1 May 1839
REIBER
  George Frederick, of Hamburgh, Erie Co. - 26 Oct. 1844
REID/RIED
  Alexander, of NYC, grocer - 3 Mar. 1835
  William, of City of Albany, formerly of G.B. - 14 Dec. 1836
  William, of Bergen, Genesee Co. - 5 Apr. 1831
REILLY
  Bridget, of NYC - 9 May 1844
  Garret, of Troy, Rensselaer Co.; took incipient measures 16 June
    1836 - 10 Mar. 1836
  John, of NYC, born in U.K. - took incipient measures 25 Mar.
    1844 - 4 Apr. 1844
REIMER
  Frederick William, of NYC - 5 July 1845
REIS
  Martin, of Monroe Co, late of Germany - 26 Oct. 1835
REITZ
  Elizabeth Barbara (wife of Francis A. Reitz), of NYC - 10 Apr.
    1845
  Francis A., of Brooklyn, Kings Co., baker - 6 Aug. 1833
RELLICT
  Henry, of NYC - 22 Aug. 1845
REMY
  Peter, of NYC, looking-glass maker, born in town of Columbid,
    Dept, of la haute Saone, France; took incipient measures in
    Marine Court in NYC on 5 Dec. 1835 - 2 Sept. 1836
REN
  John, of Lockport, Niagara Co., native of Co. Kerry, Ire. - 1
    Aug. 1842
RENAULD
  Peter A. H., of NYC - 12 Aug. 1836
RENAUT
  Charles Alexander, of Le Roy, Jefferson Co. - 19 Oct. 1836
RENDELLS
  Louis Robert, of Brooklyn, Kings Co. - 5 Oct. 1827
RENEHAN
  Matthew, of Huntington, Suffolk Co., native of Ire. - 3 June 1840
RENNIE
  Adam, of Albany - 8 Aug. 1846
  William, of Albany - 3 Aug. 1846
RESEVEAR
  Thomas, of Rochester, Monroe Co. - 3 Apr. 1843
REVLY
  Thomas, of Oneida Co. - 19 Feb. 1833
REY
  Nicholas, of NYC - 22 Feb. 1837
REYNOLDS
  Charlotte Rebecca (widow of Emanuel Reynolds), of NYC - 14 Apr.
    1847
RHODES
  Mary (wife of Joseph A. Rhodes), of Williamsburgh, Long Island -
    (sworn in NYC) 16 Oct. 1845
RICE
  Mary Ann (wife of James Rice, of Southfield, Richmond Co. -

RICE (continued)
  Mary Ann (continued) - (sworn in NYC) 24 Nov. 1845
RICH
  David, of Onondaga Co. - 12 Dec. 1832
  William, of Onondaga Co. - 12 Dec. 1832
RICHARD
  Etienne, of NYC, late of Rouen, France - 30 Mar. 1837
  John, of Livingston Co. - 13 Feb. 1833
RICHARDS/RICHARD
  Catharine, of Deerfield, Oneida Co., late of Guernsey - 3 Nov.
    1835
  Charlotte, of NYC - 11 Sept. 1844
  Edward, of Marey, Oneida Co., formerly of Wales - 27 June 1840
  George, of NYC, native of U.K. - 6 Mar. 1828
  Jane (wife of John Richards), of NYC - 14 Mar. 1846
  John, of Schuyler, Herkimer Co. - 12 Nov. 1832
  Lewis, of NYC, slater - 1 Mar. 1826
  Richard, of Brooklyn, Kings Co. - 19 June 1827
  Thomas B., of NYC, iron founder - 2 Mar. 1826
  William, of Williamsburgh, Kings Co., harness-maker - 7 Apr. 1847
RICHARDSON
  Ellen, of NYC; about 15 years ago she came to NYC with her hus-
    band, since deceased - 20 Dec. 1844
  George, of Otsego Co., native of Eng. - 12 May 1836
  James, of Albany - 27 Apr. 1833
  John, of Albany - 27 Apr. 1833
  Robert, of Watervliet, Albany Co. - 14 Nov. 1836
  William, of Coeymans, Albany Co. - 29 Mar. 1837
RICHELIEW
  William, of Newburgh, Orange Co. - 12 Apr. 1847
RICHERT
  Theobold, of Erie Co., native of Birckld, Grand Dukedom of Hessen
    Darmstadt in Germany; came to U.S. 16 June 1844 - 30 Aug. 1844
RICKCORDS
  John, of Bennington, Genesee Co. - 24 Sept. 1838
RIDLEY
  William, of Rochester, Monroe Co. - 24 June 1846
RILEY
  John, of Rochester, Ulster Co. - 12 Mar. 1839
  Mary, of NYC, for some years a res. of U.S. - 14 Dec. 1844
  Michael, of NYC - 4 Feb. 1826
  Michael, of Montgomery, Orange Co. - 22 Mar. 1834
RIMLINGER
  Michael, of Manlius, Onondaga Co. - 9 Oct. 1833
RIORDAN
  Michael, of Poughkeepsie, Dutchess Co. - (sworn in NYC) 17 May
    1847
RISK
  James, of Albany - 6 Oct. 1830
RITCHIE
  Daniel, of Oneida Co. - 29 June 1837
RITTER
  Sophia, of Buffalo, Erie Co., subject of Duke of Waldeck - 23
    July 1845
RIVERS
  Charles, of Minden, Montgomery Co. - 24 Jan. 1844
ROAB
  John, of Rochester, Monroe Co. - 10 June 1840
  Lorenz, of Rochester, Monroe Co. - 10 June 1840
ROACH
  Elizabeth (wife of John Roach), of NYC - 6 June 1846
  James, of Brooklyn, Kings Co. - 2 Aug. 1827
  Samuel, of St. Lawrence Co. - 25 Aug. 1826
ROBB
  Amelia, of Rochester, Monroe Co. - 3 May 1844

New York Alien Residents, 1825-1848

ROBB (continued)
  Mary Antoinette, of NYC, widow - 7 July 1830
  William, of Saratoga Springs, Saratoga Co. - 30 Mar. 1839
ROBE
  John, of Albany - 3 June 1845
ROBERT
  Thomas, of NYC, baker - 25 Jan. 1827
ROBERTS
  David, of Oneida Co., formerly of Merionethshire, Wales - 15
    Mar. 1831
  David E., of Brooklyn, Kings Co. - 14 Mar. 1839
  James, of NYC - 25 Mar. 1836
  Jane, of Steuben, Oneida Co. - 14 Mar. 1831
  John, of Lewis Co., native of Eng., age 55 - 20 Apr. 1832
  John, of Lockport, Niagara Co. - 3 Oct. 1836
  John B., of Rochester, Monroe Co. - 8 Sept. 1837
  Robert, of Leyden, Lewis Co. - 26 Feb. 1840
  Thomas, of Onondaga Co. - 18 Apr. 1837
  William, of New Hartford, Oneida Co. - 20 Dec. 1832
  William, of Leyden, Lewis Co. - 29 Dec. 1847
ROBERTSON
  James, of Easton, Washington Co. - 9 Sept. 1830
  John, of Fairfield, Herkimer Co. - 2 Feb. 1836
  John, of Oswego, Oswego Co., native of Wiltshire, Eng. - 18
    Oct. 1836
  John, of Warren Co. - 18 July 1838
  William, of Brooklyn, Kings Co. - 5 Apr. 1841
ROBINSON
  Isaac H., of Syracuse, Onondaga Co. - 30 Aug. 1844
  James, of Troy, Rensselaer Co. - 19 July 1839
  James, of Albany, born in Co. of Down, Ire. - 10 July 1845
  John, of Albany - 26 July 1832
  John, of Wayne Co. - 27 Sept. 1831
  John, of NYC - 9 Aug. 1834
  John, of Erie Co. - 7 Dec. 1835
  John, of NYC - 18 Oct. 1842
  John, of Palmyra, Wayne Co. - 24 Jan. 1838
  Joseph, of NYC - 20 Jan. 1835
  Matthew, of Monroe Co. - 11 Dec. 1832
  Robert, of Ontario Co., age 35, native of Ire.; has resided in
    U.S. more than 16 years and in the State of N.Y. for about
    9 years - 20 Feb. 1835
  Robert, of Troy, Rensselaer Co. - 20 July 1839
  Susannah, of NYC - 25 Sept. 1845
  Thomas, of Cohoes, Albany Co. - 10 Dec. 1845
  Thomas, of Virgel, Cortland Co., born in G.B.; emigrated to the
    U.S. 4 years ago - 20 June 1837
  William, of Genesee Co. - 4 Feb. 1834
ROBISON
  John T., of Williamsburgh, Kings Co. - 1 May 1837
  Thomas, of Wayne Co. - 23 May 1832
ROBSON
  Isaac, of Oneida Co. - 24 Mar. 1837
  William, of Oneida Co. - 24 Mar. 1837
ROCHE
  Maria (wife of Edward Roche), of NYC; arrived in U.S. 20 May
    1836 - 29 May 1844
RODENHURST
  Richard, of Oneida Co. - 2 June 1834
RODGERS/ROGERS
  Alexander, of Albany - 13 Mar. 1845
RODGERS
  Robert, of Onondaga Co. - 11 July 1840
RODH
  John, of Lewis Co. - 8 Oct. 1845

95

RODON
  Elizabeth Sloe, of NYC - 10 Sept. 1839
RODWELL
  John, of Williamsburgh, Kings Co., mason - 28 Feb. 1835
ROEDER
  John Conrad, of NYC - 26 May 1835
ROFF
  Peter, of Lewis Co. - 22 Sept. 1834
ROGERS
  James, of Le Roy, Jefferson Co. born in Kingston, Upper Canada,
    in 1808; removed to N.Y. in 1830 - 5 Sept. 1838
  Rebecca (wife of Thomas Rogers), of New Rochelle, Westchester
    Co. - 1 May 1846
  Richard, of Jefferson Co. - 3 Nov. 1832
ROGGE
  Henry Hermann Adolph, of Minden, Montgomery Co. - 26 Sept. 1836
ROHR
  Samuel, of Rochester, Monroe Co. - 20 June 1835
ROLFE
  John, of Brooklyn, Kings Co., late of G.B. - 10 Oct. 1833
ROLIN
  Pierre Francois, of NYC - 25 Sept. 1840
ROLLASON
  James F., of NYC; declared intention 29 Aug. 1837 in Marine
    Court - 30 Aug. 1837
ROMEGE
  George, of Wayne Co. - 28 Sept. 1830
ROOS
  Simon, of Erie Co. - 4 Mar. 1835
ROPATER
  Henry, of Ephrata, Fulton Co., from Hanover, subject of his late
    Britannic Majesty; came to U.S. on 15 Aug. 1831 - 14 Jan. 1839
ROSE
  James, of Brooklyn, Kings Co., grocer - 28 July 1825
  Thomas, of Lyme, Jefferson Co. - 4 Mar. 1835
ROSEWARNE
  John, of Canandaigua, Ontario Co. - 17 May 1831
ROSS
  Alexander, of Hudson, Columbia Co. - 9 Nov. 1831
  Alexander, of Poughkeepsie, Dutchess Co., subject of U.K. - 18
    Nov. 1845
  Charles, of Newburgh, Orange Co. - 27 Apr. 1835
  Charles, of NYC, baker, residing at northeast corner of Avenue 6
    and Eighth St. - 21 Jan. 1842
  Charlotte, of Canandaigua, Ontario Co. - 17 Nov. 1831
  George, of NYC - 4 June 1836
  Henry, of Newburgh, Orange Co. - 27 Apr. 1835
  Joseph, of the town of Crawford, late of the town of Montgomery,
    Orange Co. - 24 Mar. 1831
  Lucy (widow of William Ross), of Castleton, Richmond Co. - 27
    Feb. 1843
  Mary, of Rochester, Monroe Co. - 17 Dec. 1836
ROSSIRE
  Anthony C., of NYC - 18 Nov. 1842
ROTH
  Lewis, of Rochester, Monroe Co. - 3 Sept. 1839
ROULSTON
  Andrew, of Dekalb, St. Lawrence Co., late from Ire. - 17 Nov.
    1837
ROUNDLEY
  John, of Skaneateles, Onondaga Co. - 30 Sept. 1841
ROUSE
  Philip, of Ephrata, Fulton Co., subject of Hessen Castle; came
    to U.S. about middle of Aug. 1831 - 20 Apr. 1839

ROWE
  William, of Monroe Co. - 6 Oct. 1837
ROWLAND
  John, of NYC - 26 May 1842
ROY
  Tiebaux, of Western, Oneida Co. - 3 Aug. 1827
  William, of NYC, merchant - 10 Oct. 1827
REUBENS/RUBINS
  Henry, of Erie Co. - 2 Mar. 1835
RUBERT
  John, of Lewis Co. - 19 Sept. 1843
RUBY
  Anthelme, of NYC - 22 Feb. 1834
RUDDOL
  Thomas, of City of Albany, formerly of Wiltshire, Eng. - 27 Aug.
    1836
RUEDY
  John Jacob, of Erie Co., native of Gaechlingen, Switzerland; came
    to U.S. 16 June 1844 - 30 Aug. 1844
RUFF
  Mathias, of Le Roy, Jefferson Co., late of Hohenzollern Hechin-
    gen, Germany - 13 July 1833
RUMMEL
  Andreas, of Rochester, Monroe Co. - 17 Nov. 1847
RUMPLER
  Gabriel, of NYC - 8 Jan. 1845
RUSHER
  Joseph, of Brooklyn, Kings Co., furniture and cedar storekeeper,
    late of G.B. - 14 Apr. 1834
RUSSEL
  Robert, of NYC, formerly of G.B. - 2 June 1841
RUSSELL
  Andrew, of Kingston, Utica Co. - 18 Apr. 1840
  Archibald, of NYC - 3 July 1840
  George, of NYC - 10 Feb. 1829
  James G., of Bloomingdale, NYC, teacher - 18 Aug. 1838
  John, of Kingston, Ulster Co., merchant - 28 Oct. 1841
  Matthew, of NYC - 2 Feb. 1835
RUSSER
  George Frederick, of Buffalo, Erie Co., late of Grand Dukedom
    of Baden, Germany - 18 June 1835
RUTHERFORD
  Archibald, of Burlington, Otsego Co., late of the Parish of Hou-
    nam, Co. of Roxburgh, Scotland - 24 Nov. 1831
  John, of Burlington, Otsego Co. - 14 Oct. 1834
RUTHVEN
  John, of NYC - 18 Sept. 1835
RUTLAND
  George, of NYC - 27 June 1835
RYAN
  James, of NYC, formerly of town of Vines Grove, Co. of Kilkenny,
    Ire. - 5 Nov. 1825
  James, of Troy, Rensselaer Co. - 5 Sept. 1836
RYDER
  James Patrick, of Greenpoint, town of Bushwick, Kings Co. -
    (sworn in NYC) 22 Aug. 1844

SABATHNEY
  George, of Rochester, Monroe Co. - 8 Nov. 1838
SABINE
  Gustavus A., of NYC, physician - 27 Apr. 1843
  Julia Anna (wife of Gustavus A. Sabine), of NYC - 27 Apr. 1843
SADD
  Samuel, of German Flatts, Herkimer Co., native of Eng. - 22 Aug.
    1842

SADGEBEER/SAGDABEE
  Joseph, of Lockport, Niagara Co. - 4 Mar. 1833
SAJAT
  Louis, of Mexico, Oswego Co. - 2 Feb. 1831
SALENGER
  Michael, of NYC - 1 July 1842
SALG
  Jacob, of Ulster Co. - (sworn in Montgomery Co.) 21 May 1845
SALMON
  James, of Madrid, St. Lawrence Co., formerly of Ire. - 7 June
    1828
  William, of Troy, Rensselaer Co. - 20 Apr. 1842
SALT
  Samuel, of Manchester, Ontario Co. - 30 Nov. 1843
SAMPSON
  Thomas, of Wayne Co. - 18 June 1830
SAMSON
  Margaret, of NYC - 24 Apr. 1845
SAMUEL
  Charles, of NYC - (sworn in Kings Co.) 14 Apr. 1831
  Fanny M., of NYC - 6 Feb. 1846
  Morris L., of NYC - 22 Jan. 1846
SANDERS
  Edward, of NYC, res. of U.S. for about 3 years past - 25 Feb.
    1845
  Joseph, of Cambria, Niagara Co. - 27 Oct. 1835
SANDHAM
  George Anson, of NYC - 9 Jan. 1845
SANDS
  John Henry, of NYC, born in G.B. - (sworn in Kings Co.) 13 Oct.
    1846
  Joseph, of NYC, merchant, formerly of Eng., res. of NYC since
    1822 - 14 Oct. 1823
SANFORD
  Robert, of Oneida Co., native of Folkston, Co. of Kent, Eng. -
    11 June 1835
SANKEY
  William T.J., of Brooklyn, Kings Co. - 21 Mar. 1836
SARGEANT
  Elizabeth, of Williamsburgh, Kings Co. - 4 Nov. 1842
  Thomas, of NYC - 9 July 1838
SATTAE
  Francis, of Monroe Co. - 4 Mar. 1836
SAUERLAND
  John A., of Riverhead, Suffolk Co., late of Prussia - 1 Jan.
    1839
SAUNDERS
  David, of Orleans, Jefferson Co., native of Monmouthshire,
    South Wales, born in 1800; emigrated to U.S. in 1823 - 8 Oct.
    1835
  George, of NYC, hairdresser - 3 Apr. 1830
  Henry, of Genesee Co. - 15 July 1843
  John, of Oneida Co. - 27 Sept. 1839
  Michael, of Waterloo, Seneca Co. - 2 June 1843
  Thomas, of NYC - 6 Sept. 1845
SAVAGE
  James, of Saratoga Springs, Saratoga Co., age 32 - 6 Dec. 1844
  Thomas, of Erie Co., native of Scotland - 10 Mar. 1834
  William, of Venice, Cayuga Co. - 20 Aug. 1847
  William Henry, of NYC - 26 Sept. 1845
SAVOY
  Charles Aime, of N.Y. State - 27 May 1833
SAVOYE
  Ulysse, of NYC - 19 Jan. 1832

SAWYER
  George David, of NYC, teacher - 11 Oct. 1844
SAYER
  Matthew, of NYC, glass-cutter - 7 Apr. 1827
SAYLES
  Thomas, of Wayne Co. - 19 Apr. 1836
SCACE
  John, of Albany, native of Eng. - 26 July 1843
SCANLAN
  Morris, of Brooklyn, Kings Co., labourer - 2 Oct. 1828
SCANTLEBURY
  Joseph, of NYC - 17 Feb. 1831
  Samuel, of Sennett, Cayuga Co. - 14 July 1841
SCARDEFIELD
  Amelia (wife of George Scardefield), of NYC - 3 Sept. 1846
SCHAPER
  Henry, of Canajoharie, Montgomery Co. - 20 Mar. 1841
SCHARER
  Henry, of Lewis Co. - 21 Sept. 1830
SCHARF/SHERIFF
  Charles, of Canajoharie, Montgomery Co., native of Germany - 6
    Mar. 1834
SCHAUTER
  John P., of Utica, Oneida Co. - 1 Apr. 1841
SCHEHL
  George, of Monroe Co. - 24 May 1836
SCHEITLEN/SCHEITLIN
  Anthony, of NYC, merchant - 29 Apr. 1835
SCHEPLER/SHEPLER
  Theodore, of NYC - 17 Nov. 1847
SCHERR
  Johann Joseph, of NYC - 21 Jan. 1848
  Michael, of Wayne Co. - 4 June 1832
SCHICKLER
  Morris, of NYC - 1 Oct. 1834
SCHIMMER
  John, of Rochester, Monroe Co. - 26 Aug. 1847
SCHINE
  Margaret, of Collins, Erie Co. - 20 Sept. 1842
SCHLEGMAN
  George, of Wayne Co. - 8 June 1837
SCHLIEDER
  Ernst Friedrich, of Croghan, Lewis Co. - 21 Sept. 1841
  Frederick C., of Croghan, Lewis Co. - 21 Sept. 1841
SCHMELTZ
  Francis A., of NYC - 15 Oct. 1838
  Joseph, of Canajoharie, Montgomery Co. - 4 June 1845
SCHMELTZER
  Valentin, of NYC, blacksmith - 1 Aug. 1836
SCHMIDT
  Bernard, of Albany - 15 Sept. 1840
  Frederick, of NYC - 7 Apr. 1836
SCHMIETT
  Catharine M., of Buffalo, Erie Co. - 9 Nov. 1844
SCHNEIDER
  Andrew, of Buffalo, Erie Co. - 14 Apr. 1836
  George, of Buffalo, Erie Co. - 22 Aug. 1831
  John, of Lyme, Jefferson Co., born in Hohenzolen, Germany -
    20 July 1843
  Martin, of Brighton, Monroe Co. - 8 Aug. 1838
  Michael, of Lyme, Jefferson Co., born in Hohenzolen, Germany -
    20 July 1843
  Peter, of Lyme, Jefferson Co., born in Hohenzolen, Germany -
    20 July 1843
  Peter, of Syracuse, Onondaga Co. - 20 Jan. 1848

SCHNEYDER
  Abraham, of NYC - 17 Jan. 1843
SCHOFIELD
  John, of Albany - 19 May 1837
SCHOLS
  James, of NYC, late of U.K. - 14 Jan. 1830
  Maria, of Brooklyn, Kings Co. - 2 Nov. 1842
SCHOOLEY
  Azaliah/Azalial, of Waterloo, Seneca Co., born in Co. of Lincoln,
    Upper Canada; arrived at Black Rock, N.Y., about 1 May 1829,
    being then aged about 24 - 9 May 1837
SCHOULER
  James, of NYC, calico printer - 2 Aug. 1827
  James, of NYC, calico printer - 10 Sept. 1827
SCHREIBER
  Phillipp, of Gates, Monroe Co. - 13 Oct. 1840
SCHREIVER
  Frederick, of NYC - 28 Apr. 1846
SCHRODER
  John N., of NYC, late of Kingdom of Hanover - 27 Nov. 1847
SCHROEDER
  Carl/Charles Frederick, of Eden, Erie Co. - 19 Feb. 1845
  John, of NYC, confectioner, born in Hanover, Germany, age now
    21 - 13 May 1847
SCHUCHARDT
  John Jacob, of NYC - 18 Nov. 1836
SCHULER
  Michael, of Wayne Co. - 28 Sept. 1830
SCHULLY
  John, of Verona, Oneida Co., late of Killoughey, Ire. - 20 May
    1825
SCHUMACHER
  Hermann Gustavus, of NYC - 27 Jan. 1845
  John, of NYC - 25 Feb. 1847
SCHWAB
  Jacob, of Wayne Co. - 28 Sept. 1830
SCHWARTS
  Frederic, of NYC - 2 Aug. 1831
SCHWERTFEGER
  Charles, of Minden, Montgomery Co. - 14 Feb. 1838
SCHWINGEL
  Christian, of Buffalo, Erie Co. - 18 Apr. 1836
SCOLARI
  John, of NYC, painter and glazier - 17 July 1835
SCORSER
  Juan, of NYC, late of Italy - 30 June 1837
SCOTHON
  Phineas, of Lee, Oneida Co. - 17 Mar. 1842
SCOTT
  George P., of Brooklyn, Kings Co., printer - 15 Nov. 1833
  John, of Erie Co. - 2 Mar. 1835
  John, of Argyle, Washington Co., born in Eng. - 19 Feb. 1845
  Samuel W., of Villanovia, Chautauque Co.; came to U.S. in 1833 -
    23 Feb. 1837
  Thomas, of NYC, leather dealer - 3 Apr. 1840
SCRYMGEOUR
  James, of NYC - 16 Feb. 1835
  James, of NYC - 2 June 1846
SEA
  Charles, of Westmoreland, Oneida Co. - 26 Aug. 1835
SEABANFEIFER
  Philip, of Erie Co. - 3 Mar. 1835
SEAGRAST
  Maria, of NYC - 27 July 1847

SEARL
  Eliza (wife of Hugh Searl), of Albany, late of G.B. - 12 Oct.
    1833
  Hugh, of Albany Co., subject of G. B. - 12 Oct. 1833
SEARS
  John, of NYC, house-painter - 2 Apr. 1827
  Thomas, of Winfield, Herkimer Co., res. of N.Y. State for 12
    years past - 25 Aug. 1845
SEATON
  Henry, of NYC, ship-chandler - 30 Sept. 1834
  Mannin, of NYC, born 19 Dec. 1807 on Island of Santa Cruz in the
    West Indies; came to U.S. in June 1837; is son of Henry Seaton,
    dec'd, who was a naturalized citizen of the U.S. - 4 May 1847
SEBASTIAN
  George, of Newark, Tioga Co. - 21 Mar. 1842
  Jacob, of Guilderland, Albany Co. - 13 Apr. 1835
SECOR
  William, of Wolcott, Wayne Co. - 7 Nov. 1842
SEGRE
  Matthew John, of NYC, late of G.B. - 6 Feb. 1835
SEIGNETTE
  Alexander, of NYC - 17 Apr. 1847
SEKREST
  Joseph, of NYC, porter, native of Kingdom of Bavaria; res. of
    U.S. from 1821 - 6 Mar. 1832
SELF
  Jane(widow of Stephen Self, late of London, Eng.), of Canajoharie,
    Montgomery Co., native of Byfleet in Surrey, Eng., late from
    Margate, Co. of Kent, Eng.; she arrived in the U.S. in 1834;
    her age is about 70 - 21 Oct. 1845
SELIGMANN/SELIGMAN
  David, of NYC, subject of Prussia - 23 Dec. 1839
  Henry, of NYC, subject of Prussia - 23 Dec. 1839
  Michael, of NYC, subject of Prussia - 23 Dec. 1839
SELLEY
  Thomas, of Rensselaer Co., native of Eng. - 12 Apr. 1837
SELLIER
  Anne Julie, of Flatbush, Kings Co., native of France - 18 Oct.
    1846
SELLWOOD
  Enos George, of Onondaga Co. - 18 Jan. 1845
  George, of Onondaga Co. - 18 Jan. 1845
SEMLER
  John, of NYC - 16 Feb. 1835
SENDEFF
  Christopher, of Turin, Lewis Co. - 18 Apr. 1837
SENIOR
  Ann (wife of Richard Senior), of NYC - 8 Mar. 1845
  Richard, of NYC - 19 Aug. 1837
SEPTEAUNT
  Francis, of Buffalo, Erie Co. - 10 Dec. 1830
SEWORTHY
  George, of Oneida Co., native of Devonshire, Eng.; for past 7
    years a res. of N.Y. - 18 Feb. 1840
SEYBIKI
  August, of Croghan, Lewis Co. - 23 Sept. 1843
SEYMOUR
  Lewis, of City of Albany - 20 Jan. 1836
SHADRAKE
  Frederick, of Buffalo, Erie Co. - 6 Mar. 1834
SHANNON
  Robert, of NYC, late of Ballina, Ire. - 2 Nov. 1830
SHAPLAND
  George, of Stafford, Genesee Co. - 10 June 1834

New York Alien Residents, 1825-1848

SHARRY
    Bridget, of NYC - 23 Apr. 1845
SHAW
    John W., of Dutchess Co., native of Yorkshire, Eng. - 5 June
        1834
    John W., of Rochester, Monroe Co. - 12 Mar. 1836
    Luke, of NYC, late of U.K. - 17 Mar. 1832
    Robert, of Onondaga Co. - 1 Mar. 1839
    Thomas, of Saratoga Co., native of Eng. - 22 Apr. 1837
    William, of NYC, late of U.K. - 18 Jan. 1832
    William, of NYC - 18 Apr. 1837
SHEA
    Michael, of NYC, labourer - 26 Feb. 1838
SHEARER
    Robert M., of Frankfort, Herkimer Co. - 15 Sept. 1830
SHEHAN
    Jeremiah, of Albany - 7 May 1831
SHEILS
    Hugh, of Oneida Co. - 11 May 1841
SHELLEY
    Samuel Thomas, of NYC - 22 Oct. 1834
SHELTON
    James, of NYC, painter - 23 June 1834
SHEPHERD
    Thomas, of City of Albany - 21 Apr. 1836
SHEPPARD
    George G., of NYC, merchant - 8 Mar. 1836
    James D., of Buffalo, Erie Co. - 17 Mar. 1830
SHERBURN
    William, of Ontario, Wayne Co. - 16 May 1839
SHERIDAN
    Richard, of Newtown, Queens Co., farmer, born in Ire.; has re-
        sided the last 7 years in the U.S. and the last 4 years in
        Newtown - 31 July 1837
    Thomas, of Rochester, Monroe Co., subject of G.B. - 25 Mar. 1830
SHERRERD
    Jane G. (widow of Archibald Sherrerd), of NYC - 29 Jan. 1838
SHERRYD
    Patrick, of NYC - 16 June 1827
SHERWIN
    Richard, of Albany Co. - 18 Oct. 1847
SHETHER
    James, of Augusta, Oneida Co. - 12 Sept. 1831
SHIELDS
    Charles, of Middleburgh, Schoharie Co., native of Ire. 28 Feb.
        1847
    Henry, of Albany Co., native of Ire. - 23 May 1834
SHILLITO
    Michael, of Buffalo, Erie Co. - 12 Mar. 1836
SHIMMINS
    John, of NYC looking-glass maker - 23 Apr. 1828
SHIPWAY
    Joseph, of Middlefield, Otsego Co. - 19 June 1838
SHIRES
    Jane, of Albany - 28 Mar. 1845
SHIRLEY
    Stephen, of NYC, gas-light-maker - 16 Feb. 1826
SHIRREL
    David, of Phelps, Ontario Co. - 1 Apr. 1831
SHORT
    John, of Albany - 12 June 1839
    Josiah, of Liberty, Sullivan Co. - 12 July 1834
SHORTISS
    Thomas, of Troy, Rensselaer Co., native of G.B.; emigrated to
        the U.S. in 1830 - 16 Dec. 1834

SHOTTER
  Spencer Wood, of Monroe Co. - 4 Aug. 1837
SHUEFER
  Hinrick, of NYC - 15 July 1847
SHUKT
  Edward, of NYC, baker, native of Northausen, Germany, subject
    of Prussia - 13 July 1838
SHUMUSK
  Joseph, of Wayne Co. - 30 Sept. 1830
SICKINGER
  Peter, of Le Roy, Jefferson Co. - 25 July 1842
SIDDALL
  Barnabas, of NYC, late of Derbyshire, Eng. - 29 July 1841
SIEBER
  Henry G., of Canajoharie, Montgomery Co., native of Germany -
    14 Aug. 1834
SIEGERT
  John Frederick Elias, of NYC - (July 1835
SIFFLET
  Claude Marie, of NYC, merchant - 22 Mar. 1828
SIGNA
  John, of Albany - 15 Feb. 1834
SIGNAIRE
  Victoire Chapany, lady - 3 Dec. 1846
SIGNEAR/SIGNAER/SYNEAR
  Joseph, of Kings Co. - 11 Aug. 1827
SILK
  James, of Niagara Co. - 28 Feb. 1835
SILLERY
  Peter, of Genesee Co. - 25 Apr. 1842
  William, of Batavia, Genesee Co. - 6 May 1841
SIMMONS
  Charles W., of NYC - 12 May 1847
  John, of NYC - 21 Dec. 1842
  John, Jr., of Saugerties, Ulster Co. - 16 Dec. 1842
  William, of Brooklyn, Kings Co - 3 Jan. 1837
  William, of NYC - 23 July 1840
SIMPSON
  George, of NYC - 18 May 1826
  Joseph, of Hamden, Delaware Co., native of Scotland - 1 Nov.
    1834
  Moses, of Onondaga Co. - 31 Aug. 1837
  Robert, of NYC, mason - 1 Aug. 1842
  William, of NYC, print-cutter, late of U.K. - 2 Apr. 1828
  William, of Hamden, Delaware Co., native of Eng. - 1 Nov. 1834
SIMPTOT
  John C., of Parish, Oswego Co. - 2 Feb. 1831
SIMS
  Robert, of Newburgh, Orange Co., formerly of Ire., res. of the
    U.S. for seven years past - 25 Apr. 1838
SINCLAIR
  Janet (wife of James Sinclair), of NYC - 3 Jan. 1846
SIVYER
  James, of Greenbush, Rensselaer Co. - 14 Sept. 1840
SKERRIT/SKERRITT
  Joseph, of Yates Co., native of Eng. - 1 Oct. 1832
SKILLIN/SKILLEN
  Hugh, of Otsego Co. - 18 Apr. 1833
SKIM/SKYM
  John, of Albany Co. - 1 Apr. 1835
SLADEN
  Charles, of Flatbush, Kings Co. - 28 Jan. 1837
SLEIGHT
  Alexander, of City of Albany, farmer - 16 May 1829

SLOAN
  John, of Henrietta, Monroe Co., British subject - 2 June 1830
SMALE
  Henry, of NYC, British subject - 24 June 1846
SMALLWOOD
  William, of Genesee Co. - 4 Feb. 1834
SMART
  Joseph, of Oswegatchie, St. Lawrence Co., born in Eng. - 5 Apr.
    1832
  Thomas C., of New Hartford, Oneida Co. - 9 Apr. 1831
SMITH
  Andrew, of NYC, merchant - 17 Feb. 1837
  Bridget, of Niagara Co. - 7 Jan. 1835
  Bryan, of Albany, laborer - 10 May 1834
  Catherine, of NYC - 11 May 1839
  Clotilda (widow of John J. Smith), of NYC - 11 Jan. 1844
  Connay, of Schodack, Rensselaer Co. - 7 May 1833
  Cornel, of Columbia Co. - 24 Oct. 1828
  Edward, of Pitcher, Chenango Co. - 14 Dec. 1830
  Eleanor (wife of Samuel Smith), of NYC - 20 Apr. 1846
  Elizabeth (widow of Andrew Smith), of NYC - 9 Dec. 1846
  George, of NYC, blacksmith - 9 June 1828
  George, of NYC, late of Scotland - 14 Nov. 1835
  George, of Collins, Erie Co. - 20 Sept. 1842
  Hiram, of Erie Co. - 3 Mar. 1835
  James, of Islip, Suffolk Co., farmer - 11 Nov. 1847
  James Allen, of Brooklyn, Kings Co. - 29 June 1835
  John, of Malone, Franklin Co., born subject of U.K. - 3 May 1832
  John, of Onondaga Co. - 4 Mar. 1834
  John, of Oswego Co., born in Eng.; declared intent in Court of
    Common Pleas in NYC on 19 Sept. 1837 - 28 Sept. 1837
  John M., of Lockport, Niagara Co. - 8 Jan. 1836
  John V., of Peekskill, Westchester Co., born in Eng., res. of
    the U.S. for about 9 years - 2 May 1840
  Joseph, of Onondaga Co. - 1 July 1839
  Lucy, of Catskill, Greene Co. - 30 July 1845
  Owen, of Albany Co. - 29 May 1846
  Patrick, of NYC, late of Ire. - 28 Jan. 1828
  Patrick, of Buffalo, Erie Co., gunsmith - 22 Dec. 1834
  Patrick, of NYC - 27 Dec. 1847
  Robert, of Delhi, Delaware Co. - 12 Dec. 1831
  Robert, of Ontario Co. - 29 Oct. 1846
  Samuel, of Pendleton, Niagara Co. - 9 Sept. 1836
  Sarah Elizabeth Allen, of Kings Co. - 5 Jan. 1837
  Thomas, of Buffalo, Erie Co. - 11 Jan. 1834
  Thomas, of Hudson, Columbia Co. - 15 Mar. 1841
  Thomas, of Troy, Rensselaer Co. - 17 Sept. 1847
  Thomas, of Clay, Onondaiga Co. - 15 Dec. 1847
  Thomas C., of Buffalo, Erie Co. - 11 Mar. 1843
  William, of Westchester, Westchester Co., res. of N.Y. for 8
    years past - 28 June 1830
  William, of Albany - 26 May 1837
  William, of Buffalo Erie Co. - 30 Jan. 1847
  William, of NYC - 12 Feb. 1848
SMITHING
  Michael, of Turin, Lewis Co. - 3 Sept. 1834
SMITHLING
  Joseph, of Lewis Co. - 22 Sept. 1834
SMITHSON
  Thomas, of Richmond Co. - 13 July 1842
SMITLING
  Francis, of Turin, Lewis Co.; application on behalf of himself
    and daughters Catharine and Margaret - 18 Dec. 1835
  John, of Turin, Lewis Co. - 18 Dec. 1835

New York Alien Residents, 1825-1848

SMYLES
  John, of Brighton, Monroe Co., native of Scotland; migrated to
    U.S. in Aug. 1835 - 3 Nov. 1835
SNAITH
  Anne, of NYC - 10 Sept. 1839
SNEBLE
  Paul, of Gorham, Ontario Co. - 17 May 1831
SNIDER
  Cloude, of Lewis Co. - 7 June 1842
SNOOK
  John, of NYC, late of U.K. - 30 June 1832
  Samuel, of Sag Harbor, Suffolk Co., native of G.B.; came to U.S.
    in 1832 - (sworn in NYC) 25 Aug. 1847
SNOWDEN
  James, of Kings Co. - 4 Apr. 1836
SOARTH
  Thomas, of NYC - 22 Apr. 1835
SOLE
  David B., of Buffalo, Erie Co. - 9 June 1847
  John T., of NYC, architect - 23 Dec. 1835
  Sidney W., of Buffalo, Erie Co. - 9 June 1847
SOMER
  Peter, of Stafford, Genesee Co., born in G.B. - 3 Dec. 1844
SOMNER
  Gotlieb, of Oswegatchie, St. Lawrence Co., late of Kingdom of
    Wuertemberg - 20 Jan, 1831
SOUDROY
  Henry, of Ephrata, Fulton Co., native of Kingdom of Hanover; he
    came to U.S. in July 1835 - 4 July 1842
SOULIER
  Achille, of NYC, professor of dancing, native of France - 23
    Mar. 1831
  Jeanne Marie Fanny Guy Achille, of NYC - 17 Sept. 1841
SOUILLARD
  Bernard, of NYC, formerly of France - 24 Jan. 1827
SOUTHERLANDT
  Charles, of Canajoharie, Montgomery Co., native of Germany - 25
    Nov. 1835
SPANGLING
  Philip, of NYC - 21 Sept. 1846
SPEERS
  Henry, of NYC, manufacturer - 13 Apr. 1831
SPENCE
  Andrew, of Onondaga Co. - 28 Nov. 1833
  George, of Buffalo, Erie Co. - 26 Sept. 1835
  Thomas, of Onondaga Co. - 28 Nov. 1833
SPENCER
  John S., of NYC - 25 Apr. 1836
SPERRY
  Thomas, of Brutus, Cayuga Co. - 17 Sept. 1832
SPICE
  Joseph, of NYC, native of Avicon, Switzerland - 22 Jan. 1833
  William Felix, of Seneca, Ontario Co. - 15 Oct. 1833
SPICKER
  Charles F., of NYC - 26 Sept. 1835
SPISE
  Charles, of Mount Pleasant, Westchester Co. - 3 Nov. 1841
SPOONER
  Hugh, of NYC, native of Eng. - 4 Apr. 1827
SPRENG
  George, of Lewis Co. - 21 Sept. 1830
SPRIGGS
  John, of Oneida Co. - 26 Aug. 1834
SPROWL
  Robert, of Tyrone, Steuben Co., subject of U.K. - 4 Jan. 1830

SQUIRE
  Samuel, of Brooklyn, Kings Co. - 9 July 1847
  Thomas, of North Hempstead, Queens Co., native of G.B. - 4 Sept.
    1834
STAFFORD
  James, of NYC, porter - 19 June 1826
  Mary (widow of Henry Stafford, late of Williamsburgh, Kings
    Co.) - (sworn in NYC) 17 Jan. 1845
STAGG
  Clara (wife of John R. Stagg), of Brooklyn, Kings Co., born in
    G.B. - 7 Aug. 1845
  John Roddam, residing in Lawrence St., between Johnson St. and
    Myrtle Ave., in Brooklyn, Kings Co., cabinetmaker - 15 Nov.
    1843
STAHL
  John, of Buffalo, Erie Co., late of France - 7 Aug. 1835
STAINER
  Edward, of NYC, formerly of Austria - 23 Aug. 1836
STAIRS
  John, of Schenectady Co. - 9 Oct. 1838
STAMMERS
  Joseph, of Hempstead, Queens Co., late from G.B. - 21 Dec. 1826
  Joseph, of Brooklyn, Kings Co. - 16 July 1835
STANBURY
  John, of NYC - 13 Feb. 1833
STANLEY
  Edward F., of NYC - 29 July 1835
  John, of Whitestown, Oneida Co. - 2 Apr. 1832
  Joseph, of NYC - 25 Oct. 1847
SANTIAL
  Thomas, of Oneida Co., native of Eng. - 4 Nov. 1834
STAPLETON
  John, of Newstead, Erie Co. - 4 Feb. 1841
STARK
  Henry, of Whitestown, Oneida Co., native of Kilsyth, Scotland;
    landed in NYC in July 1832 - 19 Nov. 1832
STAUB
  Joseph, of Buffalo, Erie Co., French subject - 10 Oct. 1842
STAUNTON
  Thomas, of Lockport, Niagara Co. - 5 Jan. 1836
STEAD
  John, of Orange Co. - 3 Jan. 1848
  Thomas, of Guilderland, Albany Co. - 17 Jan. 1832
STEAN
  John, of Albany - 21 Oct. 1835
STEEL
  George, of New Hartford, Oneida Co. - 12 Apr. 1831
STEELE
  Alexander, of Newburgh, Orange Co., formerly of Scotland - 23
    Mar. 1831
STEEN
  William, of Buffalo, Erie Co. - 25 Sept. 1835
STEFANI
  Antonio, of NYC - 29 Aug. 1836
STEINBRENNER
  Frederick W., of NYC, merchant, French subject - 21 Feb. 1827
STELL
  Michael, of Wayne Co. - 28 Sept. 1830
STEPHENSON
  William, of NYC, carpenter, late of U.K. - 11 July 1825
STERLING
  John, of Albany Co. - 25 Feb. 1847
STEVEN
  David, of NYC, cabinetmaker - 24 Feb. 1834

STEVENSON
Frederick, of Williamsburgh, Kings Co. - 4 Nov. 1847
Henry, of NYC - 23 Nov. 1843
James, of Brooklyn, Kings Co. - 5 Apr. 1841
John, of Brooklyn, Kings Co. - 5 Apr. 1841
Sophia, of Williamsburgh, Kings Co. - 4 Nov. 1847
STEWART
Elizabeth, of Groton, Tompkins Co. - 21 Feb. 1833
James, of Saratoga Springs, Saratoga Co., late of Scotland -
    31 Oct. 1835
John Thomas, of Le Roy, Jefferson Co. - 12 Dec. 1833
Joshua, of Warsaw, Genesee Co. - 11 Nov. 1840
Mary, of Saratoga Springs, Saratoga Co., late of Scotland - 31
    Oct. 1835
Mary Jane, of Jefferson Co. - 28 Mar. 1845
Robert, of NYC, subject of U.K. - 3 Feb. 1836
STICKLAND
Samuel, of Allegheny Co. - 26 June 1832
STIMMEL
Gustavus, of Hempstead, Queens Co. - 22 Dec. 1847
STINBECKER
Antone, of Diana, Lewis Co. - 4 Jan. 1837
STIRLING
Charles, of 185 Eighth Ave., NYC, one of the firm of Stirling
    and Walton, liquor merchant, born in Scotland in 1817; age now
    27; emigrated to U.S. in 1835, when aged about 15; for past
    10 years a res. of NYC - 2 Apr. 1845
STOKES
Joseph Houghton, of Niagara Co. - 10 Feb. 1847
STONE
William P., of Alden, Erie Co. - 5 June 1832
STOPPANI
Francis, of NYC, merchant - 24 Feb. 1827
STORY
Richard J., of Albany - 7 Sept. 1840
STOURVENEL
Francis, of NYC - 28 Sept. 1846
Nicholas, of NYC - 28 Sept. 1846
STRAHAN
James, of Albany - 24 Sept. 1844
STRALE
Frederick A., of Kings Co. - 8 Nov. 1842
STRASSMAN
Conradt, of Canajoharie, Montgomery Co., from Hanover, subject
    of his late Britannic Majesty; came to U.S. in Aug. 1832 - 11
    Feb. 1839
STREB
Joseph, of Rochester, Monroe Co. - 16 Apr. 1847
STREFF
John M., of Watson, Lewis Co. - 25 July 1840
STRICKLAND
William, of Gainsville, Genesee Co. - 2 Feb. 1836
STRINGER
John A., of Otsego Co. - 8 May 1839
William, of Cherry Valley, Otsego Co., late of Eng. - 26 Apr.
    1839
STRINGRELE
Augustus, of Canajoharie, Montgomery Co., British subject; came
    to U.S. about 18 Aug. 1832 - 31 July 1838
STROHM
Michael, of Wayne Co. - 28 Sept. 1830
STRONG
Michael, of NYC, late of Dublin, Ire., tanner - 7 Aug. 1830
STROUD
John, of NYC, marble-manufacturer - 4 Aug. 1834

New York Alien Residents, 1825-1848

STROYAN
  John, of Yates, Orleans Co. - 6 Mar. 1845
STUCKEY
  William, of Onondaga Co. - 30 Sept. 1847
STUDER
  Henry, of Wayne Co. - 26 Sept. 1833
STUERT
  John, of Oswegatchie, St. Lawrence Co., from Ire. - 9 Sept. 1828
STUNT
  William Henry, of NYC - 24 Oct. 1831
STURGES
  Robert, of Poughkeepsie, Dutchess Co. - (sworn in NYC) 10 Dec.
    1838
STURMAN
  William, of Buffalo, Erie Co., subject of G.B. - 1 Apr. 1843
SUAREZ
  Benita, of NYC - 7 Apr. 1847
SUCH
  James, of Jamaica, Queens Co. - 18 Apr. 1839
SULLIVAN
  Elizabeth, of Verona, Oneida Co. - 15 June 1825
  James, of Buffalo, Erie Co. - 6 Mar. 1834
  Jeremiah, of Rochester, Monroe Co. - 3 Oct. 1842
  Patrick, of Verona, Oneida Co., late of Clunsast, Ie. - 20 May
    1825
  Patrick, of Auburn, Cayuga Co. - 30 Sept. 1846
  Thomas, of Auburn, Cayuga Co. - 1 Oct. 1846
SULZER
  Andrew, of Le Roy, Jefferson Co. - 18 June 1833
  Conrad, of Le Roy, Jefferson Co. - 18 June 1833
SUMMERFIELD
  James, of Stafford, Genesee Co. - 14 Oct. 1834
SUPERNAUGH
  Michael, of Queensbury, Warren Co. - (sworn in Washington Co.)
    3 Sept. 1845
SUTTON
  William, of Peekskill, Westchester Co., physician, now in NYC -
    8 Jan. 1840
SWANSON
  James, of Niagara Co., late of G.B. - 7 May 1832
SWEENEY
  James, of NYC, physician, native of U.K.; has resided in NYC
    from 1 Sept. 1828 - 10 Apr. 1833
SWEENY
  Patrick, of Brooklyn, Kings Co. - 28 June 1827
  Patrick, of NYC, formerly of Co. of Leitrim, Ire., res. of U.S.
    since 1832; made declaration of intent 9 Dec. 1842 - 9 July
    1845
  Terence, of NYC, tailor - 8 Oct. 1827
SWEET
  William, of Buffalo, Erie Co. - 4 Oct. 1843
SWINTON
  Peter, of Castleton, Richmond Co. - 28 Sept. 1840
SYERS
  Thomas, of Greenbush, Rensselaer Co. - 15 Apr. 1837
SYMS
  John, of NYC, res. of NYC for last 15 years - 22 Feb. 1833
TAGGERT
  William, of Albany, farmer, late of Co. of Antrim, Ire. - 10
    Sept. 1825
TAGLIA
  George, of NYC - 15 June 1841
TALLEY
  Mary, of NYC - 7 Aug. 1846

TALLINGER
  Godfrey, of Lockport, Niagara Co. - 21 Feb. 1842
TANNER
  Henry Thomas, of NYC - 25 May 1837
TAPLEY
  Daniel, of Oneida Co., native of Kent, Eng. - 16 Dec. 1835
TAPNER
  John Edward, of Augusta, Oneida Co. - 12 Sept. 1831
TAPSCOTT
  Jane, of NYC - 20 July 1846
  James, Taylor, of Kings Co. - (sworn in NYC) 21 Mar. 1844
TATE
  Elizabeth (formerly Mc Cormick), of Madrid, St. Lawrence Co. -
    18 Feb. 1842
TAYLER
  John, Jr., of NYC, native of G.B. - 3 Mar. 1845
TAYLOR
  Charles, of Hartland, Niagara Co. - 6 Sept. 1837
  Francis, of Skaneateles, Onondaga Co., British subject - 2 Mar.
    1839
  George, of Ontario Co. - 5 Oct. 1833
  Henry, of NYC - 18 June 1840
  James, of Rochester, Monroe Co., born in Balleyroblen (or Balley-
    voblen?), Co. of Antrim, Ire., about 33 years ago; came to U.S.
    about 1 May 1836 - 15 Nov. 1847
  Lewis, of Skaneateles, Onondaga Co. - 6 Jan. 1841
  Peter, of Canajoharie, Montgomery Co., native of Co. of Perth,
    Scotland - 6 Mar. 1834
  Samuel, of Batavia, Genesee Co. - 16 Mar. 1826
  Thomas, of Brighton, Monroe Co., born about 1773 on Isle of
    Wight; came to America in 1823 and since then has resided in
    Brighton - 7 May 1831
  Thomas, of NYC, builder - 21 May 1833
  William, of Monroe Co. - 3 July 1834
  William H., of Williamsburgh, Kings Co., res. there for two years
    past; family is now with him; British subject - 12 July 1842
TEARNEY
  Hugh, of Wheatland, Monroe Co. - 8 Oct. 1842
  James, of Wheatland, Monroe Co. - 8 Oct. 1842
  John, of Wheatland, Monroe Co. - 8 Oct. 1842
TELFORD
  John, of Cicero, Onondaga Co. - 30 Aug. 1841
TELLO
  John Anthony, of Williamsburgh, Kings Co. - (sworn in NYC) 7
    Aug. 1847
  Manuel Pedro, of NYC - 9 Aug. 1847
TEMPLETON
  Philip, of Albany - 13 Oct. 1834
TERRIN
  John B., of Kings Co., born in France; arrived in U.S. 22 Aug.
    1832 - 27 July 1842
TERRY
  Thomas, of Buffalo, Erie Co. - 21 Nov. 1835
TESTER
  William, of Camillus, Onondaga Co. - 22 Oct. 1842
TEVLIN/TEVLEN
  James, of Troy, Rensselaer Co. - 2 Mar. 1835
THEBAUD
  Augustus J., of Fordham, Westchester Co. - 1 June 1847
THISSE
  Nicholas, of Lewis Co. - 16 May 1840
THOM
  David, of NYC - 2 July 1846
  James, of NYC, stone-cutter, late of U.K. - 2 July 1842

New York Alien Residents, 1825-1848

THOMAS
   Edwin, of Albany - 22 Dec. 1834
   Frederick, of NYC - 31 July 1845
   George, of Erie Co., native of Chester, Eng. - 19 Feb. 1845
   Jane, of Albany - 24 Feb. 1838
   John, of NYC, carrier of the New York Mirror - 5 June 1834
   John, of Albany - 18 May 1835
   John Weeger, of Rochester, Monroe Co. - 19 Aug. 1834
   Timothy, of Frankford, Herkimer Co. - 6 Oct. 1834
   William, of Elba, Rensselaer Co. - (sworn in Washington Co.)
      27 Feb. 1837
   William H., of Rochester, Monroe Co. - 19 Aug. 1838
THOMPSON
   Angelica, of Amity, Allegheny Co. - 9 Dec. 1843
   Ann, of Genesee, Livingston Co. - 5 July 1836
   George J., of NYC - 17 June 1837
   James, of Troy, Rensselaer Co. - 16 Mar. 1836
   John, of Vienna, Oneida Co. - 10 Dec. 1834
   John, of Wilson, Niagara Co. - 5 Jan. 1837
   John, of Wayne Co. - 26 May 1837
   John, of Brooklyn, Kings Co. - 9 Dec. 1846
   John, of NYC - 16 June 1847
   Joseph, of Charleston, Montgomery Co. - 27 Aug. 1844
   Margaret, of NYC, single woman - 30 Aug. 1842
   Robert, of Onondaga Co. - 27 Nov. 1833
   Robert, of Sodus, Wayne Co., born in G.B. - 16 Nov. 1838
   Sarah, of Genesee Co. - 14 June 1838
   Thomas, res. of Walkill, Orange Co., at present in NYC - 30
      Nov. 1825
   Thomas, of Little Falls, Herkimer Co., native of U.K. - 6 Mar.
      1833
   William, of Vienna, Oneida Co. - 10 Dec. 1834
   William, of Troy, Rensselaer Co., born in G.B. - 25 Mar. 1840
   William, of Ulster Co. - 11 Sept. 1847
   William Overland, of Oneida Co., native of North Runcton, Co.
      of Norfolk, Eng. - 6 Nov. 1834
THOMSON
   Jane, of NYC, single woman - 30 Aug. 1842
THORN
   James, of Troy, Rensselaer Co., res. of Troy since about 20 Dec.
      1832; took incipient measures 26 Apr. 1833 - 29 Aug. 1836
THORNE
   John, of Oneida Co., born in Eng. - 23 Sept. 1837
THRESHIE
   David Scott, of NYC - 14 Apr. 1838
THUMANN
   Charlotte (wife of Alvin Thumann), of NYC - 16 Mar. 1847
THURSTER
   Henry, of NYC - 2 Mar. 1846
THURSTON
   Joshua, of NYC, piano-maker - 29 Mar. 1831
TIERNAN
   John, of NYC, formerly of Co. of Sligo, Ire. - 16 Feb. 1832
TIGAR
   Thomas, of Erie Co. - 6 Dec. 1831
TIGHE
   Richard, of NYC, native of Ire. - 27 Mar. 1839
TILLEY
   Alexander, of Oneida Co. - 26 Mar. 1835
TILMAN
   Peter, of NYC - 4 May 1836
TIMMONS
   Thomas, of Auburn, Cayuga Co. - 7 Nov. 1845
TIMMS
   Benjamin Jervas, of NYC - 1 Feb. 1843

TIMMS (continued)
   James, of Bethany, Genesee Co. - 25 May 1836
   Mary (widow of Richard Timms), of NYC - 2 Sept. 1845
TINDALL
   George, of Sangerfield, Oneida Co. - 12 Sept. 1831
TISDALL
   Fitzgerald, of NYC, native of Ire. - 25 Sept. 1835
TISSE
   Mary, of Walton, Lewis Co. - 21 Sept. 1841
TITMORE
   Henry, of Kinderhook, Columbia Co., mechanic - 7 May 1840
TITTMANN
   Charles Edward, of NYC - 14 Dec. 1836
TOBIE
   Dominick, of Frankfort, Herkimer Co. - 13 Aug. 1842
   Martin, of Little Falls, Herkimer Co. - 13 Aug. 1842
TOBIN
   James, of Ontario Co., late of U.K. - 23 Aug. 1832
TODD
   Charles, of NYC - 2 June 1845
   Eliza (wife of Charles Todd, of NYC, gentleman), of NYC - 12 Jan.
      1846
TOMPKINSON
   Joseph, of Wayne Co. - 25 Jan. 1831
TOMLINSON
   George, of Huntington, Suffolk Co., formerly of Castle Heding-
      ham, Essex Co., Eng. - 27 June 1831
   Henry, of Huntington, Long Island, farmer - 28 Jan. 1833
   Joseph Hale, of Huntington, Suffolk Co., formerly of Castle
      Hedingham, Co. of Essex, Eng. - 27 June 1831
   Mark, of Middlefield, Otsego Co., formerly of Stockport, Co. of
      Chester, Eng. - 12 Oct. 1840
   William, of NYC - 5 May 1827
TOMSEY
   Alexander, of NYC - 3 May 1833
TOOGOOD
   James, of Skaneateles, Onondaga Co. - 30 May 1832
TOP
   John M., of Frankfort, Herkimer Co. - 6 Mar. 1846
TOPINARD
   Casimer, of NYC, late of Paris, France - 6 Aug. 1842
   Pierre Antoine, of Paulinia, Hancock Twp., Delaware Co., but at
      present in NYC - 8 Apr. 1840
TORRANCE
   James Patterson, of Cambria, Niagara Co. - 10 Sept. 1834
   John Steele, of Cambria, Niagara Co. - 10 Sept. 1834
TOSONI
   Joseph, of Albany Co. - 25 June 1836
TOURMINE
   Lucas, of NYC, shoemaker; has a wife and family; subject of U.K. -
      19 May 1828
TOUSE
   James, of Amsterdam, Montgomery Co., born in G.B.; left G.B. in
      Oct. 1836 and arrived in NYC in Nov. 1836 - 22 July 1842
TOUSENT
   John, of NYC, French subject - 20 Apr. 1841
TOVEE
   William, of NYC - 14 Mar. 1836
TOWELL
   Thomas, minister of the Gospel, of Richmond Co. - 5 Feb. 1846
TOWERS
   James, of NYC - 2 Nov. 1847
TOY
   Charles, of Buffalo, Erie Co. - 20 Oct. 1843

New York Alien Residents, 1825-1848

TRABECK
  John Baptist, of NYC - 3 Sept. 1836
TREMAIN
  John, of Elmire, Chemung Co. - 8 Sept. 1847
TRENCHARD
  Joseph, of Pittsford, Monroe Co., British subject - 9 Oct. 1837
TREUES(?)
  Audre (or Andre?), of NYC - 17 Oct. 1840
TREWHIL
  James, of Burlington, Otsego Co. - 18 Apr. 1836
TRIESNER
  Johann Ehrenfried, of Buffalo, Erie Co. - 7 Aug. 1847
TRISTRAM
  William H., of NYC - 1 May 1838
TSCHENKEUSS
  Xavier, of Rochester, Monroe Co. - 30 Apr. 1846
TUCKER
  George, of Saratoga Co. - 4 June 1841
  Joseph, of Gates, Monroe Co. - 26 Aug. 1834
TUFFS
  Sophia, of NYC - 1 Mar. 1847
TUGNOT
  George, of Putnam Co. - 22 Dec. 1845
TURCK
  Anna M., of Lewis Co. - 26 May 1842
  Margaret, of Lewis Co. - 26 May 1842
  Nicholas, of Watson, Lewis Co. - 23 May 1840
TURNBULL
  James, of NYC, gentleman - 28 Feb. 1829
  James, of Kings Co. - 26 June 1834
  Robert, of Lyons, Wayne Co. - 29 Jan. 1838
TURNER
  Charles, of Amenia, Dutchess Co., of Lancashire, Eng., and
    lately of Sharon, Conn. - 8 Oct. 1835
  George, of Winfield, Herkimer Co. - 15 Dec. 1838
  John, of Albany - 21 Mar. 1844
  Samuel, of Adams, Jefferson Co., native of Wootton Fitzpain,
    Co. of Dorset, Eng., where he was born on 4 June 1809; he
    migrated to N.Y. in Oct. 1832 - 4 Feb. 1833
  Sarah, of Albany - 20 Feb. 1846
  Susannah, of Albany - 21 Mar. 1844
  William, of New Hartford, Oneida Co., subject of G.B. - 23 Apr.
    1838
TUNSTALL
  Ann, of Brooklyn, Kings Co. - 18 Nov. 1835
  Edmund, of Brooklyn, Kings Co. - 18 Nov. 1835
TYLER
  Samuel A., of Rochester, Monroe Co., native of Northamptonshire,
    Eng., where he was born in 1777; arrived in N.Y. in June 1832 -
    3 Dec. 1832
  William, of Niagara Co. - 3 May 1836
TYLEY
  Gabriel, of Cooperstown, Otsego Co. - 6 Feb. 1845
TYRRELL
  Patrick, of Troy, Rensselaer Co. - 26 Apr. 1837
TYSON
  Matthew, of NYC, farmer - 31 Mar. 1832
  William, of Niagara Co. - 26 Feb. 1835
UBAN
  Julia (wife of John Uban, of Williamsburgh) - (sworn in NYC)
    17 Mar. 1846
UFFINDALE
  Thomas, of Lockport, Niagara Co. - 16 Oct. 1846
UNVERFETH
  Caspar Henry, of Rochester, Monroe Co. - 6 July 1842

New York Alien Residents, 1825-1848

UPJOHN
  William, of Hyde Park, Dutchess Co, late subject of William
    IV of Great Britain - 11 Feb. 1831
USHER
  Samuel, of Onondaga Co. - 20 Feb. 1839
UTH
  Adam, of Manlius, Onondaga Co. - 9 Oct. 1833
VALE
  Joseph, of Rensselaer Co. - 15 May 1837
VALENTINE
  George, Jr., of Buffalo, Erie Co. - 12 Dec. 1838
VALLANT
  Richard, of NYC - 6 Sept. 1842
VANAWAY
  William Alfred, of Galen, Wayne Co. - 14 June 1838
VAN BYLANDT
  Johanna (commonly called "Johanna Countess van Bylandt") of
    Dutchess Co. - (sworn in NYC) 3 Dec. 1845
VANCE
  Thomas, of Westmoreland, Oneida Co. - 31 Mar. 1835
VANDE LANDE
  Daniel Frederick George, of Minden, Montgomery Co. - 11 Aug.
    1838
VAN HERTTEN
  Lewis, of Deerfield, Oneida Co. - 15 Mar. 1836
VAN KINNEY
  Stephen, of NYC - 30 July 1844
VAUGHAN
  Lumon, of NYC, broker - 17 Dec. 1836
VAUX
  James, of Aurora, Erie Co., late of Eng. - 11 Oct. 1834
VERGNOL
  Rose, of NYC, single woman, late of France - 1 June 1832
VERKLER
  Rudolph, of Lewis Co., native of France - 24 May 1834
VERNIORY
  John B., of Williamsburgh, Kings Co., glass-blower - (sworn
    in NYC) 26 Oct. 1846
VERNON
  Richard, of Stafford, Genesee Co. - 9 Feb. 1841
  Samuel, of Stafford, Genesee Co. - 9 Feb. 1841
  William, of Rensselaer Co. - 10 Jan. 1844
VERREN
  Antoine Francoise, of NYC, minister of the Gospel - 24 Feb.
    1831
VICARY
  John, of Alexander, Genesee Co. - 9 Apr. 1836
VICK
  James, of Rochester, Monroe Co. - 29 Nov. 1836
VICKRAGE
  Henry, of City of Albany - 18 Jan. 1836
VIENE
  Francis, of NYC - 9 May 1832
VIGNARDONNE
  Jean Marie, of NYC - 27 Dec. 1838
VILADE
  Claude, of NYC, importer of fancy articles - 9 Jan. 1843
VILES
  Isaac, of Poughkeepsie, Dutchess Co., formerly of Bradford,
    Wiltshire, Eng. - 11 July 1841
VINCENT
  Jonathan, of Wayne Co., on behalf of his sons, Ovid and Joseas,
    both under age of 21 - 31 Jan. 1834
  Thomas, of NYC - 10 Aug. 1847

VIRGO
   Richard, of Greece, Monroe Co. - 7 Sept. 1846
VISCHER
   Andreas, of Buffalo, Erie Co., late of France - 18 Dec. 1835
VOGT
   Adam, of Irondequoit, Monroe Co. - 2 Nov. 1844
   Joseph, of Irondequoit, Monroe Co. - 2 Nov. 1844
VON NOLSTEIN
   Frederick Gerhard Ludwig Struve, of Queens Co. - 15 Dec. 1847
VON RADER
   Ursula, of NYC - Mar. 1843
VON TAUTPHOEUS(or VON TANTPHOEUS?)
   August, of Orleans, Jefferson Co., late of Wuertemberg - 8 Nov.
      1847
VOSS
   Joachim Frederick Lewis, of NYC, late of Kingdom of Hanover -
      9 Mar. 1826
VOWLES
   William, of Onondaga Co. - 20 May 1834
   William, of Sennet, Cayuga Co., native of Co. of Somerset,
      Eng. - 29 Jan. 1833
VROOMAN
   Matilda J., of Albany Co. - 10 May 1847
VUILLAUM (or VAILLAUM?)
   John Pierre, of NYC, blacksmith - 9 July 1846
VYSE
   Charles, of NYC, merchant; took incipient measures 11 Dec.
      1841 - 10 May 1845
WADDY
   William, of Buffalo, Erie Co. - 22 Sept. 1835
WADE
   John, of Hudson, Columbia Co. - 31 Oct. 1831
   William, of Westfield, Richmond Co. - 28 Oct. 1845
WAEFLER
   David, of Rochester, Monroe Co. - 3 Sept. 1839
WAGNER
   Frederick, of Croghan, Lewis Co. - 23 Sept. 1843
WAGSTAFF
   Thomas, of NYC, accountant - 14 Feb. 1831
   William, of NYC, teacher - 15 July 1826
WAIT
   Benjamin, of Cayuta, Chemung Co., miller - 23 Dec. 1845
   Hester, of Montgomery, Orange Co. - 23 Aug. 1847
WAITE
   Henry, of Williamsburgh, Kings Co. - 8 May 1846
   Richard, of Lorraine, Jefferson Co. - 20 Sept. 1830
WAITH
   William, of Albany, late of London, Eng. - 17 Sept. 1832
WAKE
   George, of Wayne Co. - 7 Jan. 1841
WAKEFIELD
   John, of Albany - 28 Oct. 1841
WALBRIDGE
   William, of Allegheny Co., native of Dorsetshire, Eng., age
      now 31 years; arrived in U.S. 28 May 1833 - 6 July 1833
WALBUCHT
   Augustus, of Frankford, Herkimer Co. - 1 Feb. 1848
WALBURN
   Gesche (widow of Jacob Walburn), of NYC - 28 Jan. 1848
WALKER
   Elizabeth T., of NYC, widow, formerly of Co. of Fife, Scotland -
      16 Apr. 1841
   Hannah, of Palmyra, Wayne Co. - 28 Sept. 1837
   James, of Palmyra, Wayne Co. - 28 Sept. 1837

New York Alien Residents, 1825-1848

WALKER (continued)
   John, of Westfield, Richmond Co., laborer - 3 Dec. 1847
   John S., of NYC, shoe-dealer - 22 Jan. 1841
   Joseph, of Geneseo, Livingston Co., gunsmith, res. of Geneseo
      since Nov. 1822, subject of G.B. - 24 Aug. 1827
   Joseph, of Albany Co. - 4 Nov. 1847
   Margaret, of Palmyra, Wayne Co. - 28 Sept. 1837
   William, of Barre, Orleans Co. - 30 Sept. 1834
   William, of Wayne Co. - 26 Sept. 1833
WALL
   William, of Albany - 19 Sept. 1832
WALLACE
   John, of Albany - 3 Jan. 1838
WALLER
   Alfred, of NYC - 23 Jan. 1845
   Jacob, of NYC - 10 Mar. 1836
WALLIN
   Samuel, of Brooklyn, Kings Co. - 9 Feb. 1833
WALMSLEY
   John, of Fishkill, Orange Co. - 9 June 1834
WALSH
   John, of Rome, Oneida Co. - 8 Sept. 1834
   John Peter, of Brighton, Monroe Co., tanner - 7 July 1835
WALTER
   Hilaire, of NYC - 29 Nov. 1843
   Jacob Daniel, of NYC - 29 Nov. 1832
WALTERS
   William, of Victor, Ontario Co. - (sworn in Court of Common
      Pleas of Monroe Co.) 25 Mar. 1839
WALTON
   George, of NYC - 4 June 1836
   Thomas A., of NYC - 20 May 1835
WARD
   Abiel/Abel, of Sangerfield, Oneida Co. - 12 Sept. 1831
   Joseph, of Buffalo, Erie Co. - 19 Sept. 1831
   Thomas, of Oneida Co. - 27 Mar. 1837
   William Henry, of Phelps, Ontario Co. - 24 Feb. 1834
WARE
   Ellen, of NYC, subject of U.K.; came to U.S. about 12 years
      ago - 7 Feb. 1848
WARING
   Edmund, of NYC, house-carpenter - 15 Jan. 1834
WARLA
   Michael, of Buffalo, Erie Co. - 23 Aug. 1831
WARNE
   John, of Auburn, Cayuga Co. - 28 Sept. 1846
WARNER
   Benjamin, of Kings Co. - 4 Nov. 1847
   Edward, of Onondaga Co. - 3 Dec. 1834
   John, of Palermo, Oswego Co., for past 6 years res. of N.Y. -
      25 Feb. 1841
   John, of Palermo, Oswego Co. - 28 June 1841
WARR
   John, of NYC, farmer - 14 Oct. 1829
WARRAM
   Thomas, of Oneida Co. - 11 Sept. 1834
WARREN
   Henry, of Elba, Genesee Co. - 25 Nov. 1842
   John, of Stafford, Genesee Co. - 25 Mar. 1834
   John, of Buffalo, Erie Co. - 7 May 1847
   Nathaniel, of NYC, glass-manufacturer - 16 Feb. 1833
   Nathaniel, of Ellenvill in town of Wawasing, Ulster Co., native
      of Bristol, Eng. - 1 July 1841
   Sabina, of NYC - 30 June 1835
   Sabina, of NYC - 22 June 1836

WARREN (continued)
    William, of Stafford, Genesee Co. - 10 June 1834
WARWICK
    John, of NYC, gold- and silver-refiner - 14 Jan. 1833
WATERS
    John D., of Smithfield, Richmond Co. - 5 Nov. 1827
WATHAM
    Edward, of NYC, British subject - 2 Apr. 1846
WATKINS
    Samuel, of NYC - 6 Oct. 1842
WATKINSON
    Sarah, of NYC, widow - 25 July 1838
    William Martin, of NYC, coach-painter, subject of G.B., for up-
        wards of 5 years past a res. of NYC - 5 July 1838
WATSON
    Leonard, of Genesee Co. - 4 Feb. 1834
    William, of NYC, late of Lurgan, Co. of Armagh, Ire. - 22 May
        1835
    William, of NYC - 10 June 1845
WATTEL
    Joseph, of Monroe Co. - 20 June 1835
WATTS
    James, Jr., of NYC, merchant - 29 Nov. 1833
WEAVER
    Lydia, of NYC, widow - 20 July 1847
WEBB
    Eleanor (wife of Thomas Webb), of NYC - 29 June 1844
    Elisha, of NYC 21 Apr. 1836
    Isabella (wife of Edward J. Webb), of NYC - 25 Aug. 1843
    John, of Camden, Oneida Co., subject of U.K. - 10 Aug. 1829
WEBBER
    George, of Hartland, Niagara Co. - 27 Sept. 1838
    Robert, of Hartland, Niagara Co. - 1 Sept. 1835
WEBER
    Frederick, of NYC - 22 June 1830
    George, of Lewis Co. - 21 Sept. 1830
    George Adolph, of Buffalo, Erie Co. - 3 July 1843
    Jacob, of NYC - 29 July 1847
    Joseph, of Monroe Co. - 15 Nov. 1837
WEBSTER
    Richard, of Hastings, Oswego Co. - 10 Feb. 1830
    William, of Oneida Co. - 18 Mar. 1835
WEGENER
    Frederick, of Queens Co. - 22 Dec. 1847
WEHN
    Dorothea (wife of Henry Wehn, of NYC, brewer), of NYC, late of
        Germany - 27 Nov. 1844
WEIR
    James, of Brooklyn, Kings Co. - 14 Sept. 1847
WEISBROD
    Henry, of NYC - 30 Dec. 1843
WEITHAN
    Louis, of Poughkeepsie, Dutchess Co., formerly of Brunswick,
        Germany - 22 Dec. 1845
WELCH
    Abraham, of Watertown, Jefferson Co. - 31 Oct. 1834
    Alexander, of Batavia, Genesee Co. - 7 Mar. 1843
    Michael, of Onondaga Co. - 7 Dec. 1839
WELDON
    William, of Champlain, Clinton Co. - 28 Sept. 1830
WELLE
    Francis, of NYC - 14 June 1843
WELLER
    Edward, of town and co. of Onondaga - 16 June 1831
    Joseph, of Onondaga Co. - 15 Mar. 1839

New York Alien Residents, 1825-1848

WELLER (continued)
  Thomas, of town and county of Onondaga - 16 June 1831
  William, of Onondaga Co. - 31 May 1837
WELLS
  Jacob, of NYC - 2 Oct. 1844
  Sarah (wife of James Wells), of NYC - 6 Dec. 1844
WELSH
  David, of Sodus, Wayne Co. - 23 Feb. 1830
  Susan (wife of Martin Welsh), of NYC - 30 June 1846
  William, of Batavia, Genesee Co., born in Co. of Armagh, Ire.;
    migrated to the U.S. in 1822 - 2 Feb. 1831
WENGIERSKI
  Augustus, of Buffalo, Erie Co., late of Warsaw, Poland - 15 Dec.
    1835
WENSLEY
  Richard T., of Albany Co. - 29 Mar. 1841
WENZLER
  Henry, of NYC - 4 Mar. 1841
WEST
  John, of Albany - 11 May 1838
  John H., of Syracuse, Onondaga Co. - 28 Nov. 1833
  William B., of Queens Co., manufacturer - 22 Nov. 1832
  William Redwood, of NYC - 18 June 1838
WESTLAKE
  George Smith, of Auburn, Cayuga Co., British subject - 13 Dec.
    1847
WESTMACOLT
  John Guise, of NYC, late of U.K. - 22 Sept. 1835
WESTON
  John, of Eagle Harbor, Orleans Co. - (sworn in Rochester, Mon-
    roe Co.) 5 Jan. 1847
  Thomas, of Westmoreland, Oneida Co. - 8 July 1834
WETSTEIN/WETSTIEN
  Zoe Evelina (wife of John Wetstein), of NYC - 3 Feb. 1846
WETTERMANN
  John B., of NYC - 9 July 1844
WHARRAM
  John, of Whitestown, Oneida Co., late of Pickering, Co. of York,
    Eng. - 2 Sept. 1831
WHEELER
  George, of NYC, tailor - 28 Nov. 1834
WHINFIELD
  John M., of NYC - 7 Dec. 1844
WHITE
  Anne, of NYC, for some years res. of U.S. - 8 Oct. 1844
  Charles, of NYC - 14 Mar. 1836
  Isaac, of Oneida Co., recently from Eng. - 16 Nov. 1840
  Jane, of Madrid, St. Lawrence Co. - 18 Dec. 1840
  John, of 189 Orange St., NYC, baker - 9 June 1834
  John, of Plattsburgh, Clinton Co. - 14 Nov. 1837
  John B., of Oneida Co., native of Eng. - 10 June 1840
  Samuel, of NYC, heretofore residing near London, Eng. - 26 Mar.
    1832
  Thomas, of Kings Co. - 22 June 1836
WHITEMAN
  Geary, of Cherry Valley, Otsego Co. - 22 Mar. 1831
  Richard, of Cherry Valley, Otsego Co. - 22 June 1835
  Thomas, of Cherry Valley, Otsego Co. - 22 Mar. 1831
WHITFIELD
  George T., of Halletts Cove, Long Island, previously a res. of
    Genesee Co. - 10 Nov. 1834
WHITING
  William, of Phelps, Ontario Co. - 4 May 1846
WHITWELL
  John, of Middlefield, Otsego Co. - 1 Apr. 1839

WICKENS
Elizabeth, of Schenectady Co. - 9 Oct. 1838
Thomas, of Schenectady, Schenectady Co. - 10 Nov. 1838
WICKHORST
Lodowick, of Sandlake, Rensselaer Co. - 4 July 1843
WIDMAYER
George, of NYC - 18 Apr. 1833
WEISSE
Gustave Francisque, of NYC - 22 Sept. 1828
WIGGINS
William, of Aurora, Erie Co. - 5 Mar. 1836
WIGGLESWORTH
John, of Geneva, Ontario Co. - 28 Aug. 1838
WIGHTMAN
Joseph, of Seneca Co. - 12 Nov. 1844
WIKA
Jeanne (widow of Lewis Wika), of NYC - 3 June 1837
WILCKENS
Jacob Frederick, of NYC - 1 Mar. 1831
WILCOX
James, of Erie Co. - 23 May 1836
WILD
Ebenezer, of Williamsburgh, Kings Co. - (sworn in NYC) 14 June
1847
Harriet (wife of Ebenezer Wild), of NYC - 28 May 1844
WILDE
Sarah, of NYC - 24 Sept. 1847
WILEY
Elizabeth, of Utica, Oneida Co., widow, native of Scotland - 19
Mar. 1842
Samuel, of Newburgh, Orange Co. - 25 Mar. 1833
WILKES
Bartholomew, of Bath, Steuben Co., age about 27 years, native of
Ire.; res. of N.Y. State since June 1831 - 18 Feb. 1834
WILKINSON
Abel, of NYC - 20 Mar. 1835
George, of Onondaga, Onondaga Co. - 12 Mar. 1845
George, of Hyde Park, Dutchess Co., formerly of Eng. - 24 June
1846
John, of Newstead, Erie Co., age 21 and upwards - 30 Aug. 1838
William, of White Plains, Westchester Co. - 27 May 1833
William D., of Richmond Co. - (sworn in NYC) 6 Sept. 1844
WILL
Frederick, of City of Albany - 11 Jan. 1836
Jacob, of Albany Co., native of Germany - 28 Sept. 1835
WILLARD
George, of City of Albany - 2 Jan. 1836
WILCOX
James, of Allegheny Co. - 26 June 1832
Joseph, of Erie Co. - 31 Oct. 1831
WILLIAMS
Andrew, of New Hartford, Oneida Co. - 26 June 1840
Bridget (wife of John Williams), of NYC - 29 Oct. 1841
Caroline, of NYC - 3 Oct. 1826
Charles, of Brooklyn, Kings Co. - 2 Sept. 1843
Elizabeth, of Williamsburgh, Kings Co. - 21 Jan. 1845
Enoch, of Newfane, Niagara Co., born in Parish of Henbury, Co.
of Gloucester, Eng., on 22 June 1799, res. of U.S. since 18
July 1842 - 26 Aug. 1845
Francis, of NYC - 1 Nov. 1847
George, of Newtown, Queens, native of G.B. - 2 Dec. 1833
George B., of NYC, late of U.K. - 24 Sept. 1847
Henry, of NYC - 3 Aug. 1847
Hutchins Thomas, of Brooklyn, Kings Co. - 11 May 1835
Isaiah, of NYC - 23 Aug. 1847

WILLIAMS (continued)
 James, of Erie Co. - 4 Mar. 1835
 John, of NYC, veterinary surgeon - 7 Sept. 1831
 John, of Brooklyn, Kings Co. - 8 June 1834
 John, of NYC - 1 Aug. 1841
 John G., of Steuben, Oneida Co. - 12 May 1830
 Owen P., of NYC, mason, subject of U.K., for many years past
   res. of N.Y. State - 4 Oct. 1830
 Walter F., of NYC - 17 July 1835
 William, of NYC, black- and whitesmith, subject of U.K. - 12
   June 1827
 William, of Sullivan, Madison Co. - 17 Mar. 1831
 William, of Rochester, Monroe Co. - 15 Mar. 1842
WILLIAMSON
 Charles H., of NYC, clergyman - 11 June 1846
 James, of Schuyler, Herkimer Co., native of Scotland - 21 July
   1834
 James, of Cold Spring, Putnam Co. - 25 July 1842
WILLSHER
 Henry, of Brooklyn, Kings Co. - 16 Apr. 1836
WILLSON
 Thomas, of Beekman Town, Clinton Co. - 13 Jan. 1832
 Thomas, of Kings Co. - 2 Jan. 1835
 William, of Oswegatchie, St. Lawrence Co., lately from Eng. -
   2 Sept. 1830
WILSON
 David, of NYC, mason - 7 Feb. 1834
 Edward, of Brooklyn, Kings Co. - 24 Feb. 1837
 Henry, of Williamsburgh, Kings Co., mariner, native of Denmark -
   (sworn in NYC) 19 Feb. 1844
 Isaac, of Ledyard, Cayuga Co., born in Cumberland, Co. of Cum-
   berland, G.B. - 21 Apr. 1834
 James, of NYC, labourer - 16 July 1844
 James Persse, of NYC - 18 Mar. 1845
 Janet, of Brighton, Monroe Co., late of Scotland; emigrated in
   1833
 John, of Brooklyn, Kings Co. - 23 May 1826
 John, of Amboy, Oswego Co. - 28 Dec. 1831
 Lewis, of Onondaga Co. - 12 Apr. 1831
 Maxwell, of NYC, carpenter - 21 Apr. 1828
 Richard, of Kings Co. - 28 Oct. 1834
 Robert, of NYC, shoemaker, late of U.K. - 17 Jan. 1825
 Robert, of Boonville, Oneida Co. - 11 Oct. 1829
 Thomas, of Flushing, Queens Co., farmer - 26 Aug. 1831
 Walter, of Williamsburgh, Kings Co. - 9 Dec. 1845
 William, Sr., of Oswegatchie, St. Lawrence Co., late from Eng. -
   10 June 1831
WINCEMON
 Godfrey, of Canajoharie, Montgomery Co. - 20 May 1837
WINCKLER
 John Stephan, of NYC, confectioner, native of Wuertemberg -
   21 Feb. 1826
WINDUST
 Ann, of NYC, widow - 24 Apr. 1834
 William, of Kings Co. - 8 June 1835
WINHAM
 James A., of NYC, carpenter - 7 Feb. 1844
WINZENRIED
 Charles M., of Erie Co., native of Buedingen, Grand Dukedom of
   Hessen Darmstadt, Germany; came to U.S. 16 June 1844 - 30 Aug.
   1844
WISEMAN
 Joseph, of Syracuse, Onondaga Co. - 17 Oct. 1842
 Maier, of Syracuse, Onondaga Co. - 17 Oct. 1842
 Maria (wife of Samuel M. Wiseman), of NYC - 9 Mar. 1840

WISEMAN (continued)
   Samuel M., of NYC - 9 Mar. 1840
WITHERS
   Henry, of Kings Co. - 23 June 1836
WITHERSPOON
   Ann (widow of John Witherspoon), of NYC - 11 Nov. 1846
WITTE
   Gustavus Adolphus, of NYC - 23 Mar. 1844
   Hermann, of NYC - 23 Mar. 1844
WITTHAUS
   Rudolph August, of NYC, merchant - 22 Mar. 1847
WOLF
   Catharine, of Rochester, Monroe Co. - 24 Oct. 1844
   John Jacob, of Frankfort, Herkimer Co. - 4 Jan. 1836
   Joseph Leo, of NYC, physician - 15 Nov. 1830
   Lewis, of Frankfort, Herkimer Co. - 4 Jan. 1836
   William Leo, of NYC, physician - 1 Apr. 1831
WOOD
   Amos, of Ledyard, Cayuga Co., born in Langtoft, Yorkshire,
      Eng. - 13 June 1834
   David, of Utica, Oneida Co., native of Kirby, Yorkshire, Eng. -
      14 May 1833
   Jeremiah, of Troy, Rensselaer Co. - 16 Oct. 1835
   John, of NYC - 27 Mar. 1838
   Leonard, of Stafford, Genesee Co. - 15 Apr. 1835
   Lucy, of NYC - 13 Oct. 1847
   Richard, of NYC - 27 Mar. 1838
   Samuel R., of NYC, late of U.K. - 21 Apr. 1837
   Thomas, of NYC, late of U.K. - 21 Apr. 1837
   Thomas William, of NYC, subject of U.K. - 27 Oct. 1846
   William, of NYC, rigger and stevedore, formerly of Pembroke-
      shire, South Wales - 30 Sept. 1828
WOODCOCK
   Richard, of Troy, Rensselaer Co., native of Coventry, Warwick-
      shire, Eng.; arrived in N.Y. State on 22 June 1836 - 8 July
      1836
WOODGATE
   Joseph, of Scottsville, Monroe Co., born in Co. of Kent, Eng.;
      emigrated to U.S. in July 1830 and has resided in Monroe Co.
      ever since - 28 Mar. 1836
WOODHAMS
   Joseph, of Westchester, Westchester Co., miller - 17 Mar. 1830
WOODHULL
   Thomas, of NYC; took incipient measures 5 Nov. 1844 - 17 Jan.
      1845
WOODS
   Eliza, of Brooklyn, Kings Co., born 12 Mar. 1823 in Liverpool,
      Eng; before 1831, at age of about 6, came to U.S. - 2 July
      1843
   James, of NYC - 17 Nov. 1840
WOODWARD
   Charles, of Brooklyn, Kings Co. - 19 Feb. 1833
   George, of Brooklyn, Kings Co. - 30 June 1835
   Thomas, of Brooklyn, Kings Co. - 19 Feb. 1833
WOOLEY/WOLLEY
   William Joseph, of Brooklyn, Kings Co. - 13 Oct. 1835
WORTHY
   George, of Moriah, Essex Co., native of Belper, Derbyshire,
      Eng. - 29 Sept. 1831
WREFORD
   Richard, of Genoa, Cayuga Co. - 24 Feb. 1845
   Samuel, of Albany, late of the U.K. - 23 Oct. 1841
WRIGHT
   Daniel, of Rochester, Monroe Co. - 22 Jan. 1836

WRIGHT (continued)
Edward, of Hudson, Columbia Co., native of Ruabon, Co. of Den-
bigh, North Wales; came to U.S. in June 1827 - 30 Apr. 1832
Frances, of NYC, single woman - 18 Mar. ^^9
George, of Albany Co. - 3 Feb. 1835
James, of Oneida Co., subject of G.B.; came to U.S. about 10
years ago - 26 Sept. 1840
John, of NYC, starch-manufacturer, native of Ire. - 6 Apr. 1825
John, of Onondaga, Onondaga Co. - 5 Dec. 1839
John, of Williamsburgh, Kings Co. - 7 May 1844
Ruth (wife of Asa Wright), of NYC - 4 Feb. 1839
Thomas, of Williamsburgh, Kings Co. - (sworn in NYC) 10 Sept.
1846
William, of NYC - 18 July 1836
William, of Onondaga, Onondaga Co. - 5 Dec. 1839
WRIGLEY
Joseph, of NYC, born in G.B. - 10 Feb. 1846
WULLIGAN
James, of Kingston, Ulster Co. - 14 June 1847
WYBORN
David, of Oswego Co. - 28 Nov. 1846
WYLIE
James, of Easton, Washington Co. - 17 Nov. 1831
YANTZIE/JANTZI
Catharine, of Watson, Lewis Co. - 9 Sept. 1834
John/H...., of Watson, Lewis Co. -
2 July 1834
YENDLEY
Francis, of Otsego Co. - 3 Mar. 1838
YEO
Joseph H., of Monroe Co. - 22 Dec. 1843
YEOMANS
Charles, of Genesee Co. - 14 June 1838
YODER
Joseph, of Oneida Co. - 18 May 1835
YOUNG
Jacob, of Lyons, Wayne Co. - 15 Oct. 1838
James, of Onondaga Co. - 4 Mar. 1839
Nicholas, of Le Roy, Jefferson Co. - 21 July 1835
Nicholas, Jr., of Le Roy, Jefferson Co. - 22 May 1835
Richard, of Oneida Co., born in Londsboro, Eng. - 20 June 1834
Robert, of Stafford, Genesee Co. - 15 Oct. 1840
Samuel, of NYC - 24 Feb. 1836
William, of Stafford, Genesee Co. - 15 Oct. 1840
William Leslie, of Brooklyn, Kings Co. - 1 Feb. 1839
ZEGLIO
Peter, of NYC - 15 June 1835
ZEHNER
Johanna (wife of Philip Zehner), of NYC - 15 Apr. 1845
ZELKEN
Nicholas, of NYC - 5 Jan. 1828
ZENDER
Joakim, of NYC - 20 Nov. 1834
ZERMATZ
Michael, of Irondequoit, Monroe Co. - 17 Aug. 1847
ZETTINGMEYER
Louis, of NYC - 19 Sept. 1846
ZIEGLER
Johannes, of Sheldon, Wyoming Co. - 17 Sept. 1841
ZIMMER
Peter, of West Turin, Lewis Co. - 2 June 1843
ZIMPFER
John, of Erie Co. - 23 May 1836
Johannes/John, of Erie Co. - 30 Apr. 1836

ZITTEL
  Pieter, of Genesee Co. - 13 Feb. 1834
ZURNER
  Charles H., of Fallsburgh, Sullivan Co. - 9 Mar. 1839
ZWICKY/ZWICKEY
  Jacob Anselm Raphaweil, of Lancaster, Erie Co., late of France -
    3 June 1835